argentina on the couch

A series of course adoption books on Latin America:

Independence in Spanish America: Civil Wars, Revolutions, and Underdevelopment (Revised edition)—Jay Kinsbruner, Queens College

Heroes on Horseback: A Life and Times of the Last Gaucho Caudillos—John Chasteen, University of North Carolina at Chapel Hill

The Life and Death of Carolina Maria de Jesus—Robert M. Levine, University of Miami, and José Carlos Sebe Bom Meihy, University of São Paulo

The Countryside in Colonial Latin America—Edited by Louisa Schell Hoberman, University of Texas at Austin, and Susan Migden Socolow, Emory University

¡Que vivan los tamales! Food and the Making of Mexican Identity—Jeffrey M. Pilcher, The Citadel

The Faces of Honor: Sex, Shame, and Violence in Colonial Latin America— Edited by Lyman L. Johnson, University of North Carolina at Charlotte, and Sonya Lipsett-Rivera, Carleton University

The Century of U.S. Capitalism in Latin America—Thomas F. O'Brien, University of Houston

Tangled Destinies: Latin America and the United States—Don Coerver, TCU, and Linda Hall, University of New Mexico

Everyday Life and Politics in Nineteenth Century Mexico: Men, Women, and War—Mark Wasserman, Rutgers, The State University of New Jersey

Lives of the Bigamists: Marriage, Family, and Community in Colonial Mexico—Richard Boyer, Simon Fraser University

Andean Worlds: Indigenous History, Culture, and Consciousness Under Spanish Rule, 1532–1825—Kenneth J. Andrien, Ohio State University

The Mexican Revolution, 1910–1940—Michael J. Gonzales, Northern Illinois University

Quito 1599: City and Colony in Transition—Kris Lane, College of William and Mary

A Pest in the Land: New World Epidemics in a Global Perspective—Suzanne Austin Alchon, University of Delaware

Series advisory editor: Lyman L. Johnson,
University of North Carolina at Charlotte

First edition
Library of Congress Cataloging-in-Publication Data:

Argentina on the couch : psychiatry, state, and society,
1880 to the present / edited by Mariano Plotkin.
    p.   cm. — (Diálogos series)
Includes bibliographical references and index.
    ISBN 0-8263-2264-6 (cloth : alk. paper) —
    ISBN 0-8263-2265-4 (pbk. : alk. paper)
    1. Psychiatry—Argentina—History.
    2. Psychoanalysis—Argentina—History.
    3. Social psychiatry—Argentina—History.
    I. Plotkin, Mariano Ben, 1961–
    II. Diálogos (Albuquerque, N.M.)

RC451.A7 A74 2003
616.89'00982—dc21

2002152231

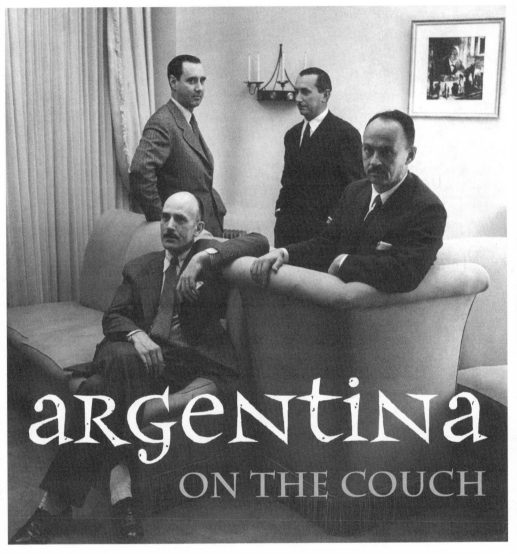

aRGentina
ON THE COUCH

PSYCHIATRY, STATE, AND SOCIETY,
1880 TO THE PRESENT

Edited by Mariano Plotkin

UNIVERSITY OF NEW MEXICO PRESS
ALBUQUERQUE

Contents

List of Illustrations

About the Contributors

Jonathan Ablard is Assistant Professor of History at the State University of West Georgia. He obtained his PhD from the University of New Mexico in 2000, with a dissertation entitled "Madness in Buenos Aires: Psychiatry, Society and the State in Argentina, 1890-1983."

Lila Caimari teaches History at the Universidad de San Andrés and is researcher at the National Council of Scientific Research (CONICET), Argentina. She is the author of *Perón y la Iglesia Católica* and has contributed articles and chapters to a number of academic journals and collective volumes. She is currently completing a book on the practices and representations of crime and punishment in modern Argentina.

Mariano Plotkin teaches at the University of Tres de Febrero and is a researcher at the National Council of Scientific Research (CONICET), both in Argentina. He lived and taught in the US where he got his PhD in History at the University of California Berkeley in 1992. His books include *Mañana es San Perón* (1994, English edition by Scholarly Resources, 2002), and *Freud in the Pampas* (Stanford University Press, 2001). He also edited several volumes and published articles in Argentine and foreign journals. His research was supported by the National Endowment for the Humanities and he received grants from the SSRC. His current research is on the history of intellectuals and social sciences in Brazil and Argentina.

Julia E. Rodriguez teaches history and women's studies at the University of New Hampshire. She is currently completing a manuscript that explores the relations between science, medicine, and the disciplinary state in turn-of-the-century Argentina.

Kristin Ruggiero is Associate Professor of History and Director of the Center for Latin American and Caribbean Studies at the University of Wisconsin-Milwaukee. Her current work is entitled "Modernity in the Flesh: Medicine, Law and Society in Turn-of-the-Century Argentina." She is the author of *And Here the World Ends: The Life of an Argentine Village* (Stanford University Press, 1988). Her research has been supported by the National Endowment for the Humanities and the National Science Foundation.

Hugo Vezzetti teaches history of psychology at the University of Buenos Aires and is a researcher at the National Council of Scientific Research (CONICET) in Argentina. He works on history of ideas in psychoanalysis and psychology. Vezzetti is a member of the editing board of the cultural magazine *Punto de Vista*. His books include *La locura en la Argentina* (1983), *Aventuras de Freud en el país de los Argentinos* (1996), and *Pasado y presente: Guerra, dictadura y sociedad en la Argentina* (2002). He has edited several volumes on the history of psychology and psychoanalysis in Argentina and published many articles in Argentine and foreign journals and magazines.

Introduction

Mariano Plotkin

In 1995, twelve years after the restoration of democracy in Argentina, General Martín Balsa, the army chief of staff, made an unexpected appearance on a widely viewed political television show and publicly apologized to the Argentine society for the crimes committed during the military dictatorship of 1976 to 1983 by the force now under his command. During those terrible years, somewhere between nine thousand and thirty thousand Argentines disappeared at the hands of the Argentine armed forces and the police. The general's "confession" and apology were indeed striking, but even more so was the language he used. General Balsa talked about such things as the need of "working through" the process of mourning and the existence of "unconscious traumas in society."

For foreign observers, the use of such terms may sound odd, particularly uttered by a military officer. For Argentines, however, those words struck a chord. The general employed language that he (or his speech writer) knew the average Argentine would understand and agree with: a language inspired by psychoanalysis. The notion of "working through," as well as the existence of an "unconscious mental level" that to some extent determines our behavior are well-worn Freudian concepts widely used by Argentines in everyday language.

Since the 1960s Argentina has become the world center for psychoanalysis. Not only have large portions of the population (and not only those belonging to the most affluent sectors) undergone psychoanalytic therapy, but psychoanalytically inspired concepts have permeated the way Argentines talk and think. From taxi drivers to soap opera stars, from politicians to generals, all speak in "psy-dialect," which has become a kind of lingua franca. The use of neologisms such as the "verbs" "psicopatear" (to manipulate someone as psychopaths would), or "histeriquear" (to seduce, sexually or not, for no immediate purpose except satisfying a pathological drive) has become common in Argentine urban slang. Psychoanalysts host their own prime-time television shows during which they discuss political and social issues. At the present time two of the most popular TV shows in Argentina have psychoanalysis as their central issue.[1] Argentina today has one of the largest communities of practicing psychoanalysts in the world, in spite of the fact that its population is only around forty million. According to some estimates, by the mid-1990s one out of approximately two hundred *porteños* (as those living in the city of Buenos Aires are known) was a psychologist who, if employed, was most probably practicing some kind of psychoanalytic therapy. Although a large number of psychoanalysts and psychologists practicing psychoanalysis live and practice in the city of Buenos Aires, which concentrates roughly one-third of the population of the country, vigorous psychoanalytic movements have emerged in the interior as well.

The culture of psychoanalysis runs so deep in Argentina that Argentines seldom reflect about it. It seems that for the average Argentine (I should say urban Argentine) psychoanalysis is part of the "nature of things," or rather, to use the words of sociologist Peter Berger, it belongs to "the world taken for granted," something that does not require or even admit questioning. However, as we all know well, nothing that belongs to the realms of culture or society is "natural." Social and cultural phenomena are not necessary; they are to be understood as "processes," unfolding over time and subject to the contingencies of history and therefore to historical analysis. The emergence of a psychoanalytic culture in Argentina is no exception. The question is, thus, what the historical analysis of such a culture tells us about Argentina, its society, its culture, and its politics.

The purpose of this volume is twofold. First, the authors aspire to introduce the historical dimension into the problem of the development of a psychoanalytic culture in Argentina. By focusing on the origins and evolution of the psychiatric assistance and on the reception and evolution of psychoanalysis the articles included in this book explore ruptures and continuities in the history of Argentines' passion for Freud. Second, the contributions included here use the history of the emergence and evolution of the system of psychiatric assistance and the diffusion of psychoanalysis as a window through which other more general topics, such as the development of the Argentine state, the process of reception and adaptation of European ideas, as well as important aspects of the social and cultural evolution of the country, can be discussed and analyzed.

In the context of Latin America the history of Argentina has been somewhat unique. After decades of bloody civil wars and following the fall of the long dictatorship of Juan Manuel de Rosas (1827–1852) it still took one decade of conflict between the wealthy Province of Buenos Aires and the impoverished interior before the national state would consolidate. The year 1862, however, marked the beginning of a new and long era of political stability (a rare phenomenon in Latin America) as well as of unprecedented economic expansion. During the last decades of the nineteenth century Argentina counted among the fastest-growing countries in the world. The fast economic growth was based on three factors: the expansion of the agricultural frontier that allowed for a dramatic increase in the production and exportation of beef and wheat; the importation of foreign (mostly British) capital; and European immigration. By the beginning of the twentieth century Argentina had become the "granary of the world." Between 1862 and 1930 millions of European immigrants arrived in Argentina attracted by the economic opportunities made available by the opening of new lands to production and by the vast program of construction work in urban and transportation infrastructure. While some of those immigrants returned to Europe, a large proportion of them stayed in the country. In 1914, more than half of the male population of the city of Buenos Aires and an even larger proportion of its working class was foreign born. In those years more than 30 percent of the population of the whole country had been born abroad. In terms of proportion to its own native population, around the turn of the twentieth century Argentina received more foreign immigrants than the United States.

The arrival of European immigrants not only was the result of economic prosperity, but also was due to deliberate government policies. The liberal elites who took power after the fall of Rosas took upon themselves the task of modernizing the country in order to bring it to levels of "civilization" comparable to those of Europe. For the Argentine elite civilization meant turning Argentina into an educated, industrious, and disciplined society that in due time would be prepared for a truly participatory and democratic political system. However, in the eyes of the social, political, and intellectual elites, greatly influenced by the pseudoscientific racist theories in fashion in Europe and in the United States at that time, the native population of the country—namely, Indians and mestizo "gauchos" (cowboys)—was a hindrance to the program of modernization. They were perceived as unable to generate a "civil society" like the one Alexis de Tocqueville had admired so much in the United States. According to members of the Argentine elite only a truly European population could create what was foreseen as a European enclave in the Americas. Juan Bautista Alberdi, a nineteenth-century publicist and inspirer of the Argentine constitution, had said, "To govern is to populate," meaning to populate with the "right people"—namely, Europeans and preferably northwestern Europeans. It is not by chance that the constitution of 1853 explicitly mandated the federal government to promote European immigration, a mandate that successive governments duly fulfilled. The history of Argentina since the 1860s through the 1920s was, therefore, a history of economic growth, European immigration (alas, not of the kind the elites had sought, but rather mostly Italians and Spaniards, followed by Eastern European Jews and Middle Easterners), and consolidation of the institutional framework of the national state. All this was promoted by the modernizing program of the ruling class. This bonanza, however, would come to an end in 1930 when the impact of the economic crisis and a pro-fascist coup d'etat led by General José Uriburu opened a long era of political instability combined with growing economic difficulties.

The massive arrival of immigrants might have solved some problems, but in turn it generated many others for the local ruling sectors. Although immigrants provided a necessary labor force, they also changed dramatically the social and cultural landscape of the country, particularly of the city of Buenos Aires, where a large proportion of the newcomers established themselves. The city was growing at a rapid pace, and the new immigrants overburdened its developing but still less than adequate infrastructure. Marginalization gave rise to increasing criminality and other social problems for which the Argentines were not prepared to cope.

Immigrants indeed enriched the culture of the country; however, customs and the vernacular were changing fast as a result of the growing influence of foreigners. These changes took place faster than the conservative sectors were willing to tolerate. Some members of the local economic and intellectual elites, the same sectors that had desperately sought the "civilizing immigrants" in the mid-nineteenth century, started by the first two decades of the twentieth century to see them as a threat. Immigrants were perceived as an economic and social threat because the most successful of them started displacing members of the traditional ruling groups from positions of economic power. Moreover, and perhaps more importantly, the newcomers were also viewed with suspicion because of the new political and social ideas they brought. Since the last decades of the nineteenth century the mostly foreign-born working class started organizing itself in unions, many of which became combative under the influence of Italian and Spanish anarchists. Around 1910, political and social violence, ranging from strikes to the assassination of public officials, followed by harsh repression by the state, became an important feature of Argentine society. In many cases the repression was unleashed before actual episodes of violence would take place. Members of the Argentine elites were victims of a "red paranoia" as early as the 1910s. Finally, some members of the ruling sectors also started seeing immigrants as agents of dissolution of the still-in-the-making national identity.

In order to confront these threats, real or perceived, a whole battery of heterogeneous legislative measures and institutions was set in place, ranging from highly repressive legislation to the creation of a system of public services; from the establishment of "patriotic education" in public schools and obligatory military service to the creation of a public system of psychiatric assistance. The idea behind these measures was to combine in a scientific way repression with integration, nationalization and discipline of the working class. "Scientific" is a key word here because of the deep influence that a set of philosophic and social ideas that proclaimed the triumph of science exercised in the thought of the intellectual elites. This set of ideas is usually referred to as "positivism."

In Argentina, as in neighboring nations, the process of modern state building took place at a time when positivism had become in fact the quasi-official ideology of Latin American elites. According to this ideology, all knowledge must be based in empirical and observable evidence leaving no room for what positivists characterized as "metaphysical speculation," meaning any kind of knowledge not based in observable facts.[2] According to positivists, society was a living and developing organism and not a collection of independent individuals. Therefore, for positivists society could be understood and operated on using the same kind of scientific methods that were appropriate for biological science. The use of biological metaphors for society was widespread. This in part explains the influence of medical doctors in the establishment of social policies and the concomitant process of "medicalization" of social issues, that is to say, the tendency of dealing with them as if they were medical problems.

At the center of those elites' idea of modernity was the reorganization of society to reflect bourgeois rationality. The full realization of this project required the exclusion of those sectors of society perceived as unable to fit into this rationality, meaning Indians, gauchos, and marginals, including people who suffered from mental disorders. Psychiatry and criminology, which developed concomitantly, occupied a central place in this modernizing project precisely because they dealt with marginalized groups, such as criminals and the insane, whose existence was perceived as an unwanted and at the same time threatening consequence of that same modernizing project. Criminality and madness were seen as products of the modern life. It is not by chance, therefore, that it was during the last decades of the nineteenth century when modern psychiatry and the public systems of psychiatric assistance developed in Latin America and especially in Argentina.

Within the field of psychiatry, the influence of positivism explains the popularity of somatic psychiatric theories that looked in the body, as opposed to in the mind, for the origin of psychiatric disorders. Among those theories, the most popular was the one known as "degeneration theory." Originating in mid-nineteenth-century France, this theory was based on the idea that mental and physical disease were passed down from generation to generation, each time in a more severe and more destructive manifestation.[3]

The presence of immigrants added a particular dimension to the idea of degeneration in Argentina. Once perceived as a coveted carrier of civilization, the European immigrant, for the reasons delineated above, came to be perceived by some members of the local elite as a pathogenic agent that would corrupt national values and the "true" Argentine "racial stock." The image of the "crazy immigrant," loaded with "stigmas of degeneration" (physical marks such as flat feet or a particular shape of the ears that, according to the theory, constituted evidence of the presence of degenerative processes), who populated the psychiatric hospitals and the prisons became a central component of the popular imagery. In the last decades of the nineteenth century Argentine naturalist novels

(many of them written by medical doctors) emphasized the importance of maintaining a "healthy Argentine race," meaning free from
foreign influence. The plot of many of those novels developed
around the horrendous consequences produced by the introduction of "unhealthy" (usually Italian) immigration. Immigrants were
portrayed as degenerates who destroyed the "healthy Argentine
racial stock."[4] As Dr. Gonzalo Bosch, longtime director of the
Hospicio de las Mercedes, the public mental hospital for men of
Buenos Aires and one of the most prestigious Argentine psychiatrists, pointed out, "[Juan Bautista] Alberdi would say: 'to govern
is to populate,' a concept typical of his era. Today we would say: to
govern is to select." For a variety of social and cultural reasons,
immigrants indeed constituted a large number of those confined
in psychiatric institutions.[5] Immigration, cultural nationalism, and
the emergent "social question," thus, all contributed to the need
for an apparatus of social reform to be set in place by the Argentine
elites. Hygienism, education, prisons, and a public system of psychiatric assistance were all component parts of this apparatus and
were important elements in the process of modernization and secularization of the Argentine state.[6] As Peruvian historian Augusto
Ruíz Zevallos suggests, the history of psychiatric medicine is an
important aspect for the understanding of the modernizing project of Latin American elites during the late nineteenth century.[7]

The history of psychiatry in Latin America in general and in
Argentina in particular also demonstrates another important cultural dimension: the reception of European social and scientific
ideas. Traditional historiography has considered the history of
ideas in Latin America as one of only secondary interest, since
Latin America has been characterized as an "importer" of ideas.
Only recently historians and other scholars began to pay serious
attention to the particular manner in which ideas are received, filtered by, and incorporated into, different national cultures.[8] This
process of reception and circulation has never been passive and in
fact constitutes a central aspect of the historical development of
ideas and scientific theories. Psychiatry, located at the intellectual

crossroads of medical science, on the one hand, and social and political concerns, on the other, constitutes a particularly rich area for the study of the reception of ideas and theories.[9] The contributions in this volume by Kristin Ruggiero and Julia Rodriguez concentrate on this dimension. The reception and circulation of ideas, however, constitutes only one aspect of the problem. Political instability, a perennial lack of funding, and the very nature of the process of state building in Latin America generated a broad gap between ideas and their actual implementation. Latin American states have in many cases generated bureaucracies more interested in their own self-perpetuation than in fulfilling the mission for which they were created. This issue is discussed in detail in contributions to this book by Jonathan Ablard and Lila Caimari for the case of Argentina.

Psychoanalytic theory based on the ideas proposed by the Viennese doctor, Sigmund Freud, put its emphasis on the unconscious and on the purely "mental"—as opposed to somatic, that is to say, related the body—origin of psychiatric disorders. According to Freud most human behavior originates in unconscious drives (most of them of sexual nature). In Argentina, because of the original emphasis on somatic psychiatry, the reception of psychoanalytic theory as a specific body of knowledge was slow at the beginning, slower than in other Latin American countries such as Brazil or Peru. While since the 1910s, for reasons explored in Mariano Plotkin's chapter in this volume, some prestigious Brazilian psychiatrists had been lecturing and writing on psychoanalysis, in Argentina psychiatrists would only start taking psychoanalysis seriously much later.

The medical reception of psychoanalysis, however, is only part of the history of its diffusion. During the twentieth century psychoanalysis has been more than a psychiatric theory in Western culture. For better or for worse, psychoanalysis has been one of the defining systems of thought in the West during the twentieth century. In spite of new scientific discoveries that may contradict parts or even all of Freud's claims, the fact is that without Freud (as without Marx), the twentieth century would have developed very differently than it did. In H. D. Auden's words, psychoanalysis became "a whole climate of opinion." Therefore, the medical reception of psychoanalysis is only half of the story of the worldwide dissemination of Freud's doctrines. The other half is provided by its diffusion within intellectual circles or broadly in what is usually termed "popular culture."

In the development of the psychoanalytic movement worldwide, it is possible to distinguish two patterns of reception of Freudian thought. Although in most cases the reception of psychoanalysis in each country took place through a combination of both patterns, one of the two usually predominated. One model of reception can be summarized as medical-psychiatric and the other as cultural. In France, for instance, until the 1960s psychoanalysis found a warmer reception in intellectual and artistic circles than in the medical profession. French doctors were reluctant to accept Freudian theory and practice. French psychology and psychiatry were rooted in a strong neurologic tradition, and psychiatrists were not inclined to accept a foreign theory whose creator, to make things worse, was not only a German speaker but also a Jew. On the other hand, literati and artists, from the writer André Gide to the surrealists, embraced psychoanalysis enthusiastically and used it as a source of artistic inspiration.

The alternative model is represented by the United States, where psychoanalysis found its first and most faithful followers among doctors and psychiatrists. Although during the 1920s and 1930s Freudism became an important component in the culture of Greenwich Village's bohemian intellectuals, and in spite of its later popularization by Hollywood, the most important path for the dissemination of psychoanalysis in the United States remained its utilization by doctors as a psychiatric technique and its formal incorporation into the psychiatric establishment. By the 1950s, psychoanalysis had become the central component in the education of psychiatrists in the United States. Psychoanalytically trained psychiatrists came to occupy the most prominent positions in American hospitals and universities. As a survey carried out in the late fifties among American doctors concluded, "The analytically trained psychiatrist is the one who is sought by many university teaching centers, community mental health agencies, and the sophisticated public. This the psychiatric residents know. There is a degree of factual basis in these realities since psychoanalytic theory is concerned with the *how* of mental functioning which provides the spring board for psychotherapy—the psychiatrist's major claim as a specialist."[10]

The Argentine pattern of reception of psychoanalysis has been unique relative to both the European and the United States experience. Until the creation of the Argentina Psychoanalytic Association (APA, hereafter) in 1942 the sectors most receptive to psychoanalysis were found within the medical profession. This does not mean that all or even a large proportion of psychiatrists adopted or even accepted psychoanalysis (although a few did), but only that psychoanalysis was discussed (for and against) mostly by doctors, as a medical specialty. Moreover, since the late 1920s psychoanalysis also had an impact on what is usually considered "popular culture": popular publications, magazines, and books for the general public.[11] Only in the 1930s did intellectual, nonmedical circles start to show interest in Freudism, while an increasing number of doctors also became interested in the discipline. Moreover, during the first few years of APA's existence, its founders, most of them holders of medical degrees, made efforts to insert psychoanalysis into the medical profession. Therefore in this respect, the early model of Argentine reception of psychoanalysis was superficially similar to the American model, except that in Argentina it occupied a much more marginal position among psychiatric theories than it did in the United States. Nevertheless, the competing somatic psychiatric theories continued to be predominant among Argentine psychiatrists for a long time. Moreover, unlike in the United States, since the 1940s the professional identity of psychoanalysts and psychiatrists developed in divergent paths. This was due to political and professional reasons discussed by Mariano Plotkin in his contribution to this volume.

In Argentina, psychoanalysts saw themselves as carriers of a modern form of knowledge that developed against the grain of the traditional somatic psychiatry practiced by the members of the psychiatric establishment. At the same time large numbers of psychiatrists opposed the use of psychoanalysis on the grounds that it was quackery and (for the most conservatives members of the psychiatric profession) subversive. Only in 1960s and 1970s and then again in the late 1980s did psychiatry and psychoanalysis converge again. In those years some progressive sectors of the psychiatric establishment were instrumental in the diffusion of psychoanalysis. By contrast, from the 1950s, psychoanalysis has occupied a central place in Argentine culture. Like in France, therefore, since the 1950s psychoanalysis became in Argentina a cultural artifact rather than a therapeutic technique.

Between 1976 and 1983 Argentina was ruled by a murderous military dictatorship. In the eyes of the generals in power any discipline or social theory that questioned "traditional values" was considered "subversive." This was true not only for Marxism but also for anthropology, sociology, and psychology in general. The case of psychoanalysis was, however, more complicated. The military regime concentrated their rage on those doctors (psychoanalysts or general psychiatrists) who had either been members of leftist political organizations, or who had participated in progressive psychiatric experiments such as "therapeutic communities," democratic communities for mental patients where the traditional hierarchy of doctors, nurses, and patients was eliminated. In spite of their British and American origins, these communities had a "communist flavor" in the eyes of the generals. At the same time, the antipsychoanalytic rhetoric of some military officers notwithstanding (one general characterized Marx and Freud as "intellectual criminals"), the psychoanalytic establishment incarnated by the APA was left unmolested. It could be said that in fact the military appropriated and used some ideas and notions originating in the conservative sectors of the psychoanalytic community in order to construct parts of their own discourse on society and to maintain the current social order. This is explored in the last part of this book by Mariano Plotkin and Hugo Vezzetti.

This volume is not narrowly focused only on Argentine history; it also seeks to offer new insights on the field of history of psychiatry and of psychoanalysis, a particularly underdeveloped area of study in Latin America. During the last three decades the history of psychiatry has developed as one of the most controversial and attention-attracting fields of historiography in Europe and in the United States. In recent years the history of psychiatry has not only generated agitated debates but also spilled over into other fields. Disputes over the rise and fall and, in general, the nature of the psychiatric asylum, the role of psychiatry as a mechanism for social and gender control, the merits of certain kinds of therapies over others and, in particular, controversies over the value of psychoanalysis, have had political, social, and cultural resonance.[12] Today, the history of psychiatry is conceptually linked to political, cultural, gender, professional, and institutional history. Although the politicization and diffusion of the history of psychiatry has taken place in the last few decades, particularly since the late 1960s, the history of psychiatry had attracted the attention of students from much earlier in the twentieth century. Important histories of psychiatry were written from the 1930s through the 1950s, providing the foundation for this emerging historiographic field.[13]

In the politically radicalized environment of the 1960s and 1970s, the early historiography of psychiatry, which emphasized the positive advances of psychiatric thought as a continuous line going from barbarism to humane science, was harshly criticized by the active academic and political left. During those decades the influence of seminal books, such as Michel Foucault's *Madness and Civilization* (1961) and Erving Goffman's *Asylum* (1961), led to the publication of influential critical works on the history of psychiatry.[14] Concomitantly, the development particularly in England and France of the politicized antipsychiatric movement, which postulated that any form of psychiatric treatment was nothing but a form of bourgeois oppression, also contributed to shape the historiography of psychiatry. The radicalized cultural environment of those decades and the common characterization of psychiatry as an instrument of social control, in a period when "liberation" (sexual, social, and political) became a key word for progressive intellectuals and militants, generated a wave of historical and theoretical works that were critical of psychiatry.[15] Most of those works, written by people who did not belong to the psychiatric profession, shared a skepticism toward the "official history of psychiatry." Many of them also shared with the antipsychiatric movement the assumption that mental diseases were essentially social and political constructions rather than disorders of somatic origin. The cause of mental diseases was thus located in society and outside of the psychiatric patient, who was perceived as a mere victim of oppressive social forces.

In those years influential leftist intellectuals, particularly in France, began to include psychoanalysis (or at least their own interpretation of it) among their analytic tools. According to French philosopher Jean-Paul Sartre, for instance, psychoanalysis could fill Marxism's blind spot by providing a theory of subjectivity. From a different perspective Marxist philosopher Louis Althusser emphasized the revolutionary potential of psychoanalysis as the science of the unconscious and of desire. The most radical leftists wanted to use psychoanalysis as an instrument for revolution by emphasizing its liberating potential. Incidentally, this perception of psychoanalysis was very popular in Argentina among politically progressive analysts. In 1971, for instance, a group of leftist analysts split from the APA, which they perceived as a conservative institution, and tried to put the discipline at the service of revolution.

Since the 1980s a "new revisionist" history of psychiatry started to emerge in part as a critical reaction to the politicization and "ideologization" of the field during the previous decades. This "new revisionism" has been deeply influenced by developments in psychiatry itself, in particular by the sharp decline in the popularity of psychoanalysis among some powerful intellectual and professional circles, as well as by the dramatic development of the neurosciences and of a new generation of psychiatric drugs. These new developments in psychiatry and the emergence of a new and more conservative ideological environment, particularly in the United States and England, led some students to revise preexisting assumptions. If in the previous decades somatic therapies (meaning those therapies that operated on the *body*, and not on the *mind* of the patient) had been considered mere instruments for social domination and oppression, in the new context they are seen by revisionist scholars in a different and more positive light.[16] Furthermore, psychoanalysis, once considered the crowning achievement of a long line of psychiatric development, is now perceived by some students as a dark parenthesis in the evolution of the discipline.[17] As it has been noted, however, the history of psychiatry is probably the subfield of the history of science in which consensus among scholars is the weakest and which generates some of the most heated debates.[18] Some of those debates, however, are more political than academic.

The history of psychoanalysis is a historiographic field in itself and can be separated from the history of psychiatry to some degree. During many decades, and starting with Freud's own writings, the history of psychoanalysis was virtually indistinguishable from the biography of its creator. Moreover, for Freud and his orthodox followers, the history of psychoanalysis is a history of the discipline's isolation, of the analyst's struggle against resistances put up by society to psychoanalysis, and of scientific heresy.[19] As the British historian John Forrester points out, "The rational reconstruction of [psychoanalytic] concepts and the personal narrative of Freud's experience as a therapist . . . are entwined."[20] But, we could ask, is it only through the biography (or the autobiography, we could say) of its creator that we can reconstruct the history of psychoanalysis? The hagiographic historiography of Freudians has provoked in recent years an "anti-Freudian" historiography in which Freud is also the center of the analysis but where his theories and practice (and sometimes him personally) are harshly criticized.[21] However, there seem to be other, perhaps more fruitful, ways to approach the history of psychoanalysis than writing new biographies of Freud.

Whereas both the orthodox history of psychoanalysis and the critical works of its detractors have placed an emphasis on the originality of Freud's thought (or, alternatively, on the total lack of it), a group of historians who could be characterized as "contextualists" have been focusing their analysis on the cultural, social, and political conditions that made possible the appearance of psychoanalysis in late-nineteenth-century Vienna.[22] The emergence of psychoanalysis, according to this version, was not the brainchild of a single isolated genius working alone, but rather was the result of a complex set of cultural, political, and social factors in a particular historical setting. Moreover, other students of the subject, such as Henri Ellemberger, have placed psychoanalysis in the broader context of other psycho-dynamic systems of psychiatric thought that were emerging in Europe at that time and that also placed an emphasis on the importance of the unconscious dimensions of the human psyche.[23] However, an analysis focused on psychoanalysis's Viennese origins would shed light on only one half of this history. The other half of the story needs to be traced outward as psychoanalysis was broadly disseminated through different countries and cultures, each quite different from nineteenth-century Vienna. A new historiography that focuses on the emergence of "national" psychoanalytic cultures started to emerge only in recent years.[24] It is clear, therefore, that a history of psychoanalysis cannot be limited to the history of Freud's circle and his followers. The analysis of different "psychoanalytic cultures" is as central an aspect of the history of psychoanalysis as the history of its concepts.[25]

In Latin America (and Argentina is no exception to the region's pattern) the history of psychiatry and psychoanalysis is still in its infancy. Only tenuous echoes of the debates that have agitated European and U.S. scholars in this field have been heard in the region. From Mexico to Peru, from Brazil to Argentina, the national histories of psychiatry or, more recently, of psychoanalysis, consist primarily of celebratory chronicles written by practicing psychiatrists and psychoanalysts who demonstrate little awareness of the historical method or of debates taking place elsewhere.[26] Although some of these histories are based on serious research, most of them are little more than a "hall of fame" for prominent psychiatrists in each country. Only since the late 1980s in the broader context of a still incipient renovation of studies in the history of science in Latin America have new works appeared that take into consideration cultural, political, and social developments.[27] This timing was not a mere coincidence. After decades of bloody military dictatorships, in the early 1980s democracy started gradually to reemerge in Latin America. The decline and eventual collapse of the military regimes encouraged Latin

American intellectuals to reexamine their nations' histories, particularly the history of the institutions they viewed as allied with the oppressors. New works on gender relations, sexuality, and prisons began to appear in the last two decades in this new environment of intellectual freedom. Encouraged by these political changes, the work of these critical intellectuals is slowly bearing fruit.

In spite of having the largest number of psychiatrists in Latin America and one of the largest communities of psychoanalysts in the world, Argentina, like the rest of Latin America, has not generated a rich historiography on psychiatry and psychoanalysis.[28] Hugo Vezzetti's book of 1983, *La locura en la Argentina*, strongly influenced by the work of Michel Foucault, is still the only book-length study of the history of psychiatry in Argentina that pays attention to the cultural dimension of the evolution of the discipline.[29] Only in recent years have new groups of young researchers emerged with an interest in the social, political, economic, and cultural aspects of the history of psychiatry. It is to be hoped that in due time they will generate new works to supplement Vezzetti's important early contribution.

Similarly, the history of psychoanalysis in Argentina received virtually no attention until the 1980s.[30] Only in the last few years have scholars outside the psychoanalytic institutions shown interest in the reception and later evolution of psychoanalysis in Argentina as historical subjects deserving consideration. This volume constitutes an effort in the direction of building a national history of psychiatry and psychoanalysis in a Latin American country.

The six chapters that compose this book are organized into three parts that each address different yet complementary aspects of the history of psychiatry in Argentina. Part I, "Degeneration, Gender, and the Construction of a Psychiatric Discourse," concentrates on the beginnings of a scientific discourse on mental disorders that emerged toward the end of the nineteenth century as a consequence of the process of rapid modernization undergone by Argentina. Julia Rodriguez's "The Argentine Hysteric: A Turn-of-the-Century Psychiatric Type" discusses the construction of a psychiatric discourse on gender by Argentine doctors and criminologists. This discourse was ambiguous in its results because it was exploited for competing progressive and conservative causes. Some progressive psychiatrists, opposing conservative Catholic ideology, promoted the idea that sexual satisfaction was a crucial dimension in women's lives. At the same time, by anchoring femininity in biology, these same doctors reinforced traditional determinist notions that claimed that nothing that women did could transcend their biology. Rodriguez also argues that in Argentina this debate concerning women's sexuality, and particularly the discussions on hysteria, constituted a fundamental factor in the process of professionalization of psychiatry as a distinctive medical specialty just as it had done earlier in Europe.

Focusing her analysis roughly on the same period as Rodriguez, Kristin Ruggiero's contribution, "Sexual Aberration, Degeneration, and Psychiatry in Late-Nineteenth-Century Buenos Aires," discusses the convergence of psychiatry and criminology in the last decades of the nineteenth century, and the reception of European theories by Argentine doctors and jurists. Ruggiero explores the tensions originating between new positivist views and older traditions in psychiatric and criminological thought, discussing them within the broader context of the relationship between science and the construction of the modern state. The chapter focuses on the case of Luis Castruccio, an Italian immigrant convicted of murder. The case attracted the attention of the most prominent Argentine psychiatrists and criminologists of the time, including José Ingenieros. Like a large proportion of the male population living in Buenos Aires at that time, Castruccio was an Italian immigrant. In line with the theories current in those years, the central point that the lawyers, psychiatrists, and criminologists involved in the case were trying to establish was to what extent Castruccio was a "degenerate," that is, someone who had a congenital predisposition to insanity and crime. The judge's determination of the "level of degeneracy" of a convict was an essential factor in deciding what, if any, punishment should be imposed. In Castruccio's case, one piece of evidence of his possible degenerate state was his alleged devotion to masturbation. What the experts who examined him tried to elucidate was if this practice could be considered as a sign of his degeneracy. In the liberal elites' project of modernization, the control of sexuality occupied an important place. Masturbation in particular was considered a vicious habit that wasted precious energy for no useful purpose other than providing depraved pleasure of those who practice it. Ruggiero uses the case as a window through which these larger themes can be examined. As Ruggiero shows, important issues such as the concept of criminal punishment itself, the social elite's attempts to control sexual impulses of the popular sectors, the increasing professionalization of the medical community and its claims for a place in the state, and even national pride were involved as well in the discussions generated by Castruccio's case.

Part II, "Psychiatric Hospitals, Prisons, and the State," includes essays by Jonathan Ablard and Lila Caimari, who elaborate from a different perspective two of the issues introduced in Part I: the forensic use of psychiatry, and the actual implementation of psychiatric theories. While Ruggiero and Rodriguez focus their discussion on the reception of ideas and on the production of discourses, Ablard and Caimari discuss the limits posed by reality to the actual implementation of some of those ideas. Using for the first time previously unavailable primary sources (archives of mental hospitals and the archive of the Institute of Criminological Classification of the Province of Buenos Aires) these authors break new ground in the analysis of the development of the Argentine state.

Ablard's "Law, Medicine, and Confinement to Public Psychiatric Hospitals in Twentieth-Century Argentina" is a study of how inefficiencies in the Argentine legal, bureaucratic, and psychiatric systems seriously compromised the legal rights of psychiatric patients. Although the need for a "scientific reform" of prisons and mental hospitals was an obsession for the Argentine elite at the turn of the twentieth century, and in spite of the proliferation of discourses and plans promoted by progressive politicians and doctors, people committed to mental hospitals by the public force (that is, the police) typically spent years there until their cases were decided or even heard by a competent judge as mandated by the law. This situation often promoted tensions between doctors and lawyers.

Whereas Ruggiero and Rodriguez place an emphasis on the processes of modernization of the Argentine state and of professionalization of psychiatry, Ablard focuses his analysis on the limits of both modernization and professionalization. As Ablard suggests, the fate of Argentine psychiatric patients reflects the limits of social control in a weak state. After discussing the origins of the Argentine system of public psychiatric assistance, Ablard analyzes the divergences between the letter of the law regarding forced commitments and the actual practice of those commitments.

Lila Caimari's "Psychiatrists, Criminals, and Bureaucrats: The Production of Scientific Biographies in the Argentine Penitentiary System (1907–1945)" offers an analysis of the tensions existing between scientists and state bureaucrats in the implementation of psychiatric and criminological theories. Scientists (doctors, psychiatrists, and criminologists) were at the center of the Argentine reformist elite of the turn of the twentieth century and occupied important official positions. José Ingenieros, for instance, was not only a reputed psychiatrist and criminologist, but also the director of the Institute of Criminology of the National Penitentiary and the chief editor of the prestigious journal *Archivos de Psiquiatría, Criminología y Ciencias Afines.*

The implementation of the experts' ideas, however, was mediated by the needs of an expanding state bureaucracy. Caimari analyzes the transformation undergone by the classificatory system of criminals proposed by Ingenieros and others. Those systems originally emphasized the psycho-pathological aspects of criminality. Ingenieros, for instance, argued that those degenerates who also suffered from psychiatric disorders (which for Ingenieros could only have somatic origins) were prone to become criminals. This biologic determinism, however, did not fit into the reformist discourse promoted by officials of the penitentiary system. "Scientific" plans for the reform of prisons presupposed the notion that criminals could be reformed. If criminality was biologically determined, then there was little room left for the reform of criminals and therefore for the scientific reform of prisons. Therefore officials in charge of applying the system of classifications placed particular emphasis on the social and economic environment as central factors for the emergence of criminal behavior. Psychiatrists, criminologists, and prison officials shared the same passion for the classification of criminals but had different interests at stake.

Finally Part III, "Argentines on the Couch," studies two aspects of the complex problem of emergence and development of a psychoanalytic culture in Argentina. The dissemination of psychoanalysis in Argentine culture cannot be fully understood without taking into consideration the role played by certain individuals who became the real "diffusers" of psychoanalytic thought. In general, those people were psychoanalysts active in different areas of culture and in the media and who enjoyed high levels of social visibility. Hugo Vezzetti's "From the Psychiatric Hospital to the Street: Enrique Pichon Rivière and the Diffusion of Psychoanalysis in Argentina" focuses on the man who was the most successful and influential of those "diffusers": Dr. Enrique Pichon Rivière. Better than anyone else, he incarnated the peculiar Argentine pattern of diffusion of psychoanalysis. Although Pichon Rivière was a psychiatrist and a psychoanalyst, he was better known for his idiosyncratic uses of Freudism and for his attempts at "taking psychoanalysis to the streets" through his unorthodox experiments. Moreover, Pichon Rivière was well connected with the avant-garde artistic community of Buenos Aires and was therefore instrumental in articulating three levels of reception and diffusion of psychoanalysis in Argentina: a popular one, a psychiatric-medical one, and one linked to intellectual circles.

Mariano Plotkin's "Psychiatrists and the Reception of Psychoanalysis, 1910s–1970s" discusses the sinuous relationship between psychiatry and psychoanalysis in Argentina from the early reception of the Freudian system by Argentine doctors, through the dictatorship that ruled the country between 1976 and 1983. Although in Argentina psychoanalysis never occupied the central place in the psychiatric establishment that it did in the United States, the public system of psychiatric assistance played in several moments a central role in the social diffusion of the discipline. The relationship between psychiatry and psychoanalysis was mediated in Argentina by a complex set of political and cultural factors that are discussed in Plotkin's chapter.

The chapters included in this volume offer a multidimensional approach to the history of psychiatry and psychoanalysis in Argentina, a country in which both disciplines developed in a unique way. The chapters provide an insight into broader developments in Argentine society and culture and into the process of state building in Argentina. Furthermore, the contributions generate a fresh discussion on a generally overlooked topic: the history of psychiatry in Latin America. The contributors hope that in the near future this book will be a point of departure for comparative works on the history of psychiatry in other Latin American countries.

part one

Degeneration, Gender,
and the Construction of
a Psychiatric Discourse

Chapter One

THE ARGENTINE HYSTERIC

A Turn-of-the-Century Psychiatric Type

Julia E. Rodriguez

In the first years of their practice, doctors in the Clinical Observation Room of the Buenos Aires city police received, studied, and treated dozens of mentally disturbed individuals.[1] José Ingenieros, one of the city's leading physicians and later director of the Observation Service, examined one such case, a suicidal young woman brought to the clinic by her distraught husband. Writing up the case in the 1910 volume of Argentina's main psychiatric journal, the *Archivos de Psiquiatría y Criminología* (Archives of Psychiatry and Criminology), Ingenieros recounted how he discovered what he believed to be the root cause of her mental disturbance: "The young woman . . . confessed that during two years of marriage she had not once experienced any sexual feelings."[2] This sorry state of affairs, according to Ingenieros, was the result of her "complete sexual ignorance," which in turn resulted from her repulsion at the sexual act. This also made her feel "inferior for conjugal life." According to the patient herself, these feelings led her to attempt suicide. She claimed she would rather die than be abandoned by or humiliated in front of her husband. The young woman's pathology was doubly disturbing to Ingenieros: not only was his patient suffering terribly, but also she was unable to fulfill her biological destiny due to her lack of sexual knowledge. Ingenieros recommended that the husband pay closer attention to his wife during the sexual act, allowing her to build up "sexual emotion." After just a few weeks, the doctor noted with satisfaction, "this simple sexual education permitted the reconstitution of a home" that had been about to collapse.[3]

The messages implicit in Ingenieros's diagnosis are surprising and contradictory. On the one hand, he exhibited an open-minded, even liberationist, attitude toward women as sexual beings. This approach was extremely unusual in a time characterized by a cultural double standard in which men were permitted to be sexually active and women were not. Although some thinkers at the turn of the century, such as Ingenieros, who fancied themselves modern and progressive, were starting to offer alternate interpretations of private behavior—new ideas solidly informed by the evolutionary theories favored by the young generation of scientists—most people rejected the application of those ideas to the sexual behavior of women. In this sense, Ingenieros could be seen as an advocate for forward-thinking sexual ideology. On the other hand, Ingenieros seemed to reduce his patient's mental suffering to her sexuality, her inability to fulfill successfully her sexual obligations to her husband. At the turn of the century, these mixed messages were also found in numerous clinical studies and published medical research on "women's diseases."

Of the reported cases of female mental pathology, the most numerous involved hysteria, which doctors (and others) believed was a commonplace women's affliction. Although hysteria in men was occasionally discussed, it was usually in the context of military performance.[4] Hysteria was a common subject of scientific and medical study in Europe, especially in France from the mid-nineteenth century. This condition seemed to capture the presumed strong links between mind and body, raising implications about will, suggestibility, and responsibility. Argentine psychiatrists, like their European counterparts, actively contributed to studies of hysteria.[5] As was true in Europe, Argentine psychiatrists professionalized their discipline, applying new scientific methods to the diagnosis and classification of patients.[6] Psychiatrists used studies of hysteria to legitimate and build their nascent medical specialization. The apparently large number of afflicted women and the assumed frequent occurrence of this disorder provided the basis for much of early psychiatric research, allowing members of this profession to distinguish themselves in the research community. Yet one of the fundamental assumptions that framed Argentine research and publications on hysteria was the belief that hysteria was "epidemic" in nature and experienced almost exclusively by women.

In this chapter, I explore the gendered theories of hysteria developed by psychiatrists at a time of great social and political transformation in Argentina.[7] I focus primarily on the major medical publications dealing with hysteria, particularly the scientific journal *Archivos de Psiquiatría y Criminología* (*Archivos*, hereafter), which between 1902 and 1913 regularly assessed cases of female psychosexual pathology, including hysteria.[8] This journal represented Argentine professionals' first significant effort to publish scientific articles in the fields of psychiatry, criminology, and legal medicine. A number of prominent scientists writing for or editing the *Archivos* (such as José Ingenieros and his teacher, José María Ramos Mejía) conducted sustained studies of hysterical patients and published their observations and analyses of these cases. These books, widely read in medical and scientific circles, provide additional material on hysteria for this chapter.[9]

Based on the medical theories analyzed here, I argue that diagnosis of hysteria in Argentine patients was characterized by culturally bound symptoms specific to that moment and to the society's larger gender assumptions. Ideas about hysteria relied not just on imported European theories but also on local assumptions about gender difference and doctors' responses to the nation's seemingly rapid ascent to modernity, with all the social pathologies that implied. I also demonstrate how Argentine psychiatrists, enjoying a growing legitimacy, contributed to changing prevailing legal discourse about women's status. While the study of hysteria helped them to promote and advance the "progressive" and "scientific" study of women's disorders, psychiatrists also—wittingly or unwittingly—helped to reinforce traditional expectations of women's behavior and capabilities.

Psychiatry and Argentine Modernity

Psychiatry in Argentina developed in the context of a society rocked by three interlocking transformations in the late nineteenth century: the explosive growth of the export economy; the subsequent expansion of urban centers and modernization; and the rapidly expanding immigrant population. On the crest of this wave of changes, a new generation of political liberals had come into power, committed to rebuilding the state and society on modern, rational grounds. The rising number of observed mental disturbances and the related phenomenon of rising crime rates appeared to be linked to the arrival of huge numbers of immigrants and to the resulting urban overcrowding and political and labor unrest. Many Argentines arrived at the dismal conclusion that mental illness and social decay or "degeneration" were somehow bound to their nation's progress.[10]

Framing the emergence of crime and mental illness as social issues was Argentina's so-called great leap forward. Measuring itself against other immigrant countries like the United States and Australia, Argentines in the late nineteenth century saw hopeful signs that they too were on the track to become an urban, industrial society.[11] The nation's unprecedented prosperity and growth was largely based on the exploitation of agricultural riches such as cattle and wheat. Foreign investment, mostly British, the construction of railroads to transport beef, and the arrival of masses of cheap immigrant laborers transformed Argentina into one of the world's foremost exporting countries. After 1880, the gross national product increased by about 6 percent per year, comparable to the most advanced industrial countries of the era. Per capita income in this period was at times higher than that in Spain, Italy, Sweden, and Switzerland and equal to that of Germany and Holland.[12] Social indicators of development such as dropping illiteracy rates and rising consumer activity confirmed the trend.

Not surprisingly, the Argentine state experienced a parallel process of stress that led to a wholesale political reorganization. By 1880, decades of civil wars and political power struggles between conservatives and liberals appeared to be resolved by political compromise in favor of the unification camp that eventually oversaw the federalization of the city of Buenos Aires, thus ending an old conflict between the national state and the Province of Buenos Aires. That accomplished, the political leadership of the late nineteenth century promoted the nation's material progress as the solution to all of its problems. The victorious liberal leaders proposed a series of social and political reforms, such as representational government, mild secularization, the protection of civil liberties, and educational improvements. Known as the "oligarchy," these new leaders fatefully married a liberal ideal of national progress to an economic system based around foreign capital, great landowners, and wealthy merchants.

The presidency of Julio A. Roca, who governed Argentina from 1880 to 1886, ushered in this oligarchic era. Roca developed his policies in close cooperation with liberal intellectuals from the Generation of 1880. He welcomed foreign capital and European immigration and eliminated Indians from the interior of the country, adhering to the program of material progress laid down by European and North American models. Yet many liberal leaders also privileged secularization, modernization, and "progress" in contrast to all that their country seemed to represent: backwardness, provincialism, and Catholicism. The ranks of this progressivist movement included public figures of all professions, who, united in their confidence, were certain that out of science and reason they could "make a great nation."[13]

The new discipline of psychiatry intervened in this national advancement project by helping to smooth the sometimes rocky path to modernization. According to many commentators at the time, modernity and urbanization had brought a host of disturbing behaviors to Argentina. The streets and other public places appeared to teem with disturbed individuals and dangerous crowds. Psychiatry, as well as its related field of criminology, appeared to provide the tools to minimize some of these unsightly blemishes on the social body. Psychiatrists and their supporters believed that bolstered by the tools of modern medicine, they could fight the pathologies of the time, much as advances in public health permitted the control of many rampant diseases a generation earlier.

After 1900, psychiatric studies of the Argentine population proliferated as doctors found new outlets, such as the *Archivos*, for their experiments and observations. These early psychiatrists enjoyed increasing resources and found a growing audience thanks to the rising status and influence of the medical and biological sciences. Along with the rapid and seemingly successful entrance of Argentina into modernity, scientific circles in late-nineteenth-century Buenos Aires experienced an explosion in their production and influence. In the last three decades of the century, previously vague approaches to the natural world began to coalesce, consolidate, and in some cases develop into full-blown scientific disciplines complete with professional organizations, research institutes, university chairs, and peer-reviewed journals. Scientists and medical doctors had enjoyed great prestige and social status for some time, but with Argentina's embrace of its role as a growing industrial economy and "cultural capital," science took on even greater importance because of its supposed ability to facilitate progress.[14]

Modern psychiatry emerged in Argentina in the last decades of the nineteenth century, promoted by a variety of popular European ideas, including positivism, evolutionary theory, and anthropometrics.[15] After 1870 most Argentine scientists embraced positivism, a transatlantic ideology that advocated "scientific" approaches to social as well as natural problems. This ideology fit the liberal, secular, and progressive worldview of most Argentine scientists who wished for a comprehensive solution to the myriad challenges facing their rapidly modernizing nation. Leading Argentine intellectuals were equally influenced by evolutionary theory. As early as the 1870s, Argentine scientists began subscribing to the idea that the study of "man" rested above all on the development of evolutionary theory and on the positivist sciences of the period.[16] Finally, anthropometrics, or the method of measuring the human body to reveal character or behavioral traits, influenced early theories of mind as well. Although propagated by a great number of European scientists in different disciplines, it was the Italian criminologist Cesare Lombroso who elaborated anthropometrics most famously as a means of identifying deviant individuals. In the words of one supporter, Lombroso forwarded the idea that "the criminal was knowable, measurable and predictable, largely on the basis of cranial, facial and bodily measurements."[17] In addition to physical stigma, Lombroso "found" in the criminal sensory and functional peculiarities, a lack of "moral sense," and other "asocial" manifestations, such as tattooing and the use of slang.

Like European and North American alienism at the time, early Argentine psychiatry favored a characteristically eclectic methodology that drew on many European schools of thought and often overlapped with hygiene, psychology, biology, and criminology. One striking feature of the new approach was its somaticism, the locating of mental pathology in the body, which persisted well into the twentieth century.[18] Studies of hysteria largely followed the research of renowned French neurologist J. M. Charcot, who used symptomological mapping of the disorder and included the recognition of bodily stigmata and the location of sensitive zones.[19]

The then-fashionable emphasis on science in Argentina, and the seeming authority of somaticism or body evidence, resulted in the medicalization of mental illness and its treatment in mental asylums in the 1870s.[20] In the newly professionalized mental institutions, positivist doctors rationalized treatment and gathered statistics of mental illnesses for the first time.[21] Along with the related new disciplines of criminology and legal medicine, psychiatry earned a place in the university. The first chair of clinical psychiatry, Lucio Meléndez, was appointed in 1886 and joined a faculty that included positions in psychology and neurology. Despite, or perhaps because of, Argentina's perceived peripheral status (as compared to Europe and the United States), the nation's psychiatrists strove to make their discipline blossom into one of the nation's most dynamic sciences.[22]

As their profession evolved and entrenched itself in universities and hospitals, psychiatrists, often in the role of professorship in a related field or a government position, undertook an increasingly active role in state affairs. They consolidated their efforts to build new mental hospitals, university departments, and offices in the police and court systems. They benefited from a growing awareness that the study, control, and containment of mental disturbances were vital to the "progress" of the nation and the "civilization" of the cities. Psychiatry was important not just as a potential new feather in the scientific cap of the rapidly developing nation; it was also important because its influence could contribute to the national discourse, defining normative behavior and pathology in a changing society. The most notable Argentine psychiatrists in this period, such as Ingenieros, were not just ivory-tower researchers but also activists in legal and state institutions. They informed state attempts to control behavior disturbing to the social order, weighing in on new courtroom procedures, legislation, policing, and prison and asylum discipline. The main contribution of psychiatrists in the first years of the twentieth century was to provide the framework for new guidelines and procedures by which mental pathology could be eliminated from the emerging modern nation, helping to civilize it in the face of great social upheaval. As is perhaps to be expected, men were the primary target of this broad project, since as a group, men were perceived as far more likely to create public disturbances, to threaten public welfare with violence, even to conspire criminally against the state. Moreover, if men abandoned their civic responsibilities because of mental illness, they might be more likely than women to disrupt the smooth functioning of society. Yet while psychiatrists played straightforward roles in policing the male citizen and his behavior, they also took a parallel interest in women, even though women did not enjoy the same status as men in the eyes of the law.

Emerging professional scientists did not develop their theories of individual pathology and responsibility in a vacuum. Rather, they were engaged in a dialogue not just with the effects of modernity but also with the new social movements associated with it, above all an emerging feminism.[23] Despite a new awareness of feminism in the last years of the nineteenth century, gender roles in Argentina remained fairly rigid. This was typical for a patriarchal society where men were the official heads of family. In addition to being the sole breadwinner, they (in theory) made all decisions at home as well as in the public sphere. Men were also responsible for the direction of political life, such as voting. Women were legally excluded from this participation. Women, however, were expected to bear and feed children and care for their husbands.[24] Their participation in the workforce was problematic; their political action was uncommon and suspect. Above all, nearly all political factions in Argentina agreed on the primary importance of mothering. Even most feminists of this period, struggling to attain more rights in and outside the family, hesitated to relinquish the special status attributed to women through motherhood.[25]

Some of the most prominent figures studying female deviance, like José Ingenieros, were social progressives who favored socialist and feminist reforms. Staunch secularists, they opposed the Catholic Church's domination of marriage and family life. Some even supported the right to divorce, still forbidden in Argentina, arguing that a healthy family could only exist if husband and wife were happy with each other.[26] Yet conservatives and progressives alike shared the same goal, bolstering the family as the basis of a strong society. They believed that crime and mental illness, whether exhibited by men or women, threatened to destroy this fundamental social unit. Even progressive scientists imbued this seemingly personal, individual problem with significance for the health of the greater society. One scholar wrote, "The question of divorce is not only of interest to the couple for whom a common life is impossible: it also pertains to their families, friends, relatives, and has repercussions on the customs of the whole society."[27]

It was the concern for women as mothers or potential mothers and as the anchors of the family that best accounts for the sheer numbers of studies about female mental illness. This preoccupation with maternal roles shaped early psychiatric studies in three important ways. First, in examining the psychic states of women, doctors attributed primary importance to women's bodies, especially their reproductive organs. In this sense, mental pathology seemed to arise from women's bodies, as much as from their minds. In some cases, a patient's reproductive organs even seemed to determine her mental functions. Second, psychiatrists often characterized female hysterics as highly sexualized, again a condition exhibited in the patient's bodily condition.[28] This sexualization ostensibly threatened what psychiatrists considered women's "natural state": marriage and motherhood. Finally, women's seeming vulnerability to their potentially pathological reproductive bodies provided evidence of their unfitness for public life.[29]

This era was also marked by an increasing surveillance of the private sphere, seen by most as the women's realm, by the state and its representatives. Psychiatrists' studies of hysteria provided an entranceway into the lives of women. For example, in the case mentioned at the beginning of this chapter, a suicidal woman consulted with a doctor at the mental health clinic of the city police—that is, with a state official—about an intensely private domestic matter. He was concerned with her individual health, but he also feared that her disease threatened the "natural order" of the domestic, reproductive family unit. In this case and many others, the doctor's intervention in the patient's problem was understood as necessary to heal a breach in the social fabric, not just to alleviate her individual suffering.

Inventing the Hysterical Subject

The psychiatric study and treatment of hysteria was important because it filled a specific gap in the state's desire to survey, assess, and police its citizens' behavior. As a seemingly definable set of symptoms, hysteria captured the attention of Argentina's most prominent medical doctors at the time, including José Ingenieros, José María Ramos Mejía, and Francisco de Veyga. Echoing the strong European interest in hysteria after 1870, but conducting research on their own local subjects, Argentine doctors wrote and distributed numerous books, articles, and doctoral theses on the topic.

According to Argentine psychiatrists at the turn of the century, hysteria was widespread, even "epidemic," in nature but exhibited almost exclusively by women. The disorder, they believed, was preeminently a diagnosis of their nation's modernity—a common side effect of modern urban stresses, which especially affected the delicate nerves of women. In explaining why women were more likely to suffer from hysteria, despite their—compared to men— infrequent exposure to "traumatic" social situations, one researcher pointed out as early as 1891 that, "Hysteria and its paralysis . . . tend to manifest themselves generally in weak, exhausted individuals or those consumed by excess or vices."[30]

So intimately related were the topics of modernity, women, and hysteria that some theorists identified urban women in particular as the most susceptible to the condition and described its presence in Buenos Aires in epidemic terms. One author wrote in 1888, "Half of all women are hysterics, and in Buenos Aires, our professor of nervous diseases [prominent neurologist Dr. Ramos Mejía], believes the number is even higher."[31] Hysteria became so popular a diagnosis that this psychiatrist, writing in a major medical journal, actually suggested that it was but "one of the varieties of a woman's character."[32] If anything, twentieth-century stresses seemed to make the situation worse. Hysteria, like crime and other disturbing social phenomena, seemed to be increasing with urbanization and the march of progress. One author wrote in 1909, "Our country does not escape the general rule: statistics demonstrate a progressive increase in mental illness in all the civilized countries."[33]

Putting such extreme views aside, I argue here that psychiatric studies of hysteria were a conscientious attempt to understand a set of symptoms confronting a new class of professional psychiatrists. By the turn of the century, the diagnosis of hysteria was in fact part of a much more systematic approach to the problems of modern womanhood. The first clinical studies of hysteria appeared in the early 1900s, largely the result of the work of a small group of physicians, neurologists, and nascent criminologists. The key figure in this new research was José Ingenieros, medical *Wunderkind* of turn-of-the-century Buenos Aires. Trained as a medical doctor, he was one of the leading neurologists, psychiatrists, and criminologists of the era. In the first fourteen years of the twentieth century, Ingenieros published two full-length manuscripts on hysteria, as well as numerous articles focused on specific cases. In his leading positions after 1900 at the Clínica de Neurología (Neurology

Clinic) at the University of Buenos Aires and the city police Observation Room respectively, he found an easily available population to test his new theories, an energetic group of colleagues, and a platform from which to publicize the new ideas. In addition to his scientific work, Ingenieros was also a political figure whose medical practice was infused with social concerns and reformist energy. Ingenieros maintained many liberal, progressive views; for instance, he supported welfare programs, the advancement of science, and the liberal-feminist vision of women's rights. Thus Ingenieros, along with his colleagues, was both a witness and participant in the introduction of new ideas about women's rights in scientific circles.

Ingenieros forwarded a typically eclectic scientific approach to hysteria. His research was based less on his original theories than on selected components of theories current in Europe. He basically held a belief in the neurological origin of hysteria—that it was a physical disease of the brain—yet he appreciated its psychological dimensions. To that, he added physiological, including genital and reproductive, factors. (Interestingly, although by 1900 Freud's well-known study of hysteria had been widely circulated throughout Europe, Ingenieros deemed it worthy of no more than a passing mention.[34]) In his 1904 book *Histeria y sugestión* (Hysteria and suggestion), Ingenieros promised to clarify the "nature and pathogenesis [origin] of hysteria, a very discussed and obscure point," which had been "muddled up by the heterogeneous doctrines expounded" by various European doctors. His conclusions were based on his personal observation of patients in the city's mental institutions and, he argued, could "complement some points which have been obscured or neglected by the classical treatments."[35] Ingenieros thus placed his original Argentine work in the context of European theory, but simultaneously introduced himself as the formulator of the next step in scientific progress in the study of hysteria. Ingenieros's evolutionary view of the "science" of hysteria included a progression from a "genital" or mystical phase in which both uterine problems and demonic possession were linked with hysterical fits. In its second phase, scientists located hysteria in the nervous system and began the clinical study of the illness. In the third, and for Ingenieros, the current phase, scientists applied "diverse psychological and physiological theories," in other words, embracing eclectic views of the disorder.[36] According to Ingenieros, he himself proposed combining the two approaches: "Psychological and Physiological conceptions of hysteria are not contradictory. . . . The first is a clinical explication, essentially descriptive. The second is a physio-pathological interpretation."[37] Embedded in his neurological conception of hysteria was a concern with psychological abnormality that would appear to dominate the study of the disease. Yet, as I will now demonstrate, despite the fundamental eclecticism of Ingenieros's (and others') methodology, these early-twentieth-century researchers ultimately traced hysteria to the body itself.

Hysteria: A Disease of the Body

Psychiatrists and other clinical observers considered hysteria to be a form of degeneration, signs of which could be located in the body.[38] In this they were adhering to the widely accepted assumptions of anthropometrics, the method locating character traits and flaws in the physical body. Argentine doctors, too, relied on biological and anthropometrical methods as they studied male and female deviants, postulating that the body could give clues to their deeper psychic states. Yet in these examinations women were embodied in a way in which men were not. In the case of women— whether criminals or hysterics—the theoretical emphasis shifted from facial features to the reproductive organs. For instance, beyond the common observations of paralysis and spasms in the arms, legs, and torso, doctors examining hysterical women also focused on their wombs, ovaries, and genitals. They fastidiously recorded medical narratives of their patients' experience with menstruation, childbirth, and other reproductive functions. The common denominator asserted in studies of hysterical women was the patient's problematic sexuality that in turn threatened the development or continued function of "normal" female behavior.

A typical case, one of Ingenieros's patients, was examined at the

San Roque mental asylum in 1903. After the requisite studies of the seventeen-year-old girl's family background, Ingenieros reported on her reproductive status. Although she enjoyed general good health, her menstrual history took a central place in the report. Despite regular menses, he linked her cycle to her mental disease. It was only eight to ten months after her first menstruation, he noted, that her first hysterical fit occurred. Additionally, it was during or after masturbation when an "irresistible desire to laugh hysterically attacked her."[39] Her second attack also purportedly occurred during menstruation. Clearly, the woman was not just "hysterical"—having fits, spasms, and so on—but also was sexually abnormal. "Since puberty," he writes, "her sexual instinct has manifested itself intensely: unable to resist its pull, she systematically satisfied her sensuality through daily titillations of the clitoris. This produced complete voluptuousness. This habit, on which we insist on referring, had a close relationship with her first paroxysm of hysterical laughter."[40] Ingenieros, like many of his colleagues, linked sexual behavior with the psychosomatic manifestations of hysteria. Relieving her sexual urge through "unnatural" means was inextricably linked to the signs of her disease; moreover, they prevented the development of a "healthy" sexuality.

The seeming commonality among hysterical subjects was a problematic sexuality that threatened the development or continued functioning of "normal" maternal behavior. This could be expressed by a hypersexuality, as in the case just mentioned, or alternatively as frigidity or fear of the sexual act. Either way, psychiatrists attributed a primary importance to women's bodies, especially their reproductive organs. Much of the published research on hysteria relied on somatic "evidence," which doctors could ostensibly observe and record. They often illustrated their published case studies of hysterical patients with photographs or line drawings, usually completed by the psychiatrist himself. These medical pictures provide us with an additional valuable source to analyze doctors' attitudes toward their hysterical patients. A glance at these medical illustrations reveals even more starkly the doctors' focus on female sexuality and reproduction in the psychiatric literature on hysteria.[41] The fact that many articles dealing with cases of hysteria were illustrated indicates the extent to which scientists located hysteria in the female body: they found it "natural" to make spectacle out of "anomalous" female bodies.[42] For instance, in *Histeria y sugestión*, Ingenieros published a photograph of his patient in her "hypnotic dream," reduced to utter passivity. Her stiff body simultaneously presented an inviting image, a body available as both a subject for the medical gaze and as a spectacle for public consumption.

Furthermore, doctors believed they could produce such catatonic states in female patients to reveal "hysterogenic zones," manifestations of their hysteria. These zones were often sexual, highlighting or emphasizing the breasts, vaginal area, or uterus and ovaries. For example, in the second image, also from *Histeria y sugestión*, Ingenieros used line drawings to illustrate his theory of the somatic manifestations of hysteria on a patient who exhibited numbness in her breast (see figure 1). This emphasis resulted in a sexualization of the hysterical patient, even when no sexual or reproductive abnormality was reported.

Other psychiatrists, publishing their findings in the *Archivos*, followed Ingenieros's lead in their representations of the hysterical body. For example, Dr. Joaquín Durquet of the National Women's Mental Asylum described the case of "M. L. C.," a hysteric whose symptoms, supposedly of psychic origin, manifested themselves in her body.[43] He also identified in his hysterical patient M. L. C. "zones" that were seemingly defined by sexual function. Durquet explained in the text accompanying an illustration, shown below (see figure 2), that "the nearly generalized anesthesia . . . is a frequent stigma of hysteria. . . . In the non-anesthetized points there is hyperthesia and hyperalgesia."[44] In locating M. L. C.'s hysterical manifestations in her body, Durquet identified the affliction with her female sex organs. In doing so, he reflected the view that hysteria was not only gendered and embodied but also intrinsically linked to sex.

The following two images (figures 3 and 4), taken from a separate article appearing that same year in the *Archivos*, exhibited the passive poses and facial expressions of the patient. Doctors provided the images to show how her "expressionless face" typically

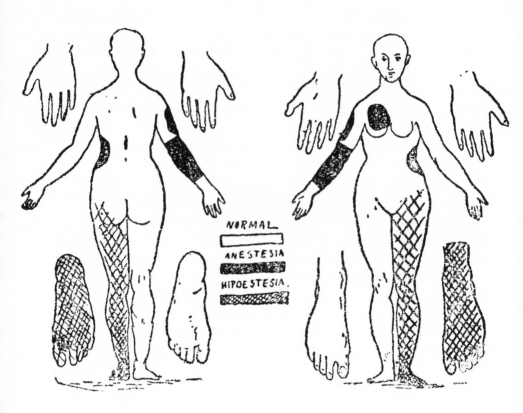

Figure 1. José Ingenieros illustrated his widely read
Histeria y sugestión with numerous line drawings such
as this one, depicting the various ways in which the
condition affected "zones" on the hysteric's body.

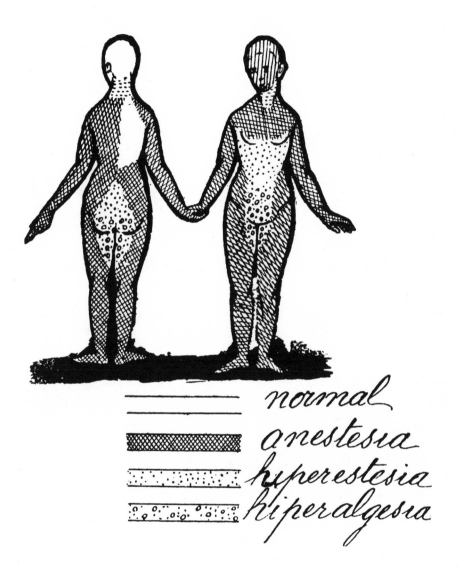

Figure 2. Joaquín Durquet's illustration of "hysterogenic zones" on the female body, highlighting the breasts, genitals, and buttocks as especially sensitive. From Joaquín Durquet, "Paraplegia histérica: Curación por sugestión," *Archivos de Psiquiatría y Criminología* 4 (1905): 306–18. Reprinted with permission.

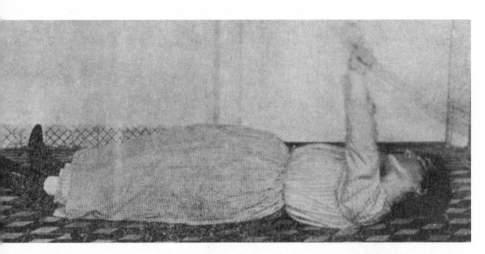

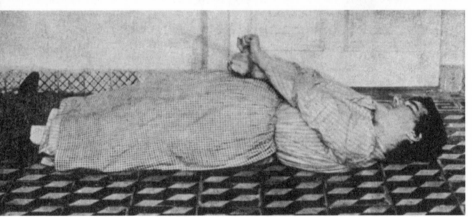

Figure 3. A hysteric in a hysterical fit; her supine
position emphasizes her supposed passivity and
helplessness. From Joaquín Durquet, "Paraplegia
histérica: Curación por sugestión," *Archivos de
Psiquiatría y Criminología* 4 (1905): 306–18.
Reprinted with permission.

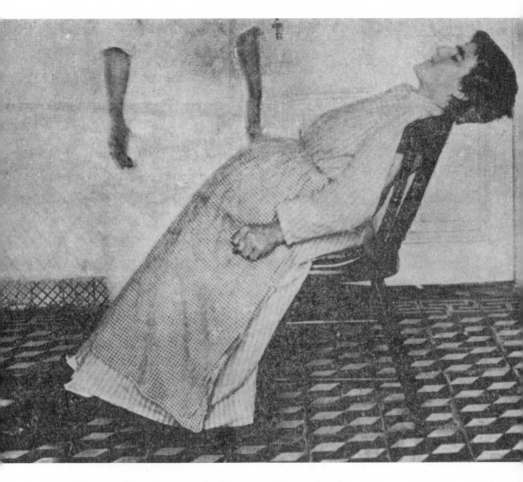

Figure 4. Here Durquet depicts the subject in her hysterical trance; the display of her stiff body and expressionless face is meant to illustrate her pathological state. From Joaquín Durquet, "Paraplegia histérica: Curación por sugestión," *Archivos de Psiquiatría y Criminología* 4 (1905): 306–18. Reprinted with permission.

"proved" the animal or atavistic features of insane subjects. Such representations illustrating the use of anthropometrical methods were similar to those used to study criminals and other male deviants. What is different in the representations of female cases is that the illustrations of hysterical women are always accompanied by reproductive or sexual histories and/or reports of bodily examinations.[45] Durquet's patient, whose hysterical symptoms were reportedly linked to epilepsy, exhibited by contrast clear signs of "degenerative stigma." Perhaps as a result of her "early initiation in sexual development," Durquet reported her to have "great development of the breasts," a small skull, small forehead, facial asymmetry, and other morphological anomalies.[46]

Subsequent issues of the *Archivos* provided additional arguments for the sexual nature of hysterics. A 1906 study examined three hysterical women, all of whom exhibited inappropriate sexual behavior. The first was a so-called impulsive degenerate exhibiting both hysterical fits and "genital impulses." Reportedly she also tended to shout "Men! Men! Men!" for hours and lunged for the testicles of any man who entered the room. In the second, the physician observed an "exaggerated sexuality." Finally, the third "had very intense exotic desires. When a man enters the room her eyes shine, she blushes, and with her tongue or other acts she offers her favors."[47] Bernardo Etchepare, author of a 1912 article entitled "Mental Imbalance, Morphinomania, and Hysteria," also saw his patient in sexual terms as he described her precocious activity involving abuse by her older relatives and subsequent habits of masturbation, bestiality, and reading pornography.[48] He also pointed out a history of related problems, including behavior at school that was "detestable." To that end, he concluded that she took on a "dominating masculine character, [she] preferred boys' amusements: soccer, running, climbing trees."[49] In addition, with the onset of her menstruation at age twelve, the patient became depressed and angry.[50] Her teen years were characterized, according to Etchepare, by continued sexual activity, periods of depression, suicide attempts, and eventually hysteria and drug abuse. In addition, her "male character" became more noticeable: she began to horseback ride, bicycle, and shoot guns. The examining doctor concluded that she was incurably mentally ill, doomed to unhappiness. Furthermore, due to her early exhibition of hypersexuality and her "male" behavior, he noted that she was probably a "psychosexual hermaphrodite," which caused her to practice homosexual acts. These representative, if not typical, cases illustrate how common it was for early psychiatric researchers to link female sexual "pathology" as defined by the mores of the time with the appearance and diagnosis of hysteria.

Hysteria and Female Suggestibility

José Ingenieros, the Argentine initiator of serious research on hysterical symptoms, intended more than a mere scientific study of the condition. He also wanted to introduce a method for curing hysteria: hypnosis. A large portion of his book was devoted to hypnotic techniques as well as their social applications. Hypnosis, or the "state of suggestibility," had acquired some legitimacy thanks to the influence of Charcot. The hypnotic trance consisted of a number of bodily states that could be scientifically measured. Hypnotic states were distinct from neurological conditions such as catalepsy and sleepwalking by the fact that only some individuals were hypnotizable, or suggestible.

Hysterics were prime candidates for hypnotic therapy since doctors believed that women, comprising the majority of cases, were more suggestible and disposed to hypnosis. In addition, women's suggestibility was seen as a useful cure for hysteria, since women were considered more gullible, with weaker wills. Theorists assumed that suggestible individuals displayed a lack of will, or in Ingenieros's words, an "ailing volition."[51] Ingenieros believed that while hysterical and hypnotic states had similar attributes, they should not be confused. He wrote, drawing on various French theories, "They are different because hysteria is born from self-suggestion and hypnotism through outside suggestion. The hysteric is active, the hypnotic is passive." Ingenieros argued that suggestible subjects "cannot govern themselves any more; [they] lack proper will, an independent ego, and normal psychic activity."[52] He also cited in 1904 the "instability" of the hysteric and "the importance of suggestion as a cause of [hysterical fits]."[53] Seeing women as suggestible and weak-willed led psychiatrists to suggest that these women were unusually gullible, unreliable, and unable to reason normally. In reducing women to their sexual identity in these studies of hysteria, and in further categorizing their volition through theories of hypnosis, psychiatrists essentially removed their female patients from the acknowledged spheres of rationality and public action. That they believed the disorder was "epidemic" implied that women were categorically unable to be fully socially responsible beyond their familial duties, at least as compared with men.

Turn-of-the-century psychiatrists, in defining the approaches to the study of hysteria, portrayed hysterical women as victims of their biological states and reduced them to all but their sexual will. Psychiatrists pursued a scientific path based on an a priori assumption that women were different than men. They believed that hysteria resided primarily in the reproductive "zones" of the female body. This line of inquiry was the only avenue taken for the study of female patients, but was not explored for men with similar mental afflictions. This approach to hysteria—a woman's disease—in fact contrasted with the creative and thoughtful way in which psychiatrists analyzed men's psychic states. In the pages of the *Archivos*, psychiatrists and criminologists explained male behavior not only in terms of psychic disturbances but also in terms of poverty, upbringing, and even political beliefs. Men's deviant behavior could be and was linked to social class, political affiliation, or power relations.[54] Yet seemingly nothing that women did, up to and including the act of committing murder, could transcend their biology. Although all men were potential cowards or criminal deserters, all women were potential hysterics.[55]

From my examination of psychiatrists' theories of hysteria, I have drawn two major conclusions. First, psychiatry's study of hysteria was a building block of the profession as a specialization distinct from other medical fields. The seeming scores of female subjects easily diagnosed as "hysterical" provided psychiatrists with the raw data of their new science and gave them roles in public institutions such as police stations and mental hospitals. Hysterical patients and the theories developed about them shaped these influential doctors' particular mapping of Argentina's challenges as it grappled with the turbulent effects of modernization. Second, psychiatrists relied on biological and sexual explanations of female difference and women's social roles in the formulation of their theories of hysteria. Thus, turn-of-the-century psychiatrists, in confronting the most widely diagnosed form of female mental illness, mediated culturally sanctioned understandings and identification of women's behavior. In the end, although nominally supportive of the more moderate wing of the feminist movement and genuinely seeking to help women suffering from a particularly feminine form of mental anguish, psychiatrists' gendered preconceptions undergirded their ostensibly objective scientific worldview. Doctors and researchers of hysteria, led by the progressives of their time, may have hoped to serve the feminist movement in their attempts to help women. But in doing so, they wittingly or unwittingly reduced female patients to their sexual and reproductive organs. The psychiatric study of hysteria, even in the hands of self-proclaimed advocates of progress for women, proved to be a dead end. It began with an assumption of sexual difference, and then carried out studies that seemed to confirm that idea. Ultimately, the hysteria diagnosis did no more than support with medical evidence the rigid sexual distinctions of the day.

Chapter Two

SEXUAL ABERRATION, DEGENERATION, AND PSYCHIATRY IN LATE-NINETEENTH-CENTURY BUENOS AIRES

Kristin Ruggiero

Alberto awoke in fear, enveloped in the fumes of chloroform. Luis was leaning over his bed and his face was uncomfortably close. Alberto moved, feigning sleep, and Luis went back to his own bed. This was in June 1888. Alberto had advertised himself in the newspaper as a servant looking for work, and Luis had hired him in early June. As the days passed Alberto became more suspicious of Luis, but did not know what to do about it. Meanwhile, Luis wooed his new servant with gifts of clothes, an iron bed with a mattress, carriage rides from Palermo to La Boca, boat trips, and nights at the theater, eventually luring Alberto into accepting a life insurance policy that made his employer the beneficiary in the case of the servant's demise. Then something went decidedly wrong. Alberto began to feel ill and suspected that Luis was poisoning him. He even accused Luis of the deed, but a doctor called by Luis diagnosed Alberto as merely having indigestion and gave him purgatives. On July 27, Luis succeeded in murdering Alberto.[1]

Alberto Bouchot Constantin and Luis Castruccio were both part of the massive European immigration to Argentina in the last quarter of the century, Alberto from France and Luis from Italy. Alberto was poor and hired himself out as a servant. Luis also came from a poor background and had hired himself out as a servant during his first months in Argentina as a fourteen-year-old in 1878. One of Luis's servant positions took him to the city of La Plata, where he opened an account at the provincial bank and invested his savings in land. When he returned to Buenos Aires, he began calling himself a land agent and began to think about hiring a servant for himself, although his income was still modest. The qualifications a person needed to become Luis's servant were that he had to be male and young and able to sign his own name.

It had only taken him a few years to come up with a scheme to make his fortune in the Republic of Argentina, to "make America," as immigrants said. The scheme was that he hired young men as servants, took out life insurance policies on them with himself as the beneficiary, and then tried to kill them.[2] This was a relatively new type of crime since life insurance was a product of modernity that required a developed science of numbers that allowed the calculation of probabilities; tables of mortality; well-run civil registry offices; a government that guaranteed public security; impartial justice; a well-rooted spirit of family; and a knowledge of laws of political economy. Although the police knew that life insurance could "excite the sordid passions and serve to incite crime," the danger of becoming a victim of a scam was not widely known.[3] Certainly, Luis's victims did not have a notion of life insurance, as the young men who survived his attempts on their lives explained.

Luis's first victim was an eleven-year-old named Juan, whom he seduced by a promise to pay for his secondary schooling if he would agree to take out an insurance policy with Luis as the beneficiary, but Juan refused. Even though Luis regularly sodomized the boy and was violent with him, Juan was still in his service when this case was being heard. Luis's next target was Roman, age twenty-five, married, a Spanish immigrant, with four months' residence in Argentina. The first night in Luis's service, Roman slept on a cot, while Luis and Juan slept together in the bed. During the following days, Roman and Juan acted as Luis's servants. At the same time, however, Luis acted as more than a mere employer, giving

Roman some of his own clothes to wear and taking Roman to stroll about the city. Apparently Luis had an ulterior motive. One night Roman woke to find Luis leaning over his face. Instantly he knew something was wrong and became alarmed, although he did not realize that Luis was actually trying to murder him with chloroform. Luis fancied himself an expert in chloroform and in 1884 had prepared by copying out a great deal of information about its use from a book belonging to one of his former employers. He remembered the title and other details well enough to tell a judge on August 1, 1888, that it was the *Manual de cirujía práctica y clínica quirúrgica*, written in English by Thomas Briant and translated into Spanish by M. Baldivieso. In his testimony, Luis explained that he had copied the information in preparation for his own suicide. This could well have been true, but he certainly later found chloroform a handy tool in his insurance scheme, placing chloroform-soaked cloths under the noses of his servants while they slept.[4] In spite of Roman's alarm about the events the night before, he accompanied Luis the following day to downtown Buenos Aires for coffee and to an insurance office. Here Luis learned that Roman would have to have a medical exam before the insurance company would issue a policy. After leaving the insurance office, Luis took Roman to the library on Corrientes Street, where Luis made Roman sign a book and read something in proof that Roman was indeed literate, as he had claimed when he was hired. At the library, Roman was noticeably afraid. When Luis asked Roman to explain his fear, after they had returned home, Roman dissembled, saying that he did not like to sign his name. Luis grew angry and told Roman that he should get used to signing his name because he would also have to sign the insurance policy. He further stated that if Roman did not want to do as he was told, he had better leave. "He called me cowardly," Roman later told the judge. "He said that he would settle the matter with my uncle," implying that Roman would be bound to accept his uncle's orders. That night, Luis was apparently in a better mood and took Roman to the theater. The next night, Roman went to his uncle's house to tell him what had been happening and that he suspected that Luis was a bad man. "My uncle told me that I should go back to Luis's house and take what was mine and then leave. When I did this, Luis got mad and took away the clothes he'd given me."[5] Gifts of clothing, trips to coffee shops, and other outings were Luis's way of ingratiating himself with his chosen victims and earning their trust. Having come into Luis's employ with little more than one suit of clothes and his life, Roman fortunately escaped with both, unlike Luis's next target, Alberto Bouchot.

Suspicious though he was, the third victim, Alberto Bouchot, went along with Luis's insurance scheme. Under pressure from Luis, he tried to convince himself that the policy was beneficial to him. Luis later claimed, in fact, that the idea of the life insurance policy had been Alberto's. In fact he (Luis) claimed that he had agreed only on the condition that Alberto's sister still in France be given to him as a wife. As future brothers-in-law, the insurance policy made sense, explained Luis. Alberto actually borrowed 80 pesos *moneda nacional* from Luis in order to be able to pay for the insurance policy that cost a total of 200 pesos. Confused about the whole venture, Alberto wrote that he was making the insurance policy in favor of Luis because of money that Luis had loaned him. The letters that were signed by Alberto are telling. In one, dated July 6, 1888, Alberto promised his sister, Elena Bouchot Constantin, to Luis and said that from then on he and Luis were brothers-in-law and promised to take out a life insurance policy. In a second letter, dated July 20, 1888, Alberto stated that if he should die before the marriage of his sister and Luis took place, Luis had the right to claim Alberto's insurance. And further Alberto wrote, "I want to be buried simply, with no pomp. Put my body in the poor section [*lugar de los pobres*] in Chacarita [a large working-class cemetery in Buenos Aires]."[6] After his failed attempts, Luis had learned a thing or two about murder. Since Luis, modern, scientific, and educated, had met with failure twice before and again in June with Alberto using his original method of chloroform to commit murder—because his victims had woken up before he could carry out his plan—he shifted to arsenic as his instrument of murder. Luis secured arsenic on July 17 using a falsified prescription, and for the rest of the month fed small portions to Alberto daily. Alberto began to feel sick, as if he were being poisoned. At first Luis chided him for thinking such a thing, and Alberto apologized. But as Alberto's condition worsened, Luis, ever the caretaker of his small staff of servants, took Alberto to the doctor and was present at the examination. The doctor's report stated that Alberto was young, tall, well formed, with a good constitution. This perhaps should have led the doctor to suspect that something was wrong. However, he found many other characteristics of Alberto that perhaps undermined any suspicion that something was amiss. He noted that Alberto had trouble speaking Spanish. He also found that his eyes were cloudy and that his face was red similar to a drunk's face. The doctor found that Alberto did not like answering questions, that his replies were monosyllabic and bad willed. The doctor thought that Alberto had a mental condition, or that he was a misanthrope who was deeply displeased with life, sad, and hypochondriacal. On July 21, the doctor treated Alberto for his complaints of stomach and head pains, lack of appetite, nausea, persistent constipation, intense nervousness, and moral depression.

> I ordered a treatment of lemon purgative for him with 30 grams of German brandy [*aguardiente*] to take twice with a half hour in between. I visited him again on July 23rd; he was in bed, in pain and vomiting. I prescribed a potion of Riviero, and pieces of ice and mustard plasters on his abdomen. For the gastric problems and fever, I ordered ten pills of a centigram of opium extract each and ten centigrams of sulfate of quinine each, to take every two hours to relieve the pain. For the day after, I prescribed a solution of pepto-cocaina Gibson [see figure 5]. The patient improved and even went to a function at the Politeama dance hall. I was called again on July 27th, but I didn't think it was serious and I wasn't feeling well myself, so I didn't go. The next day, I heard that Alberto had died.[7]

The explanation for Alberto's fatal decision to cooperate in Luis's scheme can perhaps be found in his trusting nature, his dire economic situation and as a result his need to link up with a more successful immigrant, and his lack of understanding of how life insurance policies worked.

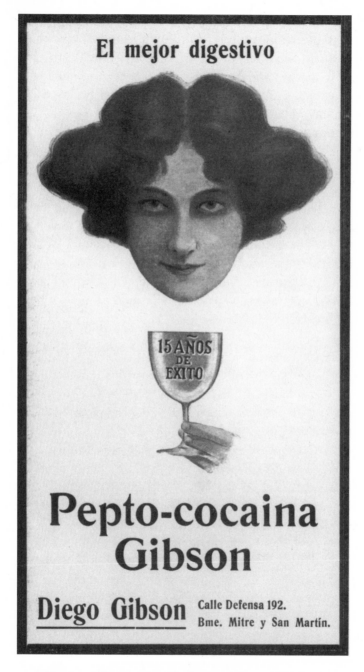

Figure 5. Advertisement for Pepto-cocaina, *PBT* 86
(1906), 102. Reprinted with permission.

After reporting the death to the Civil Registry, Luis wrote immediately to the insurance company announcing his brother-in-law Alberto's death and informing the company that Alberto would be buried in Chacarita between 5 and 6 P.M. on July 28. If an insurance agent wanted to verify the death, he could come to Luis's house prior to the burial. Luis was able to bury the body before the legal period of twenty-four hours had expired because he had convinced a doctor to falsify the time of death. The doctor had agreed to do this because he accepted the sincerity of Luis that he (Luis) could not bear to have the body of his servant in the house overnight. Being reluctant to pay out the insurance money, the insurance company insisted on an investigation. Alberto's body was exhumed on August 1, in the presence of several medical doctors, the administrator of the cemetery, and Luis. Chemical exams were performed on the organs. Luis testified this same day, as did his servants Juan and Roman and the pharmacist who had sold Luis the arsenic. Luis confessed to the police on August 6 that he had obtained arsenic and asphyxiated Alberto. An autopsy of Alberto's body was done on August 7, 1888, and Luis was arrested the same day. As he explained to the police, referring to his smothering of Alberto, "I killed him like Othello killed Desdemona; I didn't let him suffer." Later, he retracted his confession and blamed Alberto's death on his excessive use of alcohol.[8]

The cold-blooded nature of this crime, which was not based on any quarrel or passion that would have alerted the victim to danger, was so shocking that many people felt as the state prosecutor in the case did, that Luis deserved the death sentence, which the prosecutor requested on October 13, 1888.

In the late nineteenth century, the courts still preferred sending criminals to the penitentiary rather than to an asylum. However, the very horror of this crime also made other people want to leave no stone unturned in trying to discover what would make a human being do such a terrible thing. With the influence of new psychiatric and criminological theories, there was pressure to look at criminals as sick individuals, so the examining court doctors took an entire year to deliberate over Luis's physical and mental condition. After reading the doctors' report, the defense attorney for Luis Castruccio wrote to the judge of the criminal court in the Province of Buenos Aires in February 1889:

> I know, Judge, that you do not believe in putting insane people [*locos*] in asylums if they have committed crimes. But I maintain that Luis needs the balm of the asylum, not the scaffold. The chain of his disease started with his two uncles' mental illness, his father's suicide, and Luis's attempt to do the same. All of this meant that he had a congenital predisposition to insanity. This predisposition was converted into an illness very quickly by his masturbatory vices [*vicios onanistas*], his sick abstention from coitus, and his liking of pederasty. He perfectly fits the positivist school's and Cesare Lombroso's description of the morally insane in that he has no repugnance for his act and no remorse. I have the deepest conviction, Judge, that Luis is a degenerate who turned to crime obeying the impulses of his sick brain. I understand that he is a dangerous individual, but I cannot accept that he be killed. I cannot accept that four bullets be put into the chest of a demented person. I request that his case be judged according to Article 81, clause 1 of the Argentine penal code which exempts him from punishment.[9]

The ideology that formed the basis of the defense attorney's plea to the judge was positivism. It was the underpinning of the other theories mentioned in the above quote: moral insanity, degeneration, Lombroso's criminal anthropology, and even masturbation. Medical and criminological theories based on positivist doctrine and new methods of measurement, observation, photography, and sensitivity testing were hallmarks of the criminal trials in the later nineteenth century. Although the actual legal codes were not changing as fast as the new medical and criminological sciences and had not incorporated positivist theories, positivism had in fact become the dominant ideology of Latin America in this period. Before the positivist reconceptualization, crime had been viewed as an individual discreet act produced exclusively by the individual's free will and, therefore, resulted from a failure of moral responsibility.

Punishments were fixed and proportional to the crime and were intended to punish the crime rather than the criminal. With positivism, crime came to be viewed as a pathological expression of an individual's illness, which had little or nothing to do with his or her free will or moral responsibility. The criminal was viewed as diseased and as a potential victim of the multitudinous ills circulating in modern societies. He or she was, in Lombrosian terms, a regressive type of savage, a "born criminal."

In his studies of the natural history of delinquent men and women, Italian criminologist Cesare Lombroso thought that he had discovered that certain somatic and psychic characteristics distinguished born criminals. This method of identifying delinquents was not just a revival of eighteenth-century phrenology, where the shape and size of a person's cranium was examined by touch to diagnose their intelligence and character. Rather, the positivist school relied on an extensive network of relationships between a person's brain, psyche, and character and the anatomical structure. The measurement of the cranium remained important, but added to this method were examinations of the face, hands, reflexes, and even moral sense. The crucial parts of the human body believed by anthropological criminology to show either the progress or degeneration of the species were the head, hands, and the skin's sensitivity. The head of one born criminal, a contemporary of Luis, for example, was described as being covered with abundant and coarse skin that recalled the "excessive skin of certain animals" and as exhibiting a "mixture of Neanderthal and simian characteristics."[10] Other features of born criminals were said to be a narrow forehead, prominent eyebrows, and a wide, flat face with visible asymmetry. A thin mouth and lips; a long, curved nose; fleshy and asymmetrical ears; asymmetrical teeth; and small eyes were also features of these criminals. Like simians, their fingers were said to have flat and thick extremities, and the space between the thumb and forefinger was narrow. Finally, born criminals were said to lack sensitivity in the fingers, the tip of the tongue and nose, the nape of the neck, the end of the metacarpal, the ball of the thumb, and the lower forearm.

There was great enthusiasm for positivism in Argentina. For some, the new science had "revolutionized" the judicial and police

Figure 6. Education and physionomy: a chart showing various "types" of personalities based on head structure. From *PBT* 3 (91) (1906): 93. Reprinted with permission.

sciences because it offered a unique method of observation and classification of criminals, a broad analysis of the factors involved in criminal acts, a linkage between penology and the biological sciences, and a more rational scheme of punishments (see figure 6). Positivism was also described by some enthusiasts as a "rejuvenation," a more modern concept of the phenomena of life that moved jurisprudence closer to the physical sources of life and away from crime as a juridical abstraction.[11] The causes of crime were now viewed as living elements that could be identified both in the individual and in the environment.

Although Argentine positivism and criminal anthropology developed somewhat in tandem with these innovations in Europe, these sciences also had the characteristics of independent movements. There were even some areas in which Argentina's embrace of positivism outstripped Europe's. The turn of the century witnessed a surge of publishing in the sciences in Argentina. Many scientific institutes were established, such as the Institute of Criminology at the National Penitentiary in 1907, which was perhaps the first in the world to systematically study prisoners with the new scientific methods. Argentine psychiatrists' enthusiastic acceptance of positivism even earned the notice of the daughter of the influential Lombroso. In a letter to her father, published in 1908, Gina Lombroso wrote that Argentine society was more receptive to Lombrosian ideas than even Italy itself.[12] As positivist beliefs took over the field of criminology in Latin America, the biological and social sciences of anthropology, medicine, and sociology were increasingly used to analyze crime in a more complex and nuanced manner than previously. Thus, when the court-appointed doctors in Luis Castruccio's case finally made their report of their examination of Luis to the judge on July 5, 1889, apologizing for the year that this took, they alerted the judge up front that the seriousness and bizarreness of this case had demanded that they use positivist theory in their medical assessment of Luis. "Medical examination of Luis Castruccio, performed in Buenos Aires using the system of anthropometry [an analysis of the human body based on measurements and their

proportions], report filed in July 1889, suspect charged with the
murder of his male servant Bouchot in July 1888."[13]

> Physical exam: "light beard, dark clear eyes, thin eyebrows, chest-
> nut hair, normal expression. Small ears that do not have the form
> of jug handles; the pitch of his chin is four centimeters. His cra-
> nial index is 75, which means that he has a longish head (dolicho-
> cephalic). There is no cranial asymmetry. The measurement of the
> thorax yields the figure of 93; with his arms open, he measures 5
> feet 5 inches [1.67 meters], his height is 5 feet 3 inches [1.62
> meters], meaning that his arm spread is 2 inches [5 centimeters]
> greater than his height. His teeth are perfectly implanted; the vault
> of his mouth presents a completely normal formation, without any
> anomaly. His hands and feet in relation to his height are in pro-
> portion. He has appropriate sensitivity to pain. The clinical exam
> of his organs in the thoracic and abdominal cavities shows com-
> plete integrity and generally a perfect physiological state. From the
> sexual exam, we can say that Luis is a complete man. His genital
> organs are complete and his penis is fairly well developed.

What all this added up to, consonant with the medical and criminological theories of the period, was that Luis did not exhibit any
of the signs of the so-called born criminal.[14]

The rest of the examining doctors' time on this case was spent
on trying to identify just what *had* happened in Luis's life to remove
his ability to reason, and thus not be responsible for the murder
that he had committed. Three things that the doctors had to work
with were Luis's family's mental instability, his abhorrence of coitus
and women, and his possible habit of masturbation.[15] Luis told the
doctors about how his father had committed suicide in 1884 by
lying in front of a train and that his uncle had hung himself in a
mental hospital in Genoa, Italy. His misanthropy began at an early
age. At age fifteen, he made a vow of abstinence as a protest against
his father's refusal to allow him to enter the priesthood and his
insistence that he emigrate to Argentina. In Luis's own words, his
objective was "to cut out at the root [his] procreative powers and
extinguish completely [his] branch . . . eliminating completely the

power of love." Coupled with this was a hatred of women. In his suicide plan of 1887, he left a note bequeathing his property to the Italian Hospital in Buenos Aires on the condition that the funds not be used to support the women's ward, because, as he explained, women were "harmful and antipathetic."[16]

The pieces of the puzzle were beginning to add up for the medical doctors. Luis's past was strewn with incidents linking his masturbation to a predisposition to insanity. Here was a patient who claimed that he was chaste, but who obviously had had frequent sex of some sort because the foreskin of his penis was large and elastic; who hated women; and who had insanity in his family. The doctors concluded that Luis had gained his sexual pleasure through masturbation, or a combination of male partners and self-masturbation. And they also concluded that the penchant for masturbation was a sign that his family's insanity had also affected him.

The common medical wisdom was that masturbation was one of the many conditions and activities that could cause the molecular disturbance of the cerebral mass known as insanity. Also included in the list of causes were excesses of temperature, alcohol, or prostitution. Heredity, consumptive illnesses, wounds and blows to the head, bad digestion, tobacco snuff, ambition, pride, fear, love, anger, shocks, vicissitudes of family and fortune, humiliations, hypochondria, epilepsy, melancholy, and uterine furor also posed threats. Although more research has been done on women's insanity as connected to the perceived instability of their reproductive organs, as in the preceding chapter on hysteria, men too were seen by doctors as suffering from "abnormalities" in their generative lives, as Luis's case shows. In Luis's lawyer's plea in 1889, Luis was presented as having had a congenital predisposition to insanity, a predisposition that was converted into illness very quickly by his masturbatory vices, by his morbose abstention from coitus, and by his taste for pederasty, a vice that doctors viewed as a form of dementia.[17]

Consistent with the medical theories of this time, the doctors believed that the practice of masturbation could negatively influence a person's mind and body and could thus provide a possible extenuating circumstance for criminal activity. First, onanism was discussed by medical professionals as an actual disease or disease state that could mitigate responsibility. Masturbation, in particular a perceived excessive masturbation, was a common enough phenomenon to appear as an entry in popular medical manuals. Typically the discussion listed its symptoms as difficult digestion, paleness, weakness, recurring illness, trembling limbs, involuntary erections of the penis and ejaculations, loss of memory, kidney pain, head pain, cough, consumption, and hypochondria. A final effect— insensibility to reason—was especially important for the argument that masturbation was an extenuating circumstance when assigning criminal responsibility. The treatment suggested by the manuals was to have the patient stop masturbating. They also recommended that masturbators be separated from bad company and that they avoid obscene books and conversations on sexual topics. Experts promoted the vigilant surveillance of schoolchildren of both sexes to identify likely victims of this obsession.[18]

Second, masturbation was viewed as an organic and behavioral sign of hereditary degeneration that might lead to more serious diseases in the masturbator and to the committing of unwanted criminal acts. Similar to the attitude toward mental fatigue, it was asserted that masturbation reduced the brain's energy and weakened the body, thus increasing the chances of hereditary degeneration appearing in susceptible individuals. According to doctors, onanism left children with a weak personality and no initiative, and adults fatigued and dulled.[19] The picture in this literature presented the inveterate masturbator as a person with a weak spirit, physically fatigued and unable to fend off inclinations to crime. Although masturbation was a common phenomenon and not thought to necessarily lead to crime in every case, Luis was particularly affected by it because he had engaged in it excessively and had not tried to curb it, probably because of his inherited degenerative flaws. These flaws were evidenced by the presence in his family of suicide and insanity. The combination led him down the path to violent crime. Not only had masturbation affected Luis, according to the doctors, but also it was held to be a potential cause of degeneration in future generations in his family. If Luis had had children, these children, according to the theory, might well have been even more incorrigibly criminal than Luis.

Third, this habit was considered to be a symptom of some of the ills of modern society. Luis, for example, symbolized a negative stereotype of the immigrant's single-minded pursuit of quick wealth. Buenos Aires's crime statistics indicated to many observers that the city's high level of delinquency was a direct consequence of European immigration. Moreover, the majority of these immigrants were, like Luis, members of the Latin "race," which was considered by some observers to be biologically more apt to commit bloody crimes. Luis also symbolized the perceived evils of modern innovations. He had adopted life insurance as the basis for a scam to make money without having to engage in manual labor. Needless to say, this type of entrepreneur was not deemed of long-term benefit to the emerging nation of Argentina. Luis also symbolized the "new machine-age man" who manifested the moral numbness of what was considered contemporary materialistic society. Without normal human sentiments, Luis was useless as a prospective citizen and family man. Finally, to some observers Luis symbolized the perceived lack of morality of positivism, which denied the existence of human free will. He was the perfect embodiment of the positivist school's "apologetic" view that criminals made "sick" by habits such as masturbation should be allowed to atone for their crimes in asylums rather than jail.

By the end of the nineteenth century, psychiatrists had determined that excessive masturbation could no longer be thought of as just an undesirable act. As Argentine jurist and statesman Luis María Drago argued, while masturbation might start out as a voluntary act, it often later became an automatic or habitual act. Drago said that excessive masturbation originated with a degeneration, or at least a change in the nutritive functions of the modular brain centers—a degeneration that was nothing more than the "adaptation of organs to new functions, an abnormal form of equilibrium in the disequilibrium."[20] Thus, a normal person could, through excessive masturbation, bring about a degenerative change in his own organs. Evidence that the act of masturbation had made the transfer in psychiatrists' minds from a mere "vice" to a "perversity" to which everyone was susceptible seemed to be demonstrated by the case of a young Argentine doctor who had sought medical help for his problem. The man had begun masturbating at age seven. He did so with "frenzy," and even "intensified the aberration during puberty," according to the medical report. At age fifteen, he had to undergo medical treatment for malnutrition that was attributed to his masturbation. In spite of the man's preference for masturbation, he had given it up ten years before his visit to the clinic, because of changes in his "moral and scientific ideas." Determined to take up coitus, he remained unable to have normal sexual relations with women. Coitus for him "stopped being an act of the genital flesh and became a purely cerebral representation, so that he was copulating only with his brain." The clinical report repeated several times with fascination this transformation of a physical act into a mental act. Not plagued by any neuropathic condition and having no degenerative antecedents, the man's aberration could only be attributed to his frequent masturbation.[21]

This doctor's condition presented a danger because psychic substitutions for physical acts were seen as causing mental exhaustion that could in turn cause physical manifestations that were uncontrollable, such as the "masturbatory look" that could cause an unexpected erection and ejaculation. Argentine psychiatrist Lucas Ayarragaray described the "look" in 1902 as "masturbating the victim." Ayarragaray's patient, a Spaniard, age thirty-five and single, was excited by men and repulsed by women. He had sworn to five years of chastity in the hope of controlling his "illness," but had become insomniac and dispirited. Aggravating his condition was his incessant masturbation, which according to the psychiatrist was draining his mental energy. Understanding that he was ill, he had come to Ayarragaray's clinic at the National Hospital of the Mentally Ill in 1902 complaining about being victimized by a masturbatory sexual obsession. What he experienced as the "look" began when another man looked at his eyes and then at his genital area. Once aware of this "look" the patient experienced a painful sensation of anguish. To counteract the spell or curse [*maleficio*], the patient would attempt to stare back, but this did not always work. Commonly he would experience an "ejaculation with voluptuous spasm." The incident that had finally brought the man to Ayarragaray was his accidental ejaculation in a barbershop, when the barber had brushed against the man's clothes and given him the "fatal" look. Ayarragaray's diagnosis was that the patient was an "unfortunate" mental degenerate. The issue for society was whether obsessions such as this one were temporary or permanent, and whether they could evolve into other psychopathologies that might be dangerous, that is, that might even lead to crime.[22]

Although most of the research in this period focused on male masturbation, women's masturbation was also a medical issue and was almost taken as a new topic of scientific research. Argentine psychiatrists such as A. Morales Pérez and Ayarragaray, for example, revealed their curiosity about the novelty of women's masturbation in the case reports they published in the early twentieth century. Interestingly, women voluntarily presented themselves as patients at these clinics. On the one hand, perhaps it was the case that women's desire to be "cured" overcame their concern about protecting their modesty that one sees in doctors' examinations of women in other circumstances. On the other hand, Morales Pérez wrote up his case studies with some bit of amusement about the modesty of these female patients. He was amused by what he thought was their dissimulation and he was suspicious that they were victims of hysteria. A young woman who visited the clinic, accompanied by her mother, reported that she had used a hairpin to scratch the white worms in her anus and that the hairpin had gotten stuck. When the doctor could not find the hairpin, she then told him to try her vagina, but the elusive hairpin remained undiscovered. The doctor reported that at this point he had thought he was probably dealing with an "imaginary thing, typical of hysteria." Then the woman suggested trying her urinary tract. When the doctor finally found the hairpin there, he asked her why she had not told him that it was there in the beginning.[23] Unfortunately, we are not given her response. Equally uncomfortable with her masturbation, but equally willing to seek help from a male doctor, this time Ayarragaray, was a French woman, age forty, and in her second marriage. Profoundly embarrassed by both her first and second husbands' preference for "masturbation with the tongue," this woman had to wear a veil, even in the privacy of her home, if there were other people present. Ayarragaray, apparently not concerned with distinguishing the agent of the masturbation, reported that "this practice against nature" had caused a nervous depression and a tendency toward isolation and quarrelsomeness in his patient. Her husbands' preference for masturbation was "mental torture" for her; "everything made her blush" and "she couldn't stand to be around anyone."[24]

The reason why psychiatrists were concerned about perceived excessive masturbation was because of the perceived phenomenon of degeneration. Degeneration theory, from which the "modern" concern about masturbation arose, had become widely accepted among European psychiatrists in the second half of the nineteenth century and was seen as an explanation for previous unsuccessful psychiatric cures.[25] The professional reputations of Frenchmen Benedict August Morel, who formulated the theory, and Valentin Magnan, who modified it, were well known in Argentina. Morel's starting point had been his interest in an apparent increase in mental disease in the post-Napoleonic crisis period, which he attributed to degeneration in both the healthy and the sick populations.[26] To answer the question of how an entire, moderately healthy multi-generational family could degenerate, Morel identified six categories of causes of degeneration, in which masturbation figured twice. First, it was believed that alcohol intoxication, an insufficient or bad diet, a marshy environment, epidemias, and violations of the laws of hygiene could cause degeneration. Second, degeneration could also be caused by the social environment, that is, by bad housing and work conditions, poverty, alcoholism, and venereal excesses. Third, a previous morbid disease in a person's history, such as epilepsy, hysteria, or hypochondria, in which lesions of the nervous system had occurred could lead to degeneration. Fourth, degeneration could be caused by "moral" disease, that is, vices such as masturbation and other sexual aberrations. Fifth, congenital diseases or diseases acquired in infancy, such as atrophies, hydrocephalia, ossification of the cranial sutures, convulsions, tuberculosis, blindness, congenital muteness, and so on could cause degeneration. And sixth, degeneration could be caused by hereditary influences, which could also be influenced by masturbation and which it was useless to try to fight, which is why many psychiatric treatments had failed.[27]

Figure 7. Advertisement of an aperitif making fun of Darwin's theory, "Prodigious Confirmation of Darwin's Theory," *PBT* 3 no. 92 (1906): 99. Courtesy of the Archivo General de la Nación.

Valentin Magnan, coming along after Charles Darwin had published his work on the evolutionist concept of the struggle for life
and survival in 1859, applied this biological theory to degeneration.
Just as certain species were less fit to survive, so were certain people
who were predisposed for degeneration. Degeneration was a true
pathological state that made a person mentally and physically inferior in the struggle for life because the body suffered an imbalance
and was afflicted with episodic syndromes, such as obsessions,
impulsions, and delirium, and suffered from a lack of harmony
between different organic functions. Most alarmingly, he argued,
the degenerative condition would end more or less rapidly in the
"annihilation of the species."[28] (See figure 7.) Clearly masturbation,
as a sexual aberration that could predispose people to degeneration,
was potentially harmful both to individuals and society.

Porteño psychiatrists found Morel's and Magnan's categories
quite applicable to Buenos Aires, especially in its late-nineteenth-
century role as a magnet for European immigrants. Crowded ten-
ement houses *(conventillos)* harbored both moral and physical
contagions with their lack of good air, light, and water; the city
lacked sewers; fetid odors came from the slaughterhouses, meat
packing plants, and cemeteries. Marshy areas breathed ill health.
Epilepsy, hysteria, and hypochondria produced lesions of the nervous system. Moral disease, sexual aberrations, and prostitution
spread by contagion. No wonder, wrote Argentine public hygien-
ist and politician Eduardo Wilde, that people in unhygienic cities
had more girl babies than boys! It was the reverse in the healthy
countryside, where more boys were born. Likewise, parents with
"bad and dissolute habits" tended to have more girls, whereas
people of upstanding morality had more boys. Wilde's remarks
refer to the belief that physically and mentally weaker people
tended to have weaker children, that is, female children.[29] Diseases
such as gout or alcoholism in one's ancestor, for example, could be
the source of an entire family's demise. Subsequent generations
were said to likely manifest neuropathologies, gallstones, dyspep-
sias, obesity, insanity, and criminality. (See figure 8.)

Degeneration theory became widely accepted in Argentina,
and in the United States as well, because the theory could be used

El progreso de la higiene escolar

12 de marzo de 2007—Llevo á Alfredito á la escuela donde lo primero que hacen es entregarle una libreta de «salud».

15 de marzo de 2007—Llevo á Alfredito al Instituto de Higiene Escolar, donde le examinan los pelos, los dientes, la sangre, los esputos y la epidermis.

20 de marzo—Lo miden.

3 de abril—Lo pesan.

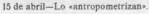

15 de abril—Lo «antropometrizan».

25 de abril—Le examinan la agudeza visual.

Figure 8. Comic strip entitled "Learning Hygiene." From *PBT* 3 no. 85 (1906): 22. Reprinted with permission.

El progreso de la higiene escolar [23]

4 de mayo—Le prueban el sistema nervioso.

20 de octubre—Lo mandan á pasar un año al campo.

20 de octubre de 2008—Lo mandan á pasar un año á la orilla del mar.

Desde el año 2008 al 2025, lo vacunan contra el sarampión, la escarlatina, el tifo, la difteria, el cólera, la disentería, la tuberculosis, la peste bubónica, etc., etc.

15 de marzo de 2026—Mi hijo tiene 24 años y los médicos, suspendiendo los cuidados higiénicos, acaban de dar por fin autorización para que aprenda á leer.

Figure 9. Comic strip entitled "Learning Hygiene (pt. 2)." From *PBT* 3 no. 85 (1906): 23. Reprinted with permission.

to identify actual and even potential criminals and because countries with high levels of immigration feared a rise in criminal
activity. The advantage of degeneration theory was that degenerates were presumed, according to the theory at least, to be easily
recognizable from their physical signs. Psychiatrists who claimed
the ability to tell police and judges who was "normal" and who was
"pathological" were seen as invaluable to the justice system. This
was one of the reasons that psychiatrists became regulars in court
proceedings as expert witnesses.[30] Masturbation was viewed as one
of the key identifiers of degeneration. For example, in a case from
1888, forensic psychiatrists introduced evidence that a man accused
of murder suffered from masturbation in an attempt to attenuate
his punishment.[31] Although the judge decided to disallow the
excuse of masturbation, this case and others like it reflect the fact
that courts were becoming more accustomed to the attempts of
doctors and criminologists to relate crime to mental illness and to
degeneracy. In the most extreme view of anthropological criminology, there were no criminals; there were just sick men and
women who could be identified by physical signs and treated in asylums rather than jails.

This is precisely what Luis's defense attorney tried to use to get
his client off the hook for his crime. Using psychiatry, the attorney
argued that Luis suffered from what psychiatrists called "moral
insanity," in distinction to the type of insanity denoted by a clear
exhibition of insane features. As elaborated by Lombrosian theorists, the morally insane were defined as persons unable to "allow
their natural morality to surface." Their lack of a moral sense made
them reject what was "beautiful and good." Even though they spoke
about "honor, order, religion, philanthropy, morality, justice, and
patriotism," they completely lacked the ability to feel these sentiments. It was the same with the affective faculties. While the
morally insane might say that they felt sorrow for someone, they
were really "indifferent to others' misfortune" and were, on the
contrary, motivated by an "exaggerated egoism." Morally degenerate, without a vestige of any affective faculty, the morally insane
succumbed to "bizarre and contradictory judgments, . . . cruelty and
evil." In addition, in terms of degeneration, the morally insane were

"truly prejudicial to the collectivity" because they succumbed to the influence of "morbid heredity and the environment." Because they did not "have the necessary elements to establish moral liberty, . . . they could not be held responsible for their acts."[32]

There were two areas in which Luis fit the positivists' description of moral insanity. Citing as his authority Luis María Drago, the defense attorney noted first that Luis, like all morally insane people, felt no repugnance for the crime before he committed it, and second he felt no remorse afterward. This "moral dullness" or lack of any moral sentiment could have been exacerbated by his habit of masturbation, since masturbation was viewed as weakening the mind. In fact, Drago, whose schedule had been too tight to accept the position of defense attorney for Luis, later addressed some remarks directly to Luis's case in his study of prisoners, declaring Luis morally insane—in Lombrosian terms, a person who "floated between dementia and good sense."[33]

Luis's lack of repugnance and repentance, his lack of any moral sense, grief or affective faculties, and his cruelty; his cold premeditation of his goal to gain financial advantage for himself by murdering his victim and cashing in the insurance, all seemed, at least to Luis's defense attorney, to support the plea of moral insanity. Luis even compounded his status as morally insane. Far from showing repugnance for his crime, Luis repeated his scheme several times before succeeding in killing one of his victims. And far from showing grief, his last concern as he was being led off to prison was that he would not receive the insurance money. His only expression of sorrow for his victim, Alberto—that he had hurried the death scientifically so that his victim would not suffer—obviously benefited Luis.[34]

The psychiatrists came up with a different evaluation of Luis. The first proof for them that they were not dealing with a morally insane person was that Luis did not "look" like a born criminal, that is, he lacked the physical signs of one. The second item of proof for the psychiatrists was that Luis had had a motive for his crime. Morally insane people, in contrast, usually lacked motives for their crimes. Instead of motives, their actions were not criminally conscious and were prompted by delirium and pathological hallucinations that were then translated into aggressive acts. The third item of proof was that Luis seemed to have control over his intellect in that he had total memory, association of ideas, judgments, satisfactory answers, and eloquence. Fourth, Luis did not have "morbid heredity." Although Luis's family background clearly provided fertile ground for morbid heredity, the doctors interpreted Luis's testimony about the suicides by family members and his own insistence that his actions were insane as just a simulation of insanity. It was clear that Luis was a difficult person to categorize, as were so many criminals.

The escape from this dilemma was provided by an important Lombrosian principle that held that not all born criminals exhibited the physical traits of such. It seemed as if he were merely morally insane. But in fact, physical traits or not, Luis was really a born criminal. This was an important distinction because if it could be proven that Luis was morally insane, as his defense attorney argued, then Luis could conceivably be sent to an asylum rather than to jail. The reason that Luis could not be categorized as insane, the psychiatrists argued, was that he had the intellect that provided him with the moral freedom to hold him completely responsible for his crime. The doctors' speculation that Luis might have been an inveterate masturbator, which would have indicated that he might indeed have been suffering from morbid heredity, was discarded too by the psychiatrists on the basis of Luis's intellect. The outward sign, meaning the masturbation, of inherited flaws did not match up with the observed inner quality, that is, intellect. For the psychiatrists, the possibility that Luis was addicted to masturbation would have been demonstrable by traces on his "intellectual level and his cerebral functioning."[35] On the contrary, the doctors saw in him satisfactory intellectual capacity. The psychiatric report became the basis for the judge's upholding of the original sentence of death for Luis in September 1889. "Nothing in the doctors' report," the judge wrote, "favors Luis. Thus, the plea of insanity does not hold. Article 95, clause 1 of the penal code holds. The sentence is death."[36]

In the appeal that was immediately filed in October 1889, the defense attorney focused on the fact that the medical doctors had not provided absolute proof that Luis was sane, a requirement for the imposition of the death penalty. Essentially, the doctors said that the ability to know if a person was insane was an unresolvable problem for contemporary science, thus providing enough doubt, argued the defense attorney, to revoke the death sentence. These scientific doubts were confirmed, said the defense attorney, by a French psychiatrist's experiments.[37] This psychiatrist had tried to distinguish a delirious idea from a logical one, and the experiments had proven "surprising and almost embarrassing" when no difference between crazy and logical ideas could be noted. Given this level of uncertainty about what was sane and what was insane, the defense attorney argued that the death sentence was totally unjust. Luis's attorney insisted that in all his dealings with his client, Luis had shown a high level of insanity. "To put Luis in with the group of the insane who are confused with criminals—criminals who have their intellectual faculties complete and thus have enough moral liberty to establish complete responsibility for their crime—is wrong," argued the attorney, "because rather than favoring the criminal, which is what the court must do by law in the case of doubt, this prejudices him." Even if Luis was not insane, the death sentence should be revoked, argued the defense attorney, on the basis of the inconsistencies in witnesses' testimonies and the conflicting reports from the autopsy of Alberto Bouchot. "No matter how vehement the suspicions," argued the attorney, "suspicions are not enough to send a criminal to the scaffold. And if suspicions were not enough in the past, as we know from legislation, they are even less acceptable now in our times in which a higher and complete civilization has torn down the scaffold and raised on top of it the penitentiary, where a criminal, sane or insane, can redeem himself through Christianity and science."[38] The attorney's point was that Luis would not have been condemned to death in times of less civilization, so he should not be condemned in this period of greater civilization. Moreover, according to Luis's attorney, it would have been especially inconsistent to have his client condemned to death when the courts of the Province of Buenos Aires, out of a high sentiment of civilization, had rescinded other criminals' sentences of capital punishment.

In November 1889 the prosecutor's response to this appeal focused on the difference between real insanity and moral insanity. He explained the need for a severe and exemplary punishment in Luis's case of moral insanity. "Capital punishment is consistent with Luis's crime. He is not insane. He is a man without god, law and conscience; a monster who kills in cold blood with no hatred or rancor, with poison, malice and premeditation. Luis wants us to think that he is insane through heredity, but the inheritance of insanity is not inevitable." He cited a French jurist who had pointed out that while a person could inherit a tendency toward crime he could still be in a state of reason and moral liberty. The prosecutor charged that Luis's alleged moral insanity came simply from his perversity, and that his characteristics such as cruelty, lack of remorse, and loss of moral sense were typical of delinquents in general. That is, the prosecutor was arguing that there was no need to suppose that a delinquent of this type was mentally ill. He argued that even if a person originally had a normal conscience, his conscience would become deadened after he had committed numerous crimes. This was not "insanity," stated the prosecutor, but "horrible depravity."[39]

The arguments of the defense attorney and the prosecutor reflected the broader debate about the theories of positivism and criminology. The defense attorney favored the use of attenuations and exemptions from criminal charges outlined by positivists. He also reflected a growing abhorrence toward the death penalty. The prosecutor, by contrast, insisted on the traditions contained in Argentina's civil and penal codes. The civil code only recognized the different types of dementia. The penal code, on the contrary, allowed only insanity originating from a definite intellectual disturbance, as an exempting cause of criminal responsibility, along with somnambulism, imbecility, and drunkenness (Article 79, clause 1). The law did not then admit presumed moral insanity. In other words, the Argentine penal code, along with other national penal codes, did not recognize the perversion of the emotions, moral sensations, and sentiments as an independent state; rather there always had to be some disturbance of a person's reason. Thus, moral insanity could not be used for a claim of irresponsibility except when it was accompanied by an intellectual disturbance. Regarding the death penalty, the prosecutor's view was that the penalty was in the code and that, although it was "painful," it was also "legitimate and in certain cases indispensable." As an earlier jurist had written, no other penalty was sufficient expiation; no other penalty satisfied the alarms and horrors that crime created in society.[40] By the mid- to late nineteenth century, this seemed to many Argentines to be an old-fashioned idea.

Like the prosecutor, the five appeals court judges did not share their period's enthusiasm for less punitive treatment of criminals. In fact, the judges' written opinions provided a focused attack on positivism and anthropological criminology, seeing them as symptomatic of the evils of the new materialistic age. When the judges of the appeals court sat down to deliberate Luis's case in December 1889, they began the meeting by reviewing their charge. They had to address the usual four questions of whether the crime had been proved and the author of it discovered; how the crime should be classified; whether there were attenuating circumstances; and then what the punishment should be. They knew that the crime was homicide done with premeditation and treachery and by means of poison and that Luis was the murderer. Regarding the issue of moral insanity, which the defense attorney had introduced following the "modern Positivist School," the original judge asked for a medical examination to see if Luis was mentally ill. This exam found no evidence in Luis of the anthropological traits presumed by the new school. This led the doctors to conclude that Luis was not morally insane, but by a strange inconsequence, their conclusion was that if cruelty and so on indicated moral insanity, even when the subject did not have the conditions that this school had established, Luis was morally insane. The fact that the doctors had been less than conclusive generally annoyed courts, as happened in Luis's case. The appeals judges ignored this bit of medical indecisiveness and focused instead on the fact that the moral insanity claim of Luis was not corroborated by the doctors' exam. Further, scientists had not yet fully proven the criminal type as a scientific fact. In fact, Lombroso himself had doubts about his own theories. In sum, positivist anthropological criminology was still just a theory, whose precepts had not yet been incorporated into any penal code. If the scientific school responsible for developing the theory had not even been able to fully characterize moral insanity, then how could a court of law, asked the judges, adopt that theory as a guiding principle in criminal cases.[41]

Since moral insanity was not part of the penal code, the judges had to follow the law, not speculative theories. The courts could not recognize excuses that were not enumerated in law. It was precisely for this reason that moral insanity could not be accepted as a circumstance exempting a person from punishment. Moreover, the judges went further and attacked the positivist school itself for ignoring the human spirit and focusing instead on the organs and functions of the body. Positivists made a complete abstraction of the spirit, they wrote, and privileged instead the alterations of the body, especially in the brain, which they considered to be the ruler of human life. This theory, the judges argued, was a materialistic one totally incompatible with Argentine law. On the contrary, Argentine law rested on free will and moral order. The judges' decision in December 1889 to uphold Luis's death sentence was unanimous.

In the Argentine judicial system, the death sentence had to be carried out within twenty-four hours of the sentence. The only chance for reprieve during this period was from the president of the republic himself, and that is what happened in this case. President Juárez Celman commuted Luis's death sentence to an indeterminate term in the penitentiary for three reasons. The president's first explanation for commuting the death sentence had to do with his recognition that certain female sentiments were beneficial to society. Moved by the "noble sentiment of piety," a group of distinguished Argentine women *(damas)* had submitted a petition in favor of Luis and it was the president's judgment that such a noble sentiment should not be denied.[42] The women were motivated more by a general opposition to the death penalty than any sympathy for Luis. This reason is also interesting because it may indicate a pattern of the use of women's petitions as a way to justify clemency.

The president's second justification was that, although the "public vindictiveness would not be satisfied with the death sentence commuted to penitentiary," he felt confident that Luis while imprisoned would not commit another crime.[43] Therefore society was safe, even if its desire for revenge was not satisfied. The need to satisfy a desire for vengeance is often referred to in cases as a justification for the death sentence, almost as if society were still engaged in vendetta, only that it had placed the ability to carry it out in the hands of government.

The president's third reason for clemency is especially interesting since he tied it to fellowship for a neighboring country and to a generalized nineteenth-century desire to conceptualize civilization. Brazil was to become a republic two days after Luis's execution date. As one might imagine, there were grand festivities planned in Brazil, and perhaps in Argentina too, for this day of December 8, 1889. A "bloody execution" on the eve of these festivities, wrote the Argentine president, would be inappropriate, even though he believed that Luis deserved to die. An "act of clemency" would be more in fitting with the festivities for the establishment of a republic, Juárez Celman wrote. This would "increase the public rejoicing" and better illustrate the "Argentine people's and their government's sympathy for the arrival of free institutions in the United States of Brazil."[44] This was how Luis ended up in the penitentiary rather than in front of the firing squad.

Luis continued to spend his days in the penitentiary under the panoptic vision of the professionals, running through many different diagnoses, which reveal the progression of positivist, criminological, and degeneration ideas in Argentina, including masturbation. His case attracted the attention of some of the most prominent Argentine criminologists and psychiatrists of the time. Picture them peering at Luis through the glass window of the prison door. The doctors wrote that they tried to be secretive, but that Luis heard them coming. In preparation for their clandestine visit, Luis adopted an "affected and confident air, walking around in his cell with an open book in his hands, striking truly comical poses." The doctors described him as having an "effeminate way of walking and moving his body, beautiful manners, and meticulous clothing, especially in relation to the other inmates."[45] During the year that the doctors observed him, Luis reportedly became less affected, began to work peacefully in the tailor's shop, and show some sentiment for the death of Alberto Bouchot.

One of Luis's original examining doctors, Drago, had had a difficult time trying to obtain Luis's cooperation for anthropometric measurement. It was not unusual for an accused person, even a convicted person, to refuse measurement. Interestingly, Drago's description includes some details that seem to indicate that Luis did indeed have the physical signs associated with the definition of degeneracy, such as a large round head, voluminous jaws, extended eyebrows, pronounced chest, long arms, and a protuberance in the middle of his forehead. The fact that there could be such differing observations and measurements made of Luis shows one of the weaknesses of anthropological criminology, which had always been an argument against the use of anthropometry. As an observer had pointed out, sometimes measurements were made with a person's clothing and shoes on, and other times, with them removed, making for a large discrepancy in the data.[46]

Luis's case continued to attract the attention of Argentine psychiatrists long after Luis was sentenced to the penitentiary. After the Institute of Criminology was opened at the National Penitentiary in 1907, its director, José Ingenieros (see figure 9), took on Luis as one of his first subjects. Ingenieros traced the life of Luis in the penitentiary, from his first months as a "mental degenerate" to his later years when he was diagnosed as suffering "chronic polymorphous hallucinatory delirium." His mental state had deteriorated slowly and he had adapted to prison well. Desiring to reconstruct Luis's psychology, Ingenieros was finally able to get hold of the voluminous court case at the tribunal archives. His analysis was that Luis lacked any moral sense; exhibited "criminal vanity"; and lacked foresight. Regarding the lack of moral sense, the genesis of Luis's crime was common to many degenerates who were moderately intelligent, but who were "moral indigents." Of humble origin, obligated to a life of poverty, these people had acquired some education but it only served to "intoxicate their spirit, awakening in their imagination a desire for wealth." This was especially true in countries of heavy immigration like Argentina. According to Ingenieros, this desire was fatal for Luis because he was prevented from getting rich by his degenerative qualities that had been exacerbated by masturbation. Degeneration had prohibited him from

Figure 10. José Ingenieros (1877–1925). Psychiatrist, psychologist, criminologist, sociologist, and publisher. A positivist to the core, he promoted the introduction of scientific criminology in Argentina.

"making America," as other immigrants had been able to do. He could not engage in concentrated and coordinated activity and did not have the ability to live by saving and progressing. Because he was abnormal, Luis chose a different route. He did not even have the ability to try a different crime when his first scheme failed. "His sick imagination delighted in the rumination of a complicated and novel crime. His attempts to use chloroform were novelesque; he did it with the perseverance of an artist modeling from clay. He was vain; he called his crime suave, meditated and scientific." He told Ingenieros his plan to use the ten years in prison for study, but he expressed the hope at the same time that he would not have to spend more than ten years there. What Luis still regretted was that the insurance company had won the claim. Luis had had no foresight while he was planning his crime, wrote Ingenieros, and lacked any foresight about his true situation even as he sat in his cell.[47]

As he reviewed Luis's case, Ingenieros concluded that Luis's lawyer had been right: Luis was insane. But Ingenieros believed that the forensic psychiatrists were also right when they said Luis did not have the characteristics of the born criminal. Ingenieros added a third diagnosis of Luis, noting an inherited mental degeneracy, which gave him deficient intelligence and a malformed moral sense. In the penitentiary, Luis "entertained visitors with his pleasant and picaresque loquacity, and with the ingenious way he could translate aberrant ideas that characterized his mentality of degeneration." Ingenieros observed Luis first in the printing workshop where he engaged in "loud soliloquies that did not make any sense using a metal cylinder to amplify his voice." He was not an efficient worker, noted Ingenieros, although he submitted to discipline. However his mental disorder was obvious. He did not associate with other inmates and preferred his solitude and hallucinatory conversations. He seemed kind and pleasant and did his schoolwork well. He typically wrote with pompous phrases and lots of adjectives. Once, he asked if in a republic, the people were sovereign. When he was told yes, he replied that he could not conceive of sovereigns without subjects and could not imagine who might be the subjects of Argentine citizens. To know his mental defects better, the doctors asked him to answer in writing some questions that would serve for his pardon. Luis answered that Alberto had died of a natural illness, cerebral congestion, and that the doctor had said this illness had been produced by indigestion and headaches. Plus, the court doctors had said that Alberto had not been poisoned. Luis also claimed to be plagued by bad spirits, electricity, and magnetism. He wrote many requests for pardon and wanted the government to pay him an indemnification. This was why he was transferred to the Mercedes Hospice, an institution for the delinquent mentally ill, noted Ingenieros, because of his obsession with being freed.[48]

Luis thus became an example of what antipositivists feared, that is, that with criminal responsibility being undermined by psychiatric medicine, much of the criminal population would be sent to asylums. Critics of positivism warned that positivism was subversive, heretical, and scientifically nihilistic. In its denial of free will, positivism totally discounted individual responsibility and morality and reduced man to a monkey or a machine. If a person's action was just "in his nature and did not earn him either merit or demerit, then all human acts would be equal and the world would not be able to establish the difference between virtue and vice."[49] This could be the end of the world as it was known at the turn of the century.

Conclusion

In the late twentieth century, psychiatric and criminological theories are informed by beliefs more complex than the belief that masturbation is connected to degeneration. However, in the late nineteenth and early twentieth centuries, these theories were considered innovative ways to analyze human behavior. Psychiatrists and criminologists not only struggled to apply these new theories to their patients and subjects but also attempted to use them as explanations for the success or failure of entire nations and civilizations. Two of the more important caveats in this focus on the degenerative condition and its manifestations in something such as masturbation were that such theories, first, delayed the search for other factors of civilization's ills and, second, involved extremely radical cures. First, these theories could be substituted for social and environmental explanations for poor economic and social conditions, and for perhaps treatable mental disease. For example, although public hygienists were campaigning to clean up conventillos and factories in the late nineteenth century, move cemeteries outside the city center, build sewers and improve latrines, and so on, they could still say, as did one of Argentina's most famous, Eduardo Wilde, that degeneration in the constitution of the city's working class came more from workers' own vices and excesses and lack of regimen than from poor living and working conditions and the monotony of factory work.[50] Although Wilde was most likely referring to vices such as alcoholism, the habit of masturbation was certainly considered by many professionals to be an important and influential vice and excess.

Second, a cure seriously suggested for degeneration seemed to presage the atrocities of the early to mid-twentieth century in Europe. "Regeneration," the counterpart to degeneration, it was suggested, was to be accomplished not through moral improvement, but through physiological purging. That is, improvement of the "race" was no longer to be accomplished through religion, but rather now through evolution, selective marriages, and the castration of born criminals.[51] Just as purgings of the body relieved it of excess blood and so on, so would the purging of society eliminate unwanted elements and degenerates. This was considered to be nothing more than preventive medicine that, it was argued, was not limited to transmissible diseases, but rather could be more broadly applied to "preserve the human race from all causes of physical and moral degeneration."[52] The problem with allowing an individual act such as masturbation to go unchecked was that it would inevitably spread its degenerative nature to the entire "race." What was one day an individual and limited evil, it was argued, could easily be converted the next into a broad social evil. In this reality, then, there was more to be feared from degeneration than from "transitory plagues and contagions" because degeneration was more irreversible.

Ingenieros, one of Luis's closest observers, made one of the most elaborate statements on the need to eliminate degenerates. It was the "professional weakness" and "ridiculous piety" of psychiatrists, he wrote, that was undermining society by prolonging the life of incurably ill persons. Rather, he argued that medicine's function was to defend the human species using biological selection, which would preserve "the superior characteristics of the species, through the immediate and sweet destruction of incurables and degenerates." This would avoid, he wrote, social parasitism and the possibility of the hereditary transmission of bad characteristics. Although Ingenieros explained that doctors could only theorize about such prophylactic strategies at the present time, he expressed hope that doctors in the future would "educate their sentiments within a purely scientific morality that would reflect the objective conditions of the biological utilitarianism of the species." The result would be medical treatments based on "the serene and cold calculation of the interests of the species" rather than on the "altruism, piety and beneficence" that had led to the present situation of preserving the weak members of society.[53] Had such treatments been in existence and widely accepted, it is likely that they might have been applied to Luis.

part two

Psychiatric Hospitals,
Prisons, and the State

Chapter Three

LAW, MEDICINE, AND CONFINEMENT TO PUBLIC PSYCHIATRIC HOSPITALS IN TWENTIETH-CENTURY ARGENTINA

Jonathan D. Ablard

Burdened by the expenses of a private psychiatric clinic, Francisco, an Italian immigrant living in Buenos Aires, decided in March 1921 to transfer his sister Elba to the city's only public psychiatric hospital for women. In November of that same year, the director of the public hospital requested that Elba's case be legally certified—that two court-appointed doctors examine Elba, and that a judge rule that Elba's confinement was appropriate and justified. The following month, a court declared Elba mentally incompetent and her hospitalization was given post facto legal sanction. Although on the surface, Elba's path to the asylum seemed to conform to the law, in fact there were several irregularities. According to the Argentine civil code, Elba should have received her court-appointed inspection *prior* to being hospitalized. Worse still, she was in the public hospital for nine months before being examined. When Elba eventually gained her release in 1924, she quickly brought accusations against her brother. Named guardian of her estate and of her children, Elba accused him of theft of her property and mistreatment of her eldest daughter during her confinement.[1]

Figure 11. Prisoners and psychiatric patients being transported together in a train. "Presos y Locos" (Prisoners and madmen). Courtesy of the Archivo General de la Nación.

Elba's story fits into a larger narrative of the plight of Argentina's psychiatric patients both before and after her case. As recently as 1985, a team of doctors and jurists published a comprehensive study on the legal status of Argentina's psychiatric patients. The book, published in the wake of South America's bloodiest regime of the twentieth century, analyzed a recently enacted law designed to better protect persons deemed mentally incompetent. The authors, respected authorities in jurisprudence and medicine, argued that the national civil code's guarantees against arbitrary or inappropriate hospitalization were unenforceable and often ignored. As a case in point, when the military junta fell in 1983, more than 85 percent of public psychiatric patients "[had been] there for years, in many cases until death, without anyone outside the hospital being charged to defend their rights." This was true in cases where hospitalization had been necessary and also when family, spouse, or neighbors had conspired to deprive individuals of their liberty for personal gain. The authors concluded that many patients, lost to the outside world, simply became accustomed to hospital life and vanished behind asylum walls.[2] (See figure 12.)

This chapter explores the legal pathways that led everyday Argentine women and men to become involuntary psychiatric patients during the twentieth century. The desire of state bureaucrats and the elite to lock up the mentally ill, starting in the mid-nineteenth century, is beyond question; it was expressed repeatedly by doctors, legislators, and the press. Contemporary scholars have deftly analyzed the relationship between the containment of deviance and nation building and modernization in Argentina. The early impetus to build mental hospitals was grounded in humanitarian concerns and also beliefs in the social, medical, and even political danger that the mentally ill posed to the new nation. These ideas shaped medical notions of who was mentally ill and in need of hospitalization. However, individuals' pathways in and out of the hospitals were not solely a product of medical ideas but also were profoundly shaped by the ways in which medico-legal bureaucracy—the courts, hospital administrations, the police, and other public functionaries with the power to commit—functioned on a day-to-day basis. In sum, the fate of patients was as powerfully shaped by the medical and legal structures that surrounded hospitalization as by medical diagnoses that were at the core of psychiatric medicine.

Historically, and across national and cultural contexts, there have been fundamental differences in the treatment of the mentally ill and those suffering from physical ailments. The latter have generally had choices about which treatments to receive and from whom. Historian Roy Porter has remarked, "Those people suffering from serious mental disturbance have been subjected to compulsory and coercive medical treatment, usually under conditions of confinement and forfeiture of civil rights."[3] Therefore, psychiatric patients are often at risk of neglect or abuse, unless some authority outside of the hospital is charged to oversee that their stay in the hospital is warranted, that they receive humane and medically appropriate treatment, and that their release is timely.

Because of inadequate and ineffective formal legal protections, the care and confinement of psychiatric patients in Argentina in both public and private institutions often occurred without the oversight or supervision of any external authority. According to the Argentine civil code of 1871, no one could be confined to a hospital without a medical evaluation and the consent of a judge. However, hospital doctors, the police, and other officials, often with the tacit support of patients' families, frequently ignored or circumvented the law. A poorly worded legal code, hospital understaffing, and patient overcrowding conspired to deprive patients of their basic legal protections. As such, patients were liable to suffer wrongful confinement, dispossession, and social abandonment. For doctors, this state of affairs lent credence to a perceived public distrust of psychiatrists and their hospitals. In the absence of strong laws or consistent enforcement, psychiatrists enjoyed tremendous autonomy from outside regulation or scrutiny with regard to decisions to confine persons against their will.[4]

Despite the bad press, many psychiatrists were deeply concerned about these irregularities. And like their counterparts in nineteenth- and early-twentieth-century North America and Western Europe, Argentine psychiatrists and their allies tried to develop a national psychiatric network, one that would include up-to-date laws, modern hospitals, and advanced medical training.[5] Many doctors believed that the creation of viable laws to protect patients and to help professionalize psychiatry was an important part of that project. The rhetoric of doctors, and their allies in congress and elsewhere, belies the fact that much of their project to modernize Argentine society did not materialize.[6]

The absence of legal protections in the asylum also reflected broader questions of citizenship and rights. Until the 1940s, the overwhelming majority of those in asylums were foreign born or were recent transplants from the Argentine countryside. Most were working class or poor; maids, construction workers, and seamstresses were the most common occupations of those confined to public hospitals. Thus, those most adversely affected by the medical and legal system came from groups that typically lacked the necessary resources to challenge it.

The fate of Argentine psychiatric patients has implications beyond the grim reality of the asylum. Political scientist Joel Migdal has reminded us that "some states have gained much more mastery than others in governing who may heal the sick and who may not; the duration, content, and quality of children's education; . . . and countless other details of human action and relationship."[7] Although the Argentine state made impressive gains in the eradication of infectious disease and social welfare more generally, numerous historians have observed that well into the twentieth century many Argentines continued to lack basic health care or labor protections.[8] Furthermore, as historian Ernest Crider concluded, the authority of national and municipal governments in Argentina had but weakly penetrated into the lower ranks of society by 1914.[9] The case of psychiatric hospitalization also demonstrates, however, that well into the twentieth century the national state continued to exert less control over the behavior not only of individual citizens but also of its own bureaucrats and professionals. As the case of Argentine psychiatric patients demonstrates, there was little regulation of Argentine society by the state.

Background of Hospitals

Starting in the mid-nineteenth century, Argentina, and particularly Buenos Aires, experienced a profound transformation of its economic, social, and political life. These changes were largely the result of the country's growing importance as an exporter of primary goods. As the economy flourished toward the late nineteenth century, Argentina attracted increasing numbers of immigrants, many of whom settled permanently in urban rather than rural areas. The initial creation of mental asylums and their later modernization were to a large extent a response to Argentina's changing social, demographic, and economic landscape and were strongly tied to the belief that social instability and mental disorder went hand in hand.[10] Although Argentina gained effective independence from Spain in 1816, the next four decades were characterized by civil war between regionally based caudillos. In 1852, the most powerful of these leaders, Juan Manuel de Rosas, fell to forces who supported national unification of Argentina and its reorientation toward European and North American models of economic and social development. In tandem with political consolidation, the new government wished to create institutions of social welfare. To that end it reestablished the Society of Beneficence and the Philanthropic Societies, both banned during the toppled Rosas regime, comprised of elite women and men respectively, to oversee the construction and administration of hospitals, asylums, and schools in Buenos Aires. These measures, as well as education reform and the encouragement of European immigration, were part of the larger reorientation project.

Health care, and particularly care for the mentally unbalanced, was of critical importance for the project of national rejuvenation. The new government and its supporters viewed the early decades of independence as a period of barbarism, during which racial, class, and gender distinctions had eroded. According to many observers, this had resulted in increased mental disturbance, particularly among women, and non-Europeans of both sexes.[11] Reformers understood the need to create hospitals as part of a larger project that would help Argentina to earn the reputation as a "civilized" nation. Thus, one of the first acts of the Beneficent

arroja para esa enfe r .ne d a d una proporción de 84 % en el total de falleci-mientos.

—La Socie-dad Científica Argentina ha elegido su pre sidente al se ñor teniente coronel Inge-niero don Ar-turo M. Lugo-nes, ventajosa-mente conoci-do en los cen-tros militares y de ingenie-ría, j e f e de construcciones militares. y

Patio interior de un departamento

profesor de ferrocarriles en la Facultad de Ciencias.

—Uno de los más meritorios y anti-guos empleados del ministerio de Ins-trucción Pública era el inspector de colegios nacionales señor Publio Es-

cobar. Supri-mido su empleo e n e l presu-puesto de este año, q u e d ó temporalmente separado de su cargo; pero uno de los primeros acuerdos d e l gobierno fué re-ponerle, apro-vechando l o s cambios en el personal ocasionados por los últimos nombram i e n-tos. Este acto de justicia se ha reci b i d o c o n general aplauso.

—La procesión del Nazareno que tradi-cionalmente se hace en la iglesia de San Francisco salió también este año reco-rriendo los alrededores del templo, acom-pañada por las cofradías y numerosos devotos.

Celdas de reclusión para furiosas

Corredor transformado en dormitorio

Figure 12. Views of the "Hospital Nacional de Alienadas," *PBT,* 3; 82 (1906): 56–57. Courtesy of the Archivo General de la Nación.

Society was to transfer all female insane from the city's decrepit hospital to a newly renovated colonial-era hospital. During its first year, the new asylum housed 68 women patients. During the rest of the nineteenth century, the asylum grew in a haphazard fashion.

In 1863, the Municipality of Buenos Aires opened the Casa de Dementes (House for the Demented) with 120 male patients. Starting in 1881, administration for the Casa became the responsibility of the municipal Public Assistance. In 1873, the city changed the name of the asylum to the Hospicio de las Mercedes (Hospice of Mercy), in honor of the patron saint of convicts and the insane.[12] Likewise, in 1889 the women's asylum was renamed the Hospital Nacional de Alienadas (National Hospital for the Female Insane) and placed under national authority. Finding the men's hospital to be both a financial and political burden, the city of Buenos Aires relinquished its responsibility to the federal government in 1905. As with all national health facilities, the two hospitals were administered by the Ministry of Foreign Relations and Religion until the mid-1940s. During the government of Juan Perón, 1946–1955, the hospitals were placed under the newly created Ministry of Public Health where they remained until the 1990s. In response to urban population growth, and the resultant pressure on hospital services, both hospitals built rural satellite facilities in the Province of Buenos Aires. The all-male Colonia Nacional de Alienados (National Colony for the Insane) opened in 1899, and the women's hospitals opened a similar facility in the Buenos Aires suburb of Lomas de Zamora in 1908.[13] (See figure 11.)

Although by the beginning of the twentieth century, Argentina's capital and surrounding area possessed an adequate number of psychiatric hospital beds to service the local population, there was little care available in the country's more isolated provinces.[14] Thus, in 1906 under the auspices of the director of the Hospicio de las Mercedes, the Comisión Asesora de Hospitales y Asilos Regionales (Advisory Commission on Regional Hospitals and Asylums) was created to supervise the construction of provincial hospitals. In 1914, the Oliva Colony Asylum in Córdoba Province opened and while serving the entire northwestern portion of Argentina, it also served as a place to remove excess population from the porteño psychiatric facilities.[15]

In order to understand the legal status of Argentina's psychiatric patients it is imperative to consider, if only briefly, the social historical context of the hospitals. Undoubtedly, the legal status of patients was directly influenced by social conditions inside the hospitals. The two most salient points were that the majority of the patients were foreign born and the hospitals were overcrowded and understaffed.

Since the mid-nineteenth century, Argentina's expanding export economy attracted growing numbers of immigrants in search of economic opportunity. Argentina's official policy of attracting immigrants reinforced this demographic trend. Although many immigrants came in search of land, tenure patterns in the countryside made it difficult to acquire agricultural property. As a result, most immigrants settled in the cities, particularly in Buenos Aires.[16] This demographic reality was reflected in the population of the city's asylums, where, until 1939, a majority of patients were foreign born. For this reason, among others, doctors frequently assailed unregulated immigration as being the cause of increased rates of mental and physical illness among the general populace.[17]

Immigration, as well as increasing domestic migration from interior provinces, placed heavy burdens on all of Buenos Aires's social services, particularly on its psychiatric hospitals. Despite a spate of promising reforms between 1890 and 1900, both hospitals continued to suffer from extreme overcrowding, a problem that reached its apex in the 1930s and 1940s.[18] These conditions adversely affected both the medical treatment of patients and also the ability of the hospitals to keep up with the paperwork concerning the confinement and release of patients.[19]

At the beginning of the twentieth century, most men were confined by public authorities, especially the police. During the course of the next two decades, however, confinements were increasingly effected by family members.[20] Throughout the first three decades of the twentieth century, most women were confined by household or family members. Starting in the 1930s the HNA changed its admissions procedures in response to overcrowding and there was a sharp rise in confinements by public authorities.[21]

Hospitalization and the Law

Throughout Argentina's history, men and women hospitalized for psychiatric illness generally lacked basic legal protections. Until 1983, the Argentine civil code of 1871, in conjunction with rules developed in each hospital, theoretically regulated insanity proceedings, hospitalization, and guardianship.[22] The civil code ordered that an individual could not be considered mentally incompetent without the prior consent of a judge. The civil code also prevented judges from ruling on mental competence until two medical doctors had examined the person in question.[23] Professional medical evaluations of suspected lunatics could take place in private homes, jails, general hospitals, and even the police's Service for the Observation of the Insane.[24]

Until 1968, the civil code defined insane persons as "individuals of either sex who are in a habitual state of mania, dementia or imbecility, although they may have periods of lucidity, or the mania may be only partial."[25] Either spouse, another relative, the Ministry of Minors, or, in the case of foreign nationals, the respective foreign consul could request a declaration of insanity. Any citizen could also make a request for a finding of insanity but only "when the insane person is furious, or inconveniences his or her neighbors."[26] The code called for the naming of a temporary guardian on the initiation of insanity proceedings. Should a person be found insane, his or her personal property became the responsibility of the appointed guardian. Incapacity could only be rescinded after the patient was reexamined by doctors and a judge declared the interdiction lifted.[27]

The civil code also regulated hospitalization, stating that "the insane person will not be deprived of liberty except in cases where it is feared that exercising it, he will injure himself or others. Nor can he be sent to a psychiatric hospital without judicial authorization."[28] Legally, then, hospitalization could occur only after a court of law had deemed the subject insane. As strict and comprehensive as these normative procedures and rules were on paper, often they had little effect on the actual practices of courts, hospitals, and the police in the hospitalization of the mentally ill. An examination of case studies, medical journals, and legislative debates illustrates that public officials frequently failed to follow the letter of the law.[29] These cases offer glimpses into the lives of women and men who fell, if only briefly, into the darkness that often lay between hospital and court.[30] For although the civil code demanded judicial authorization prior to psychiatric hospitalization, in the vast majority of the insanity proceedings reviewed here, patients had already been in the hospital for lengthy periods of time before their case came before a judge.

Involuntary placement in a psychiatric hospital accounted for the overwhelming majority of confinements. Whether accomplished through proper legal channels or not, the process posed serious threats to individuals' civil rights, financial well being, psychological condition, and physical health. This was particularly so if the confinement occurred without judicial oversight. Aside from losing personal freedom, commitment potentially meant the loss not just of property, but de facto custody of children, housing, and social standing.

One of the most common legal irregularities was the delay between a person's hospitalization and its approval by a court of law. By law, patients were to be inspected prior to hospitalization. Archival material indicates, however, that not only did the hospitals admit patients without examination, there were often delays of months and even years before a court approved the hospitalization. Aside from their technical illegality, delays also carried the implication that no public authority outside of the hospitals was aware of the patients' physical confinement.

In August 1924, Josefina D., a twenty-three-year-old native of Argentina, asphyxiated her five-week-old baby. The police immediately remanded her to their psychiatric observation facility, from whence, on the order of two staff doctors, she was placed in the women's hospital in October 1924. Little is known of her life in the hospital, save a brief mention that the isolation felt by all patients was perhaps worse for Josefina because she was deaf and her speech was difficult for doctors to understand. It appears, nonetheless, that Josefina adapted to hospital life and was considered obedient and helpful with chores. In 1937, the city's Office on Youth and Legal

Minors informed the hospital that formal proceedings to establish the subject's insanity had never been carried out. Thus, only in October 1937 did court-appointed doctors examine her and find her insane.[31] Josefina's experience was not an isolated case; Silvia O. was confined in 1932, but her case did not go before a judge until 1937. Carolina M., who accused her father of sexual abuse, waited four years before her 1943 confinement was approved by a court.[32]

Patients also frequently experienced protracted delays between the moment when a hospital determined that they were fit to be released, and when a court verified that decision and effected the release. José P., suffering from "mental confusion caused by alcoholism," was sent to the Hospicio in July 1925. By September the same year hospital authorities communicated to the court that he was fit to leave. Yet the following month, the Hospicio sent an identical communication to the court.[33] Thus, the patient, whose ultimate fate is not mentioned in the document, remained hospitalized due only to delays by the court. A Russian sailor, whom the police sent to the Hospicio after a bout of heavy drinking, faced a similar dilemma. Hospicio director Domingo Cabred was obliged to request that the courts lift the sailor's interdiction not once but twice.[34] The Federal Police similarly sent Samuel J., a thirty-four-year-old Czech, to the Police Observation Unit for the Insane after he was arrested for disrobing in public.[35] From there, the police sent Samuel to the Hospicio. In March 1935, forensic psychiatrists communicated to the court that they had judged the subject mentally competent and recommended his release. However, his judicial record shows that he was not released until June 1935, two months later. Another Czech, Carlos Luis, endured similar complications. The Federal Police brought the thirty-eight-year-old day laborer to the Hospicio in March 1932 for reasons not made clear in his file. Yet five months later, in August, the Hospicio communicated to the court that Carlos Luis "was in condition to be released." In October the same year, however, the Hospicio was forced to notify the court that the patient was still in its care. In their letter to the judge, Hospicio administrators noted, "Since as of this date we have received no resolution in favor of Carlos Luis' release and because his medical improvement persists, I reiterate to your honor, the request that was made in the cited note."[36] Then, in May 1933, the Hospicio repeated for a third time its request to have Carlos Luis's case resolved. Six days later, the court approved his release. For Paulina C., an Argentine-born maid committed by her employers in 1933, there was a six-week delay between the HNA's declaration that she was cured and her release from the hospital.[37] Delays seem to have been even more common for patients in rural hospitals, because of the greater difficulty of bringing outside inspectors and patients together.[38]

The delays experienced by these patients had serious consequences. In times of overcrowded and unsanitary hospital conditions, they jeopardized the health and safety of the inmates. After a two-week delay following a finding by the medical examiners that he was mentally competent, Francisco N. addressed himself to the court: "On December 28 [1946] medical examiners determined that I was cured, and ready to be released. As is public knowledge, we [hospital patients] are crammed together and poorly fed. I request my speedy release. Remaining in the Hospicio during this past month has caused me irreparable damage."[39] Francisco's complaint about the situation of the hospital is consistent with official reports of deterioration in all national mental health facilities. Likewise, his words mirrored concerns of hospital administrators who were well aware that many families refused to place relatives in their institutions during periods of overcrowding because they feared for their safety and health. In a report for 1913 and 1914, the director of the HNA noted, "Daily we face numerous persons who refuse to resign themselves to hospitalizing a loved one in the indigent wards and who also lack sufficient resources to place the relative in a private institution."[40] Finally, as was demonstrated by the case of Elba, weak judicial oversight may have facilitated opportunistic confinements by families and neighbors of patients.[41] The issues of timely reporting and release were not mere technical questions; they were profoundly important to the well-being of patients. (See figures 12 and 13.)

Irregularities influenced not only the length of hospitalization but also possibly the outcome of medical examinations. The hospitals were notorious for their overcrowded and unhygienic wards. In these conditions, a patient's mental state and physical appearance would deteriorate between the time of confinement and the medical examination. This, in turn, might have prejudiced the inspecting doctors and led to the judgment that a person was insane.[42] In some cases, the impact of unnecessarily long confinements may have been aggravated by persistent ideas of degenerative heredity, which held that physical evidence manifested itself on the bodies of the mentally ill.[43] Insanity proceedings demonstrate that doctors were quick to find evidence of degeneration and often did not even bother to note the precise condition or its significance.[44]

Attempts at Reform

The precarious legal situation of patients has been, and remains, a subject of great interest for psychiatrists, lawmakers, social critics, patients, and the general public in Argentina. Since the 1870s, doctors and parliamentarians decried the lack of legal protection for these wards of the state.[45] Many argued that the situation weakened Argentina's claim as a civilized and advanced nation and pointed out that the republic lagged behind Western Europe, the United States, Great Britain, and even some neighboring republics in providing legal safeguards for psychiatric patients.[46] The absence of proper legal controls over hospitalization was also a matter of professional concern, and many psychiatrists argued that laws should protect them from accusations of wrongful confinements.

Legislative initiatives to better protect patients, as well as critiques of these problems published in medical journals, provide us with a picture of the condition of psychiatric patients in twentieth-century Argentina and also how psychiatrists viewed the problem. The proposals and debates around the question of patients' legal rights help to explain why so many patients fell into a legal no-man's land. The first attempt to craft legislation for the treatment of the mentally ill came from Emilio R. Coni. One of the founders

Figure 13, above. Psychiatric patient being taken away at the Hospicio de las Mercedes. From the article "Una hora en el Hospicio de las Mercedes" (One hour at the Hospice of Las Mercedes), *Caras y Caretas* 26; 1300 (September 1, 1923). Courtesy of the Archivo General de la Nación.

Figure 14, left: "Egolatrous," *Caras y Caretas* 37; 1864 (June 23, 1934). Courtesy of Archivo General de la Nación.

of the Asistencia Pública for the city of Buenos Aires, Coni's legislative proposal is found in his 1879 *Código Médico Argentino*. Although the section devoted to psychiatric legislation was never put before congress, it served as the basis for many future proposals.[47] Coni called for regulation of all private and public psychiatric facilities through the offices of the municipal Asistencia Pública.[48] He also developed guidelines for admission and release of patients who sought to prevent abuses by either public authorities or families of patients. Each admission, for example, was to be accompanied by medical certificates, and hospitals were required by law to keep close track of admissions and releases.[49]

Dr. Antonio Piñero, director of the Hospital Nacional de Alienadas, penned the first actual piece of legislation to be presented before congress in 1894. His effort, and that of the Hospicio's director, Domingo Cabred, reflected a broader movement to reform the treatment of psychiatric patients.[50] Although no mention was made of Coni's earlier proposal, the themes addressed are quite similar. Piñero called for the creation of a commission to inspect hospitals to better ensure prompt reporting of admissions and releases. Piñero also recognized that in many emergency hospitalizations doctors and other public authorities ignored the civil code because there was no time to obtain court sanction. Recognizing the unwieldy nature of the code, his proposal therefore allowed for persons to be confined prior to a judge's approval, provided that the proper authorities were notified within three days.[51] In 1906, Piñero, now working in private practice, reintroduced the 1894 legislation. He noted a paradox in Argentina: criminals' due process protections were more secure than that of the mentally ill.[52] The majority of psychiatric hospitalizations, therefore, were illegal.[53]

Piñero's congressional sponsor, deputy Félix M. Gómez, argued that the civil and constitutional rights of the presumed insane went unprotected in Argentina. Gómez noted that the lack of adequate legislation with regard to the mentally ill might be excused to the relatively late formation of the Argentine state. Nevertheless, Argentina was clearly behind most of the world in terms of the development of comprehensive legislation. Gómez continued:

"We face a problem of our sociability, which is that as many as 98 percent of the insane locked away in our asylums are there illegally. The dispositions contained in Titles X, XI, and XIII of the civil code, which pertain to insanity, are dead letter in the majority of cases with regard to the treatment, confinement and the exercise of guardianship of the insane."[54] For Gómez, the question of national pride was a central concern, because in its lack of such legislation Argentina had fallen behind not only the nations of Western Europe but also the neighboring republics of Chile and Brazil, as well as the United States.[55]

As with other questions of psychiatric care, doctors and reformers tended to look to Europe, and later the United States, to gauge progress in Argentina. During the presentation in 1894 of Cabred's legislation, for example, deputy Eliseo Cantón noted with sadness that Argentina ranked far behind Western Europe with regard to legislation in defense of the mentally ill. France, England, Wales, and even Spain had passed laws regarding the confinement and care of the insane. Cantón noted, by contrast, that with regard to such legislation Argentina ranked with the more backward nations of eastern Europe.[56]

Starting in the 1920s, overcrowding and decay of public psychiatric hospitals led to heightened scrutiny of patients' rights by both the print-media and members of congress.[57] Critics increasingly recognized that overcrowding contributed to delays in the legal processing of patients. Responding to such concerns, Radical Party deputy Leopoldo Bard offered legislation to regulate confinement and treatment in psychiatric institutions in 1922. His proposal allowed for a variety of confinements, including emergencies, while it also sought to guarantee the physical safety and civil rights of patients. Influenced by a broader eugenic discourse, Bard argued that the national government was obliged to protect the property, reputation, and civil rights of the presumed insane and to safeguard citizens from the mentally ill, who, because of family resistance or loopholes in the laws, evaded psychiatric confinement.[58]

Hospital conditions also motivated national deputy Guillermo R. Fonrouge to request in September 1926 that the government investigate the legal status of patients held in national psychiatric facilities. Fonrouge pointed to the lack of regulatory statutes or procedures for the hospitals, as well as to rumors of husbands using hospitalization to punish their wives. Rather cryptically, Fonrouge cited a "semiofficial" report that calculated that of the "3,700 patients at the Hospicio de las Mercedes, 80 percent, that is, around 3,000 have been deprived of their liberty without the knowledge of any civil judge." The sheer number of patients with unresolved legal status was striking and spoke to the problem of overcrowding. Fonrouge went on to enumerate the now familiar violations of Articles 140 and 482 of the civil code.[59]

Private-hospital patients also suffered from the lack of proper judicial oversight. The issue came to the public's attention when a wealthy businessman was confined to a private clinic by his son in 1928. The confinement did not proceed quietly, and the father's employees and other businessmen started a boisterous campaign to free the man.[60] The following September, national deputy Aníbal Mohando cited the case when he proposed a bill to regulate the practice of medicine in private psychiatric clinics. Mohando observed that while the probity of these doctors was beyond question, nevertheless, "these clinics operate with complete liberty of action, without any efficient control by the National Department of Hygiene."[61]

Despite these indictments of hospitals' legal practices, psychiatrists were far from united on the issue of how to protect the rights of their patients. The thorny question of professional privilege, for example, complicated the issue of court involvement in hospitalizations. A December 1926 newspaper editorial by Adolfo M. Sierra, a well-regarded psychiatrist, criticized the various legislative proposals of Bard, Fonrouge, and Mohando. One of his principal arguments was that obliging doctors to communicate hospitalizations violated the penal code's rule of medical confidentiality. Likewise, Sierra noted that anyone claiming wrongful confinement could have legal recourse to the penal code's kidnapping statute. Optimistically, Sierra concluded that psychiatric patients already enjoyed adequate legal protection under existing statutes.[62]

Sierra continued this line of argument in a 1930 medical journal article. He observed that the major problem was the absence of regulations guiding admissions policy for private clinics. By contrast, Sierra noted that confinement to public facilities was characterized in fact not by lawlessness, but by excessive legal formalism.[63] At the Hospicio and its colony, for example, "There is a lawyer, on salary, who exercises a priori the function of guardian of the hospitals' patients; said lawyer must give notice of all confinements to the corresponding judge." At the state-run HNA, by contrast, there was no lawyer; instead the director of the establishment served as the patients' guardian and had to report their confinement within twenty-four hours to the judge.[64]

Sierra's position seemed untenable in the face of the experiences of many doctors who worked in the public sector, particularly as conditions in public hospitals grew more critical during the 1930s and 1940s. Dr. Máximo Agustín Cubas, a staff doctor at the overcrowded and poorly staffed Oliva asylum in Córdoba Province, was particularly vexed by the legal issues that rural asylums faced.[65] Cubas, writing in the hospital's quarterly journal in 1935, argued that certification of the insane (the formal process of establishing insanity prior to confinement) was plagued by bureaucratic and professional routine where paperwork was often signed off on with only careless reviews.[66] Similarly, many of the doctors working outside of the hospital who provided certificates of insanity often did not directly examine the patient prior to signing the papers.[67] It was not uncommon for family members to deposit someone at the colony and send medical certificates to the director well after the fact.[68]

Such problems were more acute in the rural asylums such as the Oliva colony because of the relative shortage of physicians in the countryside. These shortages compounded the fact that by law hospital doctors could not sign certificates of insanity on their own patients. The other problem that rural asylums faced was that owing to poor transportation networks in the countryside, suspected lunatics were often housed in local jails until there was a sufficient number to warrant their collective transport to an asylum. In these cases, police medical inspectors often would simply extend the certificates of insanity to all detainees, regardless of whether their condition remained serious. Cubas went on to note that as a consequence, "many times individuals arrive here in a state of perfect mental lucidity who may have suffered temporary mental confusion brought on by mere intoxication or similar causes. During their time in jail, which often lasted months, they get better. Yet, because the individual arrived [to the hospital] with a medical certificate of insanity, the hospital is obliged to maintain them for a period of time to make sure the episode is over."[69]

When finally released, the former patient would likely face social marginalization and also be a target of police scrutiny. This increased the likelihood that he or she would return to the institution. As was common in the psychiatric literature of the period, Cubas also expressed concern that countries at the "vanguard of humanity" had passed adequate legislation protecting their insane. Thus, the task of creating better laws was necessarily connected to Argentina's international reputation as a civilized country.[70] Furthermore, Cubas was quick to observe that without proper legal outlines for hospitalization doctors and administrators were exposing themselves to legal action by patients or former patients.[71] Thus, for Cubas, patients' legal rights involved not only protection of individuals, but also of national reputation and professional privilege.

Conrado O. Ferrer, also a doctor at Oliva, reiterated the issue of doctors' liability in a 1938 journal article: "Because of the lack of a law of the insane, interned mentally ill persons find themselves deprived of liberty by virtue of guidelines which have been established by practice, but which lack legal force. Thus our current incarceration would be considered a criminal act of arbitrary kidnapping and the directors of hospitals would be sanctioned by the Penal Code."[72] Ferrer's concern with arbitrary hospitalization reflected both a concern for professional legitimization and patients' rights. Argentine psychiatrists' work was tainted, according to Ferrer, by its susceptibility from unscrupulous families, irresponsible police forces, and a shortage of qualified specialists. To save the hospitals and medical practitioners, reform legislation was required.[73]

After decades of severe overcrowding in all national psychiatric hospitals and legislative inertia, promise of change arrived with the creation of the Ministry of Public Health in 1946 under the government of Juan Perón. At least on paper, the new government appeared committed to deep and lasting reforms of Argentina's public institutions, especially its long-neglected hospitals. The ministry's first director, the well-regarded neurosurgeon Ramón Carrillo, faced enormous challenges. In the realm of psychiatry, Carrillo directed his attention to the repair of the hospitals and also to regularizing thousands of patients' legal status. In a July 22, 1949, speech Carrillo noted that on assumption of the ministry, he had discovered that in national psychiatric facilities patients' legal paperwork was in total disarray:[74]

> In the Ministry of Public Health we have psychiatric establishments that house 15,000 patients, the majority of whom have been admitted without the authorization of a judge. In other words, we have a situation in fact, at the margins of the civil code, since the code requires prior judicial authorization to intern a supposedly insane person. We have not been able to initiate all of the corresponding proceedings as there are an infinitely larger number of patients than available judges. In the past year, as I believe, the Official Curatory of the Insane, with great effort and few resources, has been able to get 1,000 to 1,200 insanity judgments in a vain effort to correct a situation that has been neglected for years.[75]

According to Carrillo, at the root of these entanglements lay the civil code that was out of date and ineffectual in both medical and legal terms. Article 482, which required judicial authorization to commit someone, and Article 140, which stated that an allegedly insane person could not be so declared without prior judicial review, were impractical. In essence, the requirement of prior judicial authorization produced large numbers of extralegal hospitalizations, because neither the courts nor the hospitals had sufficient personnel to keep up with paper work.[76] Once confinement had taken place, it was easy for patients' cases to be forgotten by outside authorities.

Carrillo proposed to resolve this situation through a reform of the civil code and the creation of a national health code in order to, among other things, provide a more precise legal definition of insanity. His revised terminology read as follows: "The interdiction for mental illness only occurs when the person is above the age of 12 and cannot function normally in his personal life nor manage his personal or business affairs, because he suffers from such an affliction."[77] Carrillo astutely noted that for judges, what was relevant was whether "the sick person can manage their affairs, conduct themselves normally and engage in relationships with others. It matters much less to them whether a person is manic, demented or imbecilic, or if he has lucid intervals at the moment of characterization."[78] Carrillo thus sought to create a law that would facilitate communication between doctors and judges.

Carrillo further argued that the insane should always be given the right to speak before a judge during commitment proceedings: "Under the actual system, the mentally ill person, represented totally by the guardian, cannot speak before the judge. As it is, if the ill person does not have a well-intentioned guardian who brings him or her before the judge, the latter will not have the opportunity to hear from the patient."[79] In most cases judges rarely saw the subject of the insanity proceedings personally, since in Argentina commitment hearings, as well as most legal proceedings, were conducted through written documents and not with oral argument.[80] The matter was also of concern to patients. Celia B., confined to a private hospital by her parents in 1949, pleaded with the presiding judge that she be allowed to present herself before the court to demonstrate her sanity.[81] Carrillo's modified Article 147 would have required the presence in court of the person under question and the person requesting the insanity proceedings. Likewise, Carrillo urged that Article 144, which governed who could initiate proceedings, needed to be restricted.[82]

Carrillo's belief that the laws themselves were contradictory and often unrealistic was echoed by other doctors. In his 1946 proposal to regulate hospitals, psychiatrist and legal scholar Nerio Rojas elegantly explained the deficiencies in the current legal status and treatment of patients. Essentially, the Argentine civil code lacked flexibility. No one could be placed in a hospital without prior judicial authorization, and there was no provision to allow temporary hospitalization. Therefore, when an individual was brought to the hospital and required emergency attention, the hospital had two options. It could either turn the person away, thus putting the patient or others at risk, or it could violate the civil code by admitting the individual immediately. If the hospital followed the latter course of action, court doctors would inspect the subject after his or her confinement. Rojas also reminded his fellow congressmen that his legislation sought to resolve two sides of the confinement problem. On the one hand, admission raised a possible charge of *secuestración* (abduction), a danger that he felt had been exaggerated, but nonetheless, needed to be addressed. On the other hand, if the individual were not admitted, "There is the danger of the insane person who is both free and without help, or poorly monitored, because of negligence or ignorance on the part of his or her family, of whom little is said."[83]

In his classic legal medicine textbook, Rojas reiterated to his readers that the problem of the protection of the insane had been overstated. "The practice of confinement, inspection of establishments, the situation of the psychiatric patient, hospitalized or not, but not the interdicted, are not legislated here. It is a sad state of affairs, which is usually overcome for good or bad, thanks to regulations or the good faith or honesty or experience of doctors and family."[84] Although expressing faith that those with the power to confine would exercise it responsibly, Rojas dismissed as hyperbolic the notion that wrongful confinement frequently occurred: "I will not bother discussing the supposed 'abduction' of sane people, another of the popular prejudices favored particularly by lucid insane persons whose psychosis is unknown or denied by him and by his friends or family who often work from their own interests."[85] Rojas reminded readers that while abuse occurred to many disabled persons, there were already penalties on the books for crimes against the liberty of a person.

Conclusion

The failure of successive governments to pass comprehensive legislation or to enforce existing laws was consistent with the overall history of social legislation in Argentina during the twentieth century.[86] The deficits in public mental health, both in terms of legal protections and the quality of care, are clear. What remains more conjectural at this point is the reason that laws protecting patients never passed. There is some indication that the directors and owners of private clinics opposed passage of any legislation that would have interfered with their professional autonomy, particularly the issue of medical confidentiality. Recently, for example, Eduardo Cárdenas, a family judge in the city of Buenos Aires, explained the failure of a century of legislative proposals. "None managed to pass into law, thanks to the resistance of economic interests of the private clinics, *obras sociales*, and the resistance to change among certain sectors."[87] Cárdenas's analysis finds its echo in early allegations that psychiatrists in public hospitals often moonlighted in private hospitals and that they benefited from poor regulation of the profession.[88]

Although it is difficult to provide a more concrete explanation of why Argentina experienced no reform of confinement practices, archival sources point to the reasons that existing laws and regulations were not always followed. Simply put, overcrowding and understaffing made it difficult for public hospitals to keep up with the paperwork necessary to follow the letter of the law. Material conditions, then, aggravated the fact that the civil code only covered the institutionalization of persons already under the supervision of a judge; there was no legal procedure for emergency short-term hospitalizations.[89] Historian Cynthia Jeffress Little concluded that as the patient population at the Hospital Nacional de Alienadas grew at the turn of the last century, the "entrance exams must have been cursory at best."[90] Her hypothesis is borne out by archival evidence; the administration of the HNA complained in the 1920s and 1930s, for example, that it was difficult to hire and retain a sufficient staff of doctors.[91] Likewise, by the 1940s, in what was probably not an isolated incident, the director of the HNA complained to a presiding judge that he was able to serve as guardian of the patients' persons, but not their properties due to enormous caseloads.[92]

Furthermore, there is evidence that the hospitals attempted to follow the letter of the law, but were overwhelmed by the task. Monthly internal reports from the HNA demonstrate that hospital administrations might have spent a sizeable amount of time communicating the status of patients to the courts. Despite great effort, administrators were not equal to the enormous task. In August 1920, for example, the HNA sent 52 official reports on the mental status of patients to the courts, and an additional 246 letters to the relatives of patients. In that same month, the HNA received 103 new patients. At a minimum 51 of these women did not have their cases communicated by the hospital to the presiding judge. In September 1920, there were 122 admissions but only 44 communications to the courts.[93] The gap between admissions and cases reported to the courts indicates both a degree of effort on the part of hospital administration to apply the law, but also a failure to maintain adequate communication with the courts.

Legal delays may have also resulted from hospitals' policies, which worked so that the authority requesting hospitalization had the power to terminate it. For example, Article 67 of the regulations of the Hospicio de las Mercedes stated that a person who had been sent to the hospital by public authorities could only be released on order of those same authorities.[94] This issue remained vital into the 1980s and speaks to the problem of how well the Argentine legal bureaucracy functioned. Although the only reference to this problem comes from the 1980s, the extent of legal stasis makes the analysis worthwhile:

> In the majority of the cases, the police acted in collaboration with family members, and they did not consider themselves responsible for the hospitalization. They therefore did not inform the judge of their actions. Nevertheless, in the hospital the person was considered as interned by the police, and was not allowed to leave until the hospital had received judicial authorization which never arrived since no judge had been apprised of the case.[95]

The mental health network of Argentina was governed more by the whims and vagaries of a poorly funded medico-legal bureaucracy than by an efficient state apparatus. Due to an odd and tragic set of conditions, most Argentine psychiatric patients entered psychiatric hospitals without the benefit of the legal protections guaranteed to them by the civil code. In addition to the absence of effective safeguards, there was widespread failure to observe and enforce existing laws and regulations. On one level this was a result of unwieldy laws. Shortages of professionals and staff only further hampered compliance with legal and medical protocols.

Argentine psychiatrists and their congressional allies had sought to regulate and order the process by which individuals were confined to and released from hospitals. Their activities were tied to both nationalist and professional objectives. For a number of reasons, psychiatrists' work nevertheless remained largely unregulated, and they operated with great autonomy, their authority to confine or release persons going largely unchecked. However, this freedom came at a price. As proponents of legal reform had argued, public opinion tended to view psychiatrists as possessing excessive and arbitrary power to decide who was sane, who was insane, and who should be locked up. It is no surprise, then, that questions about the undue power of psychiatrists in Argentine society continue to be raised to this day by both laymen and professionals.[96]

Involuntary psychiatric hospitalization in Argentina provides a unique perspective into the day-to-day operations of the Argentine state and compels us to reconsider the capacity of state functionaries to exercise diligence over citizens. The case of Argentine psychiatric patients also serves to remind historians of the importance of studying not simply the rhetoric of social policy and legal reform, but also its actual implementation.[97] For several generations of scholars, Michel Foucault's description of the Panopticon—a prison design that allows the guards to carefully monitor each prisoner—has been an attractive metaphor to explain the historical experience of psychiatric patients.[98] The Argentine patient, however, suffered not only from the burden of psychiatric scrutiny but also from invisibility and abandonment. The Hospicio de las Mercedes and the Hospital Nacional de Alienadas, as well as rural institutions, were places where patients' lives were rigidly controlled. But they were also places where patients were lost from the outside world, and sometimes from the hospitals themselves.[99]

Chapter Four

PSYCHIATRISTS, CRIMINALS, AND BUREAUCRATS

The Production of Scientific Biographies in the Argentine Penitentiary System (1907–1945)

Lila Caimari

Without knowing my feelings, my parents suggested that I marry a good man, with a better economic situation; and since my parents were so good and I was used to sacrificing myself to help their good home which had so many difficulties, I decided to accept.

I worked for six months in a wool business, and I liked to alternate this job with my favorite amusements, such as reading, playing soccer, dances and watching films, which I did quite often.

I remember my sixth grade teacher, Srta. Beatriz Rey. The refinement that characterized her and her superior culture left this beautiful memory that I want to invoke today.

Instituto de Clasificación de la Provincia de Buenos Aires, Historias Criminológicas, #341, 27, and 3,598

These fragments from three autobiographical testimonies do not come from patients lying on a therapist's couch, nor from Catholics whispering their thoughts to a confessor, nor from letters addressed to close friends. These are the words of three convicted thieves, dressed in striped uniforms, telling their life stories to a team of criminologists from the Argentine penitentiary system. How and why these individuals, caught trying to steal money, ended up describing their teachers, romances, recreational habits, and family relationships to these prison officials is what this chapter attempts to explain. To do so, it is necessary to examine certain scientific ideas of the late nineteenth century, when new theories altered the study of criminality to embrace psychiatric concepts and practices, thus opening the door for research projects that involved an unprecedented emphasis on self-examination by convicted offenders. This chapter will also follow the metamorphosis of these criminological precepts as they shifted from the scientific field to be applied in the context of the penitentiary bureaucracy of the modern Argentine state. In other words, I will attempt to explain how stories about teachers, amusement preferences, or failed marriages could be viewed as information that determined if an inmate would remain in prison or be released.

To Modernize is to Classify

Between the end of the nineteenth century and the beginning of the twentieth, positivist criminology fundamentally swept aside previously dominant ideas about crime. According to the leaders of this science, the best way to fight this problem did not lie in the study of crime per se, but rather in perfecting the tools for understanding the nature of each criminal. As in medicine, where doctors were shifting the emphasis from the study of diseases in general to the study of particular cases, criminologists (many of whom were also medical doctors) emphasized the study of individual criminals at the expense of the study of crime as one of the foundations of their new science. Knowledge about the infinite particularities of each offender would lead, they believed, to a scientific definition of the causes of criminality. It would also lead to the elaboration of new sentencing practices that would reflect the special needs of each case. This individualization of the study and treatment of offenders was intimately linked to another element of the new criminological thought of the period: the concept of *dangerousness*. Dangerousness, the *potential* inclination toward antisocial impulses in each individual, was defined by many variables. It was the chief mission of criminology to defend society from individuals with these impulses by determining the dangerousness of each offender, as well as his or her chances for rehabilitation. In the society imagined by criminologists, people would not be punished for what they had done, but rather for what they were.

Of course, this approach was not an Argentine invention. Local specialists had followed closely the evolution of the Italian school, where the scientific study of the criminal had been defined by Lombroso in the foundational text of positivist criminology, *L'uomo delinquente* (1876). Early theory was later modified by Lombroso's disciple, Enrico Ferri, and by members of the "French school" of criminological thought, whose analysis of "criminal man" emphasized environmental considerations over congenital determination. The Argentine adoption of these ideas was profoundly shaped by a context of rapid changes taking place in both the state and in society. European immigration grew spectacularly, and so did big cities like Buenos Aires. Linked to these changes was a remarkable increase in the crime rate (reflected in the new police statistics of the large cities), which led political elites to look to the young science of criminology for ways to calm the nation's many anxieties. This political leadership belonged to a generation remembered in Argentine history as the men of "peace and administration." As such, they were already in the midst of an unprecedented expansion of the national state apparatus, as well as an ambitious public works program, and had definite ideas about the potential contributions of science to the art of governing. Thus criminologists found both the moods of politicians and national budgets predisposed to support their ambitious demands for the modernization of punishment. In fact, certain initiatives in this regard, such as the highly publicized dedication of the imposing Penitentiary of

Buenos Aires in 1877, were in place even before this generation of criminologists gained ascendancy.

Criminology was born as an "official" science in more than one sense: not only was it linked to the state as one part of nation building, but also it was dependent on its financing and involved with its leadership's role in public administration. The intellectual leaders of positivist criminology were also the directors of the programs and institutions that implemented and enforced the proposals of the same scientific publications that they themselves wrote for and edited. United in their search for solutions to the problem of crime, scientists and statesmen, doctors and bureaucrats, all worked to turn this change in the analysis and treatment of offenders into another manifestation of Argentine modernity.

Criminology fit naturally within the state's expanded use of statistics, an expansion reflected in the multitude of new official studies of this society undergoing such rapid change. Researchers today have been left with a dense record in the form of countless reports on social conditions: censuses of various kinds, statistics about education, urbanization, and sanitary conditions, and detailed official bulletins. Government publications were illustrated by a wealth of graphs, charts, and tables: visual ways of representing data that may be seen also as metaphors for the increase in knowledge about society that was generated and stored by the state. These representations were multiplied ad infinitum as the "avalanche of numbers," and they generated in turn an avalanche of classificatory systems to represent those numbers.

The classificatory fashion of this period was remarkable among criminologists. This was a natural result of the founding theories of the new science: the expansion of individual studies for each offender produced a parallel expansion of the ways to systematize this new knowledge, especially important since classifications were meant to support concrete institutional decisions. Entire scientific careers were devoted to the elaboration of classification systems that would accurately reflect the vast diversity of the data generated by scientists of crime and that would be useful to the institutions that would apply them. In addition to satisfying the demands of science, these classification systems contributed to the intellectual prestige of their authors, while they provided therapeutic recipes for prison directors, as well as support for the decisions of judges, and grounds for the debates of legislators. Classifying was the main goal of the two Institutes of Criminology founded in the city and Province of Buenos Aires.

This project of classification of offenders according to their individual personalities and experiences was tied to another, deeper, anxiety. Within the frame of a scientific graph, the threats and pathologies of this turbulent society could be represented in the form of units and subunits, disassociating each element from its original context.[1] To classify was to bring order to a disorderly reality. In addition, to classify criminals was to bring science, order, and symbolic control to the representation of a social phenomenon that was most commonly seen as a threatening and somewhat amorphous dark force. By classifying offenders, criminologists were symbolically divesting them of some of their danger to society, thus fulfilling (on paper at least) the mission of social defense proclaimed by the new science and sought by the political class. Classifying was a way of turning the "contagious crowd"—an image shared by many at a time when medical concepts were widely used to conceptualize social problems—into harmless subjects under a microscope. It was a way of reducing the unsettling (yet fascinating) mysteries of the world of crime to clear, hierarchical categories.[2] Constant classification also reflected a more specific concern: it served as an impressive representation of still controversial scientific practices, such as the enumeration of the causes of crime, defining the intrinsic nature of the criminal, and the determination of degrees of criminal dangerousness. Typologies and classifications could reassure their consumers (both political and institutional) as well as their scientific producers.

As in other areas, medicine provided an attractive model of the relationship between therapeutic institutions and science. Like doctors who produced knowledge from the clinical examination of hospitalized patients, criminologists would generate similarly valuable knowledge from the observation of incarcerated offenders. Prisons were perceived as laboratories with seemingly boundless repertoires of criminal pathology. This is how criminologist Pietro

Gori justified his 1899 carceral-anthropological investigation:

> Visiting inmates is, among works of charity, within the canons of
> the Catholic Church. For the modern criminologist, that charity
> must be felt as a scientific duty. It is there, behind those bars . . .
> that we need to enter. . . . The material [of observation] is man:
> The man who has failed, the offender toward whom social and
> anthropological sciences have the right to direct all the effort of
> their research, far from the curiosity of the crowd and the ridicu-
> lous scruples of spiritualists.[3]

Because prisons were the ideal place to develop the new studies, it
was within the walls of the recently created National Penitentiary
that the first Institute of Criminology was founded. The Instituto's
genesis is a good example of the marriage of science and state in
this period. In 1905 the director of the penitentiary, Antonio Ballvé,
solicited the creation of a technical office for the scientific study of
inmates. Minister Federico Pinedo immediately approved the necessary funds, adding them to an already expanded budget for the
penitentiary. The direction of the new project was immediately
offered to José Ingenieros, who was sent to Europe by Minister
Pinedo to visit institutions that might provide examples to emulate.
The *Archives of Psychiatry, Criminology, and Related Sciences,* the prestigious scientific journal edited by Ingenieros beginning in 1902,
became the official organ of the Instituto, as well as the vehicle for
disseminating its scientific findings. The journal was printed in the
workshops of the penitentiary itself. Thus, the Instituto was at once
the fruit of the ideas disseminated by the *Archives,* the locus of
experimentation and promotion of such ideas, and the intellectual
as well as material producer of the new scientific knowledge
obtained from the observation of the convicts of the institution.

Psychopaths and Psychopathographs: Bureaucratic Uses of a Scientific Classification

The research agenda developed by Ingenieros for the Instituto coincided almost perfectly with the scientific mission defined by the *Archives*. Like that mission, it was ambitious, drawing on "all the studies converging on the determination of the causes of criminality," including sociology, anthropology, and psychology of each convict. Scientists would describe the various manifestations of criminality and would develop a clinical study of each criminal. As one of its directors put it, "In these medico-psychological laboratories, bodies and souls are naked, and truth is unmasked."[4] A new, uncharted field of research about the inmates opened before scientists leading these institutions. The opening of this field of study involved, by extension, an expansion of the state's knowledge about the working classes, since such was the social background of the overwhelming majority of subjects under observation. Beginning in 1907, thousands of convicts would be placed under the magnifying glass of the new scientific bureaucracy.

The successive directors of the Instituto made sure that the information obtained was collected in standardized forms that allowed the uniform organization of the data. Between 1907 and 1940, the increasing complexity of both the state apparatus and the scientific debates supporting these studies added complexity to the forms that were used. From the beginning, criminological histories aspired to exhaustiveness. Ingenieros himself designed these forms to serve as a matrix of data for different morphological, psychological, and sociological aspects of the individual. The inclusive nature of these early reports, which was a long-term characteristic of these studies, reflected the agitated state of the scientific debate regarding the causes of crime. Lombroso's initial emphasis on the congenital nature of "criminal man" had been, by then, well polished, both by the following generation of Italian criminologists led by Ferri, and by the French school that had defined its scientific identity against Lombroso's "anthropometric" techniques based on body measurements (see figure 14). Despite the long-lasting respect that Lombroso enjoyed among Argentine criminologists, it

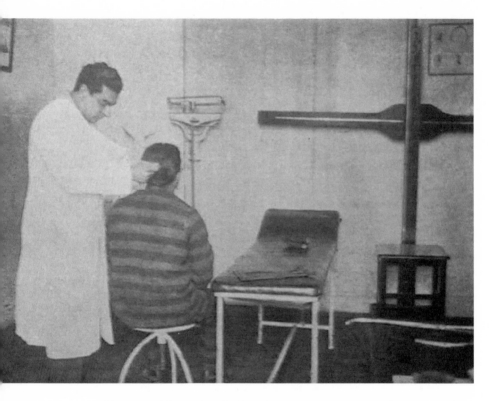

Figure 15. Measuring skulls: a doctor measures
the skull of an inmate to detect evidence of
"degeneration." Courtesy of the Archivo General
de la Nación.

was Ferri who provided the dominant model for local explanations of crime and for the institutional enforcement of criminological theory. Unlike Lombroso's, Ferri's explanations of crime combined internal and external factors, allowing models of explanation that could absorb virtually every element without the need to wait for the *unfolding* of the scientific debate.

Of course, this does not mean that Ingenieros lacked personal views about this debate. Indeed, one of his most ambitious contributions to criminology was a new system of classification that borrowed elements from a number of preexisting systems, but placed a greater emphasis on psychological factors than had any previous one. At a time when medical theories about degeneration were extremely influential in the analysis of social reality, and fears of "racial degeneration" and "moral degeneration" were shared by many social thinkers, Ingenieros wanted to prove that the criminal had specific features that distinguished him from the broad mass of "degenerates" and that these specific "criminal anomalies" resided in the psyche. According to him, criminals committed crimes because they were victims of psychopathologies. These "psychopathological factors" characteristic of the criminal were, according to Ingenieros, part of the endogenous factors of crime, like "the microbes waiting for the necessary bouillon in the environmental conditions." Even a decade later, Ingenieros repeated this conviction: "The 'specific' study of the offender—and therefore the most fundamental one—is that of the anomalies of his psychological functions."[5] The role attributed to psychological factors in the analysis of the criminal was so critical that Ingenieros referred to the birth of a new separate tradition of criminological interpretation as the "psychopathological school."[6]

Thus early scientific studies about Argentine offenders had a psychiatric-psychological bent that was bound to leave a long-term mark. It was not a psychiatrist, but the director of the National Penitentiary, Antonio Ballvé, who referred to the ideal modern prison of the future as "a great hospital of psychological clinic."[7] During the period analyzed here, all the directors of the Institute of Criminology—Ingenieros (1907–1911), Fernández (1911–1927), and Osvaldo Loudet (1927–1942)—were prominent psychiatrists.[8]

Data about psychic characteristics of the inmates, such as intelligence or emotional life, were given twice as much space as other elements in the original reports (named, precisely, as "Medical-Psychological Bulletin"). This proportion remained almost identical in the second matrix of data, used until 1927 for the observation of more than 3,500 convicts.

In order to examine the consequences that the "psychopathological" approach to the study of offenders had in the penitentiary system, I have selected three different institutional stages of these studies. Each one of them reflects the successive metamorphosis of criminological theory in the state apparatus: (1) from its scientific formulation to the use of these theories to design standardized forms (matrix) where the data about observed convicts would be kept; (2) from the design to the routine use of such a matrix by the staff of the Instituto; and (3) from this use to the elaboration of the final report by the director.

Paradoxically, the exact meaning of "psychological factors" was not made explicit in theory in any scientific article. Rather, it was defined in practice: in the actual institutional forms where they were divided into distinct elements that served to establish the lines of the standard interrogation of convicts. The examination of an offender's psyche consisted of various elements. His character was defined according to the following indicators: "mental level, self-preservation and social instincts, religious, esthetic, political and social feelings." The behavioral profile was reconstructed from information provided about domestic, professional, political, and military life, as well as the general environment and its influence. The section entitled "Psychic analytical characteristics" consisted of several subcategories: "intelligence (perception, memory, imagination), feelings (selfish, family, social), emotions, affections, passions, morality, will, and impulsiveness." This eclectic list reveals that the "psychopathological" factors used to explain criminality consisted of a surprisingly heterogeneous set of variables. Once removed from the typologies of scientific papers to institutional forms, psychopathologies turned into a collection of characteristics ranging from the political ideas to the emotional structure of the convict. Of course, it should come as no surprise that these reports included questions about political ideas, the most openly ideolog-ical area of inquiry. Doubtless, their main goal was to identify anar-chists, then perceived as the chief threat to the modernizing project, given their use of strikes and occasional violence, even assassina-tion, as weapons against the system. Indeed, anarchism was widely discussed in criminological publications.[9] If this aspect of crimi-nology was rather predictable given this science's intrinsic vocation for expanding social control, the fact that political inquiries were couched in psychiatric terminology may be less so. However, the ways in which these institutions made use of the information hidden under the label "psychological factors" is even more remarkable. This aspect is revealed only at the second level of analysis, that of the everyday production of medico-psychological reports.

Criminological histories were the result of a tense "collabora-tion" between convicts and criminological experts. Inmates were examined and interviewed by the doctors of the Instituto in an extremely asymmetric context, where the scientist had most of the power, while the convict had none. The institutional environment of these conversations, in the penitentiary itself, framed the funda-mental inequality of the exchange. Photographs taken during these meetings show convicts wearing their striped uniforms, submitting to the observation of experts wearing professional gowns and using measuring instruments (see figure 15). Doctors were conscious of the pressure exerted by this mise-en-scène: "V. T. L. lends himself to the interrogation with solicitude. He is correct, submissive, kind. . . . One can easily guess that this kindness is rooted in the respect and fear provoked in him by the experts."[10] Furthermore, convicts knew that the information obtained in these exams would be used to make decisions about their future. It is not impossible that some of them understood the implications of the questions and calcu-lated their responses carefully. It should not be overlooked that many inmates worked in the prison print shop that produced the scientific publications of the Instituto and transcribed the discus-sions of the specialists. But even when inmates knew nothing about criminology, the moral implications of many of the questions they were asked were clear enough to guide their answers. Such was the case with inquiries about past alcohol consumption, work habits, and family structure. As a rule, inmates guessed the intention behind such questions, and they attempted to underplay the role of alcohol in past life, to overrepresent their work habits, and to provide what they thought was a respectable picture of their family. The limits of this chapter do not permit a discussion of the theatrical aspects of these encounters or the strategies developed by convicts to appear "adaptable," although these dimensions must be essential to any discussion of the reliability of the data collected in these reports.[11] The object of this study is confined to the criteria applied by the observers, rather than the answers of the observed.

Interestingly, these criteria altered in their passage from criminological journals to the prison. And, as is often the case with questionnaires, they say at least as much about the intentions of the questioners as they do about those who are being questioned. Indeed, the sections set aside to define the psychic structure of the offender reveal little about this structure and more about the ideals of reform of the experts who produced the reports. The attitude of the inmate was defined according to the interviewer's judgment of his manners ("articulate," "humble," "serious") and about the use of language ("correct," "he expresses himself with great vocabulary," "poor vocabulary despite his attempts to appear cultivated," and so on). An inmate's emotional condition was measured according to two main indicators: the number of contacts between the convict and his family (frequency of visits and correspondence), and the ways in which the convict used the savings obtained through work in the penitentiary workshops. Both indicators were then used to either support or contradict subsequent information about the "sphere of volition" of the psyche, measured according to labor habits inside and outside of prison. This collection of data said little about the emotional structure of any psyche, although it did provide more objective information about degrees of integration in a family and the connection between this integration and labor and economic discipline. The interpretations that stemmed from it—either in the preliminary assessments, or in the final summary submitted by the director of the Instituto to penal and penitentiary authorities—maintained a similar perspective: "Emotional life alive: he keeps a sustained relationship with his family and contributes to their

Figure 16. Doctor interviewing an inmate in the
National Penitentiary, ca. 1920. From *Revista de
Criminología, Psiquiatría y Medicina Legal* 19
(May–June 1932): 276. Courtesy of Biblioteca
Nacional, Buenos Aires.

support with the savings obtained at the workshop"; or in another case, "Lacking any taste for work and emotional ties linking him to a home, the readaptation of this subject seems doubtful."[12]

The use of psychological categories to elaborate normative descriptions of social discipline reflected an important gap between the perception of the goal of classifications as they were provided by science and as they were used by the state. Clear signs of such a gap between the goals of scientists and those of penal authorities appear in other areas of the same penitentiary establishment. On the one hand, penitentiary authorities soon discovered that science might say things that they did not want to hear—for example, that certain offenders were congenital criminals and, therefore, nonreformable. Such an idea conspired against the very foundation of modern prison reform, which was built on the assumption that "no offender can be considered incapable of reform."[13] On the other hand, a detailed classification of the psyche anomalies associated with the criminality of each offender was not what the authorities of the penitentiary needed. This up-to-date penal institution worked, according to one of the prison administrators, as "true industrial and educating organisms." In order to organize such a system, psychopathological criteria were viewed as ultimately irrelevant, as the penitentiary director, Eusebio Gómez, showed in his rather impatient description of the classifications of "theoreticians": "It can happen, and it often does happen, that subjects with the most dissimilar criminal tendencies can manifest similar industrial vocations. . . . Criminals with the greatest psychological similarity can have very dissimilar manual skills." He went on to add: "Of course, we cannot accept the criterion of the character of those condemned because, even if it would allow a strict individualization of penal treatment, the sheer number and variety of the series it would generate would render it impossible."[14]

Assessments of inmates' work skills and discipline, rather than Byzantine chains of causality by scientists, is what the authorities of the penitentiary needed from the Institute of Classifications housed in their facilities.

By 1920, the "psychopathological classification," based on a series of questions about the criminal psyche, barely concealed an institutional use of criteria quite different than those of psychiatry. Rather, this classification scheme had become a tool in a process that distinguished individuals capable of integrating into the working classes—as imagined by the scientific/functionaries of the penitentiary system—from those incapable of doing so. In its everyday uses, psychopathological classification had evolved from a scientific system meant to arrange offenders according to the organic causes of their criminality, to a tool that generated assessments of crimes and criminals according to criteria of economic and moral acceptability. In other words, psychopathological classifications produced the definitions of the criminal that met the needs of the Argentine modern state.

Total Scientific Biographies: Assembling a Puzzle of a Thousand Pieces

The introduction of parole and probation mechanisms in the new Penal Code of 1921 produced an unprecedented demand for individual criminological histories to facilitate the decisions of judges. During these years, there was a proliferation of centers of observation of inmates and "psychiatric annexes" in the main federal and provincial prisons. These new "annexes" were meant to generate information for eventual criminological histories of the entire prison population of the country, as well as to provide data for different practical aspects of the penitentiary system itself, such as reclassification and movement of convicts, or the reconsideration of the rehabilitation therapy. This expansion of individual studies seemed to reflect the goal of "total medicalization" of the penitentiary system then being advocated by the new leader of the Instituto, Osvaldo Loudet. Loudet, a psychiatrist, hoped that this postpositivist era would expand the doctor's initial roles of anthropologist and alienist of the system, to comprise the *whole* individualized penal treatment.[15] This expansion of scientific studies coincided with an increasing "legal rationalization" of the penitentiary system, which led to the creation in 1933 of the Dirección de Institutos Penales, in charge of supervising all national prisons. Its directors were the same as those of the old Criminological Institute of Classification, indicating that these criteria of observation, applied until then only to the population of the penitentiary, were now to be applied in prisons throughout the nation.

Contrary to Loudet's hopes, however, the increasing number of reports about each individual offender failed to produce the total medicalization of the system. (See figures 16, 17, 18, and 19.) Instead, it led to the lessening of control exerted by the doctors of the Instituto over such studies, a general bureaucratizing of the research, and (as the limits of the studies grew) an increased diversity of professions involved in the process. In order to avoid the administrative chaos resulting from the exponential growth of qualitative and quantitative information, Loudet designed an ambitious matrix for all penal establishments—incidentally, a model of interrogation also used to highlight the intellectual level of its author in the main criminological publication of this time, the *Revista de Criminología, Psiquiatría y Medicina Legal,* now directed by Loudet himself.

Unlike Ingenieros, Loudet did not attempt to impose his own "author's classification" on the structure of criminological histories. His scientific project was not for that reason less ambitious, however. The new questionnaires were meant by their author to uncover the causes of crime, although in this version the logic of the causal chain was not predetermined by a particular theory. Instead, it was built from an infinite aggregate of explanatory elements obtained according to virtually unlimited criteria of inclusion. "It is in the active connection of endogenous and exogenous factors—in other words, in the combination of anthropological, physical, and social elements—that we must look for the causes of the criminal phenomenon," explained Loudet. This reflected the triumph of the "integral" approach to the phenomenon of crime defended by Enrico Ferri. Reacting against the obstinate biological determinism of Lombroso, Ferri had put forth explanations of criminal etiology whose all-inclusiveness rendered the whole of society the proper field of criminological research: "The genesis of the criminal phenomenon is not determined solely by the occasional will, the consciousness and the remote past of the criminal

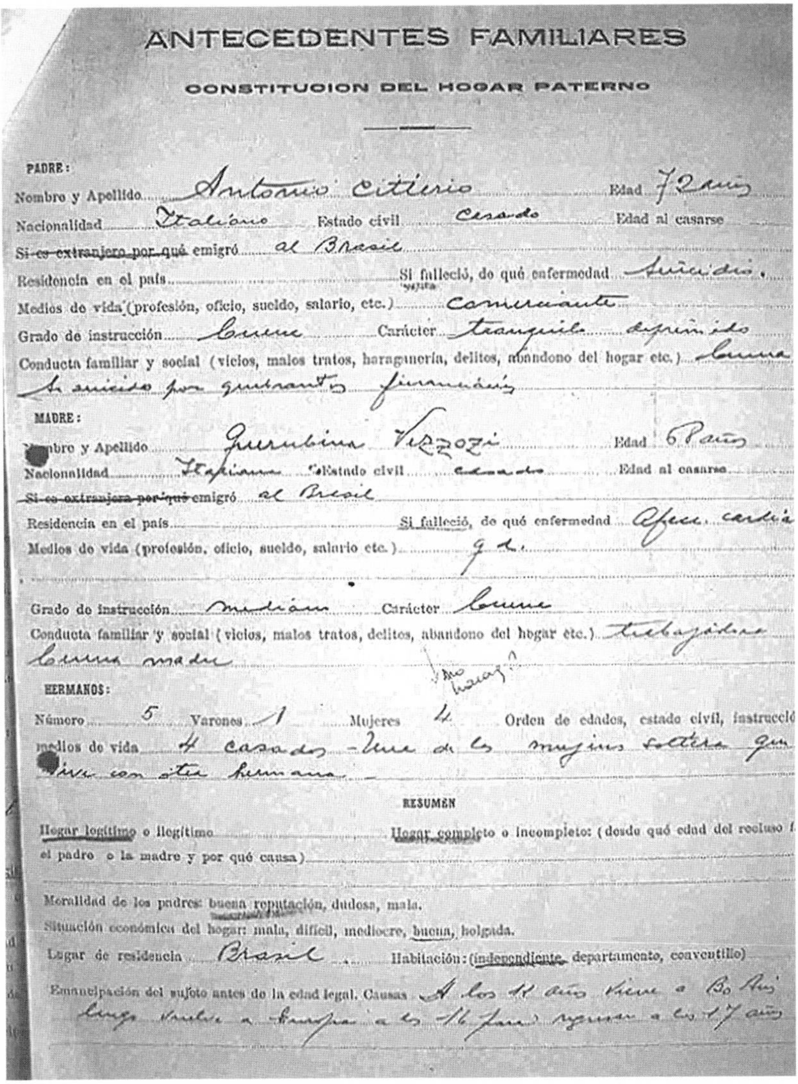

ANTECEDENTES FAMILIARES

CONSTITUCION DEL HOGAR PATERNO

PADRE:

Nombre y Apellido Antonio Citterio Edad 72 años

Nacionalidad Italiano Estado civil Casado Edad al casarse

~~Si es extranjero por qué~~ emigró al Brasil

Residencia en el país Si falleció, de qué enfermedad Suicidio.

Medios de vida (profesión, oficio, sueldo, salario, etc.) Comerciante

Grado de instrucción Buena Carácter tranquilo deprimido

Conducta familiar y social (vicios, malos tratos, haraganería, delitos, abandono del hogar etc.) Buena se suicidó por quebrantos financieros

MADRE:

Nombre y Apellido Querubina Vezzozi Edad 68 años

Nacionalidad Italiana Estado civil casada Edad al casarse

~~Si es extranjera por qué~~ emigró al Brasil

Residencia en el país Si falleció, de qué enfermedad Afecc. cardíaca

Medios de vida (profesión, oficio, sueldo, salario etc.) q. d.

Grado de instrucción mediana Carácter Buena

Conducta familiar y social (vicios, malos tratos, delitos, abandono del hogar etc.) trabajadora buena madre

HERMANOS:

Número 5 Varones 1 Mujeres 4 Orden de edades, estado civil, instrucción

medios de vida 4 casados - Una de las mujeres soltera que vive con otra hermana

RESUMEN

Hogar legítimo o ilegítimo Hogar completo o incompleto: (desde qué edad del recluso f... el padre o la madre y por qué causa)

Moralidad de los padres: buena reputación, dudosa, mala.

Situación económica del hogar: mala, difícil, mediocre, buena, holgada.

Lugar de residencia Brasil Habitación: (independiente, departamento, conventillo)

Emancipación del sujeto antes de la edad legal. Causas A los 11 años viene a Bs. As. luego vuelve a Europa a los 16 para regresar a los 17 años

Figure 17. "Family history." A form like this was used to collect data on the inmate's family. Courtesy of Instituto de Criminología de la Penitenciaría Nacional, Buenos Aires.

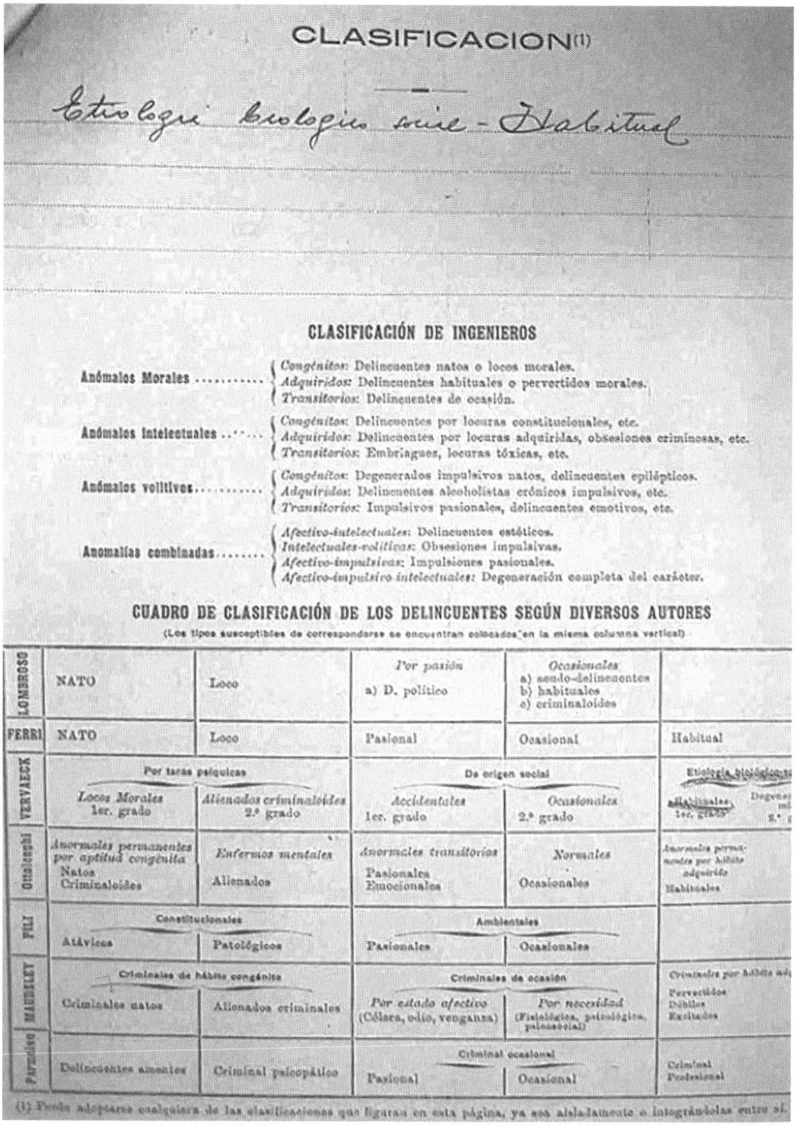

CLASIFICACION(1)

Etiologia biologica socie - Habitual

CLASIFICACIÓN DE INGENIEROS

Anómalos Morales .... { *Congénitos*: Delincuentes natos o locos morales. *Adquiridos*: Delincuentes habituales o pervertidos morales. *Transitorios*: Delincuentes de ocasión.

Anómalos intelectuales .... { *Congénitos*: Delincuentes por locuras constitucionales, etc. *Adquiridos*: Delincuentes por locuras adquiridas, obsesiones criminosas, etc. *Transitorios*: Embriagues, locuras tóxicas, etc.

Anómalos volitivos........... { *Congénitos*: Degenerados impulsivos natos, delincuentes epilépticos. *Adquiridos*: Delincuentes alcoholistas crónicos impulsivos, etc. *Transitorios*: Impulsivos pasionales, delincuentes emotivos, etc.

Anomalías combinadas........ { *Afectivo-intelectuales*: Delincuentes estéticos. *Intelectuales-volitivas*: Obsesiones impulsivas. *Afectivo-impulsivas*: Impulsiones pasionales. *Afectivo-impulsivo intelectuales*: Degeneración completa del carácter.

CUADRO DE CLASIFICACIÓN DE LOS DELINCUENTES SEGÚN DIVERSOS AUTORES

(Los tipos susceptibles de corresponderse se encuentran colocados en la misma columna vertical)

LOMBROSO	NATO	Loco	*Por pasión* a) D. político	*Ocasionales* a) seudo-delincuentes b) habituales c) criminaloides	
FERRI	NATO	Loco	Pasional	Ocasional	Habitual
VERVAECK	Por taras psíquicas: *Locos Morales* 1er. grado	*Alienados criminaloides* 2.º grado	De origen social: *Accidentales* 1er. grado	*Ocasionales* 2.º grado	Etiología biológico-s[illegible]: Habituales 1er. grado; Degene[illegible] 2.º [illegible]
Ottolenghi	*Anormales permanentes por aptitud congénita* Natos Criminaloides	*Enfermos mentales* Alienados	*Anormales transitorios* Pasionales Emocionales	*Normales* Ocasionales	*Anormales permanentes por hábito adquirido* Habituales
FILI	Constitucionales: Atávicos	Patológicos	Ambientales: Pasionales	Ocasionales	
MAUDSLEY	Criminales de hábito congénito: Criminales natos	Alienados criminales	Criminales de ocasión: *Por estado afectivo* (Cólera, odio, venganza)	*Por necesidad* (Fisiológica, psicológica, psicosocial)	Criminales por hábito ad[illegible]: Pervertidos Débiles Excitados
Parmelee	Delincuentes amentes	Criminal psicopático	Criminal ocasional: Pasional	Ocasional	Criminal Profesional

(1) Puede adoptarse cualquiera de las clasificaciones que figuran en esta página, ya sea aisladamente o integrándolas entre sí.

Figure 18. "Classification." The classification of inmates following rigid categories was considered an essential aspect of scientific administration of the penitentiary system. Courtesy of Instituto de Criminología de la Penitenciaría Nacional, Buenos Aires.

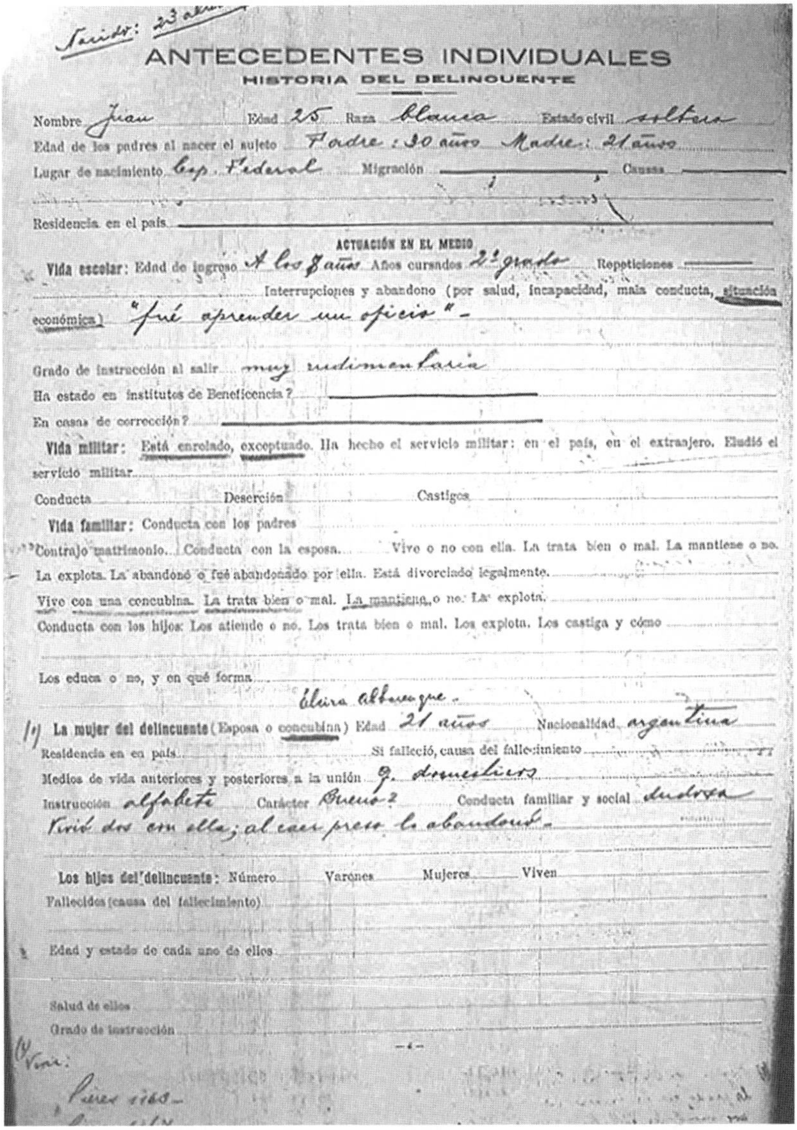

Tavidr: 23 años

ANTECEDENTES INDIVIDUALES
HISTORIA DEL DELINCUENTE

Nombre Juan Edad 25 Raza blanca Estado civil soltero
Edad de los padres al nacer el sujeto Padre: 30 años Madre: 21 años
Lugar de nacimiento Cap. Federal Migración Causas
Residencia en el país

ACTUACIÓN EN EL MEDIO

Vida escolar: Edad de ingreso A los 8 años Años cursados 2º grado Repeticiones
Interrupciones y abandono (por salud, incapacidad, mala conducta, situación económica) "fué aprender un oficio"-
Grado de instrucción al salir muy rudimentaria
Ha estado en institutos de Beneficencia?
En casas de corrección?

Vida militar: Está enrolado, exceptuado. Ha hecho el servicio militar: en el país, en el extranjero. Eludió el servicio militar
Conducta Deserción Castigos

Vida familiar: Conducta con los padres
Contrajo matrimonio. Conducta con la esposa. Vive o no con ella. La trata bien o mal. La mantiene o no. La explota. La abandonó o fué abandonado por ella. Está divorciado legalmente.
Vive con una concubina. La trata bien o mal. La mantiene o no. La explota.
Conducta con los hijos: Los atiende o no. Los trata bien o mal. Los explota. Los castiga y cómo
Los educa o no, y en qué forma

Elvira Albuquerque
(1) La mujer del delincuente (Esposa o concubina) Edad 21 años Nacionalidad argentina
Residencia en el país Si falleció, causa del fallecimiento
Medios de vida anteriores y posteriores a la unión q. domésticos
Instrucción alfabeta Carácter Bueno? Conducta familiar y social dudosa
Vivió dos con ella; al caer preso lo abandonó-

Los hijos del delincuente: Número Varones Mujeres Viven
Fallecidos (causa del fallecimiento)
Edad y estado de cada uno de ellos
Salud de ellos
Grado de instrucción

—4—

(1) Ver:
Pérez 1168-

Figure 19. "Individual antecedents." Courtesy of Instituto de Criminología de la Penitenciaría Nacional, Buenos Aires.

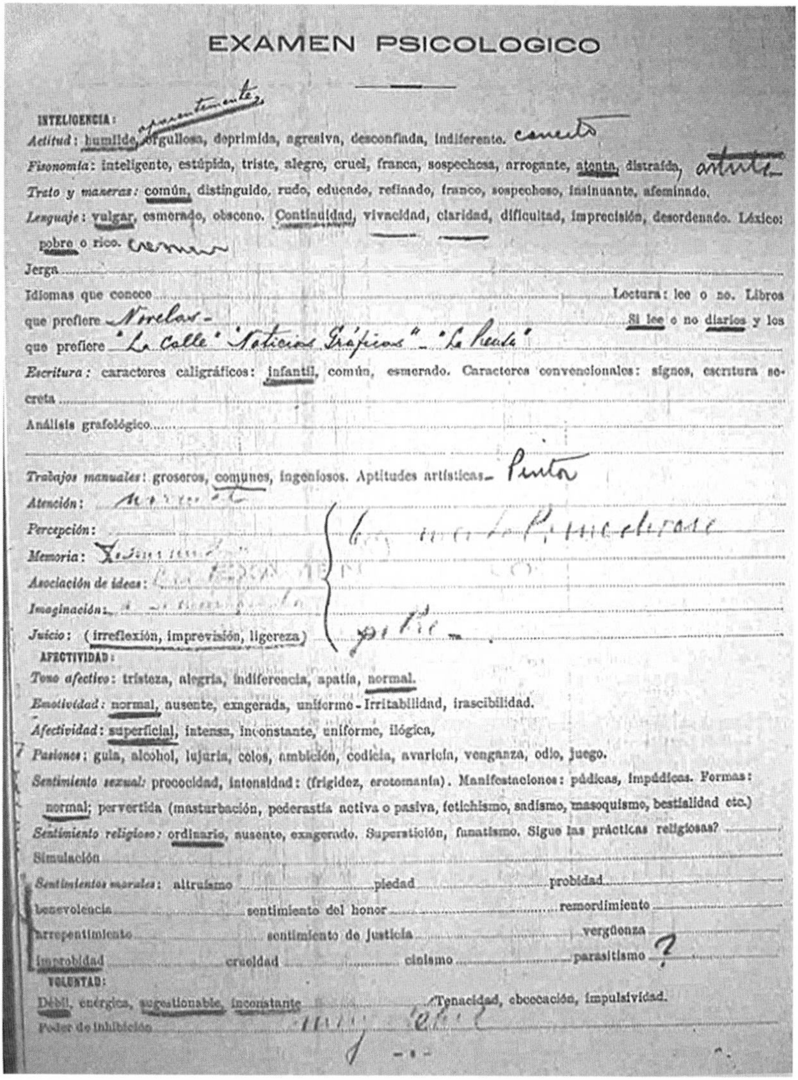

EXAMEN PSICOLOGICO

INTELIGENCIA:

Actitud: humilde, orgullosa, deprimida, agresiva, desconfiada, indiferente.

Fisonomía: inteligente, estúpida, triste, alegre, cruel, franca, sospechosa, arrogante, atenta, distraída,

Trato y maneras: común, distinguido, rudo, educado, refinado, franco, sospechoso, insinuante, afeminado.

Lenguaje: vulgar, esmerado, obsceno. Continuidad, vivacidad, claridad, dificultad, imprecisión, desordenado. Léxico: pobre o rico.

Jerga

Idiomas que conoce ... Lectura: lee o no. Libros que prefiere Novelas - ... Si lee o no diarios y los que prefiere "La Calle" "Noticias Gráficas" -

Escritura: caracteres caligráficos: infantil, común, esmerado. Caracteres convencionales: signos, escritura secreta

Análisis grafológico

Trabajos manuales: groseros, comunes, ingeniosos. Aptitudes artísticas- Pintor

Atención:

Percepción:

Memoria:

Asociación de ideas:

Imaginación:

Juicio: (irreflexión, imprevisión, ligereza)

AFECTIVIDAD:

Tono afectivo: tristeza, alegría, indiferencia, apatía, normal.

Emotividad: normal, ausente, exagerada, uniforme - Irritabilidad, irascibilidad.

Afectividad: superficial, intensa, inconstante, uniforme, ilógica,

Pasiones: gula, alcohol, lujuria, celos, ambición, codicia, avaricia, venganza, odio, juego.

Sentimiento sexual: precocidad, intensidad: (frigidez, erotomanía). Manifestaciones: púdicas, impúdicas. Formas: normal; pervertida (masturbación, pederastía activa o pasiva, fetichismo, sadismo, masoquismo, bestialidad etc.)

Sentimiento religioso: ordinario, ausente, exagerado. Superstición, fanatismo. Sigue las prácticas religiosas?

Simulación

Sentimientos morales: altruísmo ... piedad ... probidad ... benevolencia ... sentimiento del honor ... remordimiento ... arrepentimiento ... sentimiento de justicia ... vergüenza ... improbidad ... crueldad ... cinismo ... parasitismo ?

VOLUNTAD:

Débil, enérgica, sugestionable, inconstante ... Tenacidad, obcecación, impulsividad.

Poder de inhibición

Figure 20. "Psychological examination" following the classificatory system designed by José Ingenieros. Note that the technician in charge of this particular interview has underlined the categories he thought adequate for the classification of the inmate. Courtesy of Instituto de Criminología de la Penitenciaría Nacional, Buenos Aires.

and his farthest direct and ancestral heritage; *the whole society* intervenes, with its economic, moral and social organization, and with its organic defects."[16]

These "total scientific biographies"—whose standard matrix had expanded from four to twenty-six pages—attempted to remove the criminal from the "glass bell" in order to "watch him live—stimulated, moved, and agitated by the social atmosphere."[17] Each aspect of the social life of the convict—work, family, school, military service, culture, morality—was meticulously examined. This collected mass of biographical information came from two sources: the usual prison interviews with the convict, and a new "service of social research." Although data about the socioeconomic circumstances of the convict had been collected from 1924 on, such work was not formally organized until 1932, when the graduates from the new courses of *Visitadoras de Higiene Social* (social workers of social hygiene) from the medical school and the Museo Social Argentino were recruited for the project. The visits to the home and workplace of the convict were coordinated and supervised by a new figure of the Instituto, the director of the Patronato de Recluídos y Liberados, appointed to supervise parolees. As representatives of the state, the new social *visitadoras* enjoyed unprecedented latitude in their contact with thousands of working-class families. Despite occasional resistance, their gaze seems to have been more readily accepted because it was presented as the consequence of a crime committed by a family member, and not as part of an official campaign defined in terms of class or political affiliation.

The new "clinical criminological histories"—a name that reflects the model of medical clinical histories—were designed to resist the perceived negative impact of increased bureaucratization of the studies by formalizing the transcription of data. The empty spaces on the forms had been reduced to a minimum, and the majority of the questions were followed by a selection of possible responses that the interviewer simply underlined. The resulting biographies included an impressive mass of information, so broad in scope that it could be relevant to virtually all theories of criminality.[18]

The report opened with questions about the home—whether it was legitimate or illegitimate, the number of parents living in the household, their reputation, and so forth. This information was followed by biographical sketches of each parent:

> "*Father of convict J. D.:* M. D. *Age:* 64 (more or less)
>
> *Nationality:* Italian . . . ; *Married:* yes . . . ; *Age at time of marriage:* . . .
>
> *If a foreigner, reason to emigrate:* with his parents
>
> *Residency in the country:* since 1880
>
> *If he died, of what disease* . . .
>
> *Makes a living as (profession, trade, wage, salary, etc.):* cart driver . . .
>
> *Instruction level:* literate . . . *Temper:* nervous, irritable
>
> *Family and social behavior (vices, bad treatment, laziness, offenses, abandonment of the household, etc.):* incidents with the police; he (the convict) thinks that he was condemned for homicide
>
> *Mother of convict J. D.* . . . . [etc.][19]

As this excerpt shows, criminologists required quite specific data about the work history and fulfillment of family duties of mothers and fathers. The fact that the five options suggested to describe the father's performance in fulfilling such duties were negative, points to the strong assumption of an incomplete, poorly integrated family behind each offender. Similar inquiries about each of the convict's siblings followed these sketches. It was only after this profile of the family's social standing had been established that the individual biography of the inmate was introduced. In this life story, much attention was paid to past experiences in state institutions of integration (school, military service, correctional houses), allowing for the consideration of data about the cultural assimilation of the (numerous) immigrant convicts. The great number of questions about the relation of inmates with their partners (whether they supported them, married them, or exploited them) and children (whether they sent them to school and supported them), as well as the countless questions about housing conditions, the reputations of their friends, favorite leisure activities or political ideas, all of

these were pieces of the profile of the ideal male working-class citizen, its opposite, and all the intermediate combinations. The entire
range of potential portraits was anticipated—from Petiso Orejudo,
the legendary child murderer who terrified Buenos Aires in the
1920s, to the most docile worker.

Of course, not all the pieces of the puzzle were equivalent. The
most important piece was not psychological, but rather the labor
history of the convict and his family. The categorization and label-
ing—"profession or trade; skilled workman, apprentice; daily wage,
investment of the wage; number of crafts he tried to learn; causes
of the changes; works regularly, period of rest; unemployment"—
reflected the long-standing anxiety of authorities faced with the
mass of temporary rural workers who were hired intermittently and
whose labor instability was perceived as one of the main crim-
inogenous factors of poor families. The experience of the labor
therapy inside the penitentiary system was also the object of
detailed observation by criminologists. The convict's performance
in the prison workshops was an essential indicator of his capacity
to be reformed. As such, it was carefully measured according to
punctuality, attitude toward work and authority, discipline, con-
centration, neatness, reason and length of interruptions of the
work, evolution through several periods of time, wage obtained,
and a projection of a potential salary in free life. The modern prison
had been conceived as a factory of industrious citizens.
Criminological histories were the main tool to measure the success
or failure of this factory's production of such citizens.

Despite the new diversification of the professionals involved in
these reports, the decision regarding who would be able to achieve
such a transformation was still made by doctors, who completed
the remaining sections of the report with other pieces of the puzzle.
As in Ingenieros's times, the data about psychological factors was
largely adapted to the needs of the prison system. It was also
blended with the interviewer's implicit social and moral judgment
of the inmate in question. Moreover, the highly detailed data matrix
that was included suggested conclusions about various aspects of
the convict's performance during the interview. For example, moral
feelings were to be defined by underlining one or more of the

following options: "altruism, mercy, integrity, benevolence, feeling of honor, remorse, repentance, feeling of justice, shame, cruelty, cynicism, parasitism."[20] The frame provided to describe the religious feelings of the convict also says something about criminologists' view on the role of Catholicism among the working classes. Of the five words selected to characterize such feelings—"Religious feeling: regular, absent, exaggerated, superstitious, fanatical"— three were negative. The two acceptable options, "regular" and "absent" (a description that did not carry any stigma in the report), suggest toleration rather than encouragement of religion. The majority of these scientists endorsed anticlerical intellectual traditions; in fact, there were well-known socialists and even former anarchists among them. They did not want a working class dominated by a religious view of the world. The scientific articles where the role of religion in the prison rehabilitation therapy was mentioned usually warned against exposing inmates to "excessive" religion, an influence that could only lead to hypocrisy and superstition.[21] As in society, religion in the ideal prison was acceptable if it was reasonable—that is, a practice capable of instilling principles of social discipline without any accompanying fanaticism—in other words, a religion devoid of the antimodern tendencies from which these reformers wanted to free Argentine society.

Anthropometrics (the Lombroso-inspired measurements of the body) was still considered an ingredient of these studies. The pages designed for the body measurements of inmates, however, were hardly ever completed by the doctors employed by the prison system. This omission speaks eloquently about the penitentiary bureaucracy's autonomy in the selection of criteria at the expense of the patterns transmitted by the scientists, and it might also constitute a judgment about the usefulness of these measurements.

Certain aspects of the report reflect the voyeuristic fascination that the underworld of crime exerted on the scientists of crime. In a section on morphological stigmata of the "bad life," scars and tattoos were described and classified by subject ("romantic, passionate, obscene, religious, political, patriotic, criminal, mixed"). Passions and sexual habits of the convict were interrogated in great detail. In this regard, the bureaucrats in charge of the report had at their disposal a number of detailed categories for underlining: "Sexual feelings: precocious, intensity (frigidity, erotomania). Manifestations: modest, immodest. Forms: normal; perverted (masturbation, pederasty active or passive, fetishism, sadism, masochism, bestiality, etc.)."[22]

Once all the pieces of the puzzle had been gathered, a narrative profile assessing the dangerousness of convicts had to be constructed. However, what criteria were to be used at this stage was something the scientific articles did not explain. Those who faced this typically "bureaucratic" problem could use the "index of dangerousness" added at the end of the report, with two lists containing factors of greater or lesser dangerousness, respectively. In both cases, the first indicator to consider was the inmate's lifestyle before the crime—for example, "dissolute, dishonest, parasitic" or "honest, hard-working." Each list reproduced perfectly a portrait either of the unreformable criminal or the honest and repentant worker, a kind of Dr. Jekyll and Mr. Hyde of working-class citizenship in the era of massive immigration. Of course, the majority of the subjects observed were exclusively neither one nor the other, and the specific ways in which these elements were to be combined was delegated entirely to the common sense of the functionary in charge of the diagnosis. The instructions provided seem deliberately vague: "When circumstances of greater and lesser dangerousness concur, it will be determined which ones are prevalent in order to grade the dangerousness."[23]

A similar problem of synthesis arose again at the final stage of the criminal's classification. The declared goal of accumulating this wealth of information was to identify the most appropriate place for each case within the criminological systems of classification. However, the scientific production of classifications was so overwhelming, and the competition between different theories to classify so fierce, that no less than eight systems were included in the matrix. The penitentiary workers grappling with this problem could then choose their favorite model (or, more likely, the model they knew), or build a combination of classifications. This extreme eclecticism is the great paradox of the ambitious biographical project to which this prison population was subjected. Born of the turn-of-the-century faith in the transformative potential of science, criminology had succeeded in gathering scientists and state reformers around the rallying cry of individualized treatment, of considering the offender and his circumstances, and of using science to understand (and fight) the complex chain of causality that produced these crimes. But, when it failed to provide an organizing principle for the information of the "Babel reports" that resulted from these initiatives, criminology sacrificed the scientific aspirations of these biographies and relinquished the construction of the inmates' profiles to the personal impressions of the functionaries of each institution. Not only had the meaning of criminological concepts been transformed in their implementation by the state, but their theoretical force had been compromised as well. In the context of the state bureaucracy, criminological theory was blended with both the unconscious, tacit normative principles and the reformist ideals that had inspired the penitentiary project, all built on certain axioms: what a good family consisted of, what a good work history should look like, accepted ways of speaking, normal religiosity, allowed sexual practices, and so forth.

If there was one criterion of selection that prevailed throughout the whole period, imposing itself on changing scientific theories, bureaucratic reforms, and individual moral judgments, it was the potential of each individual to absorb social norms of integration. And, among all these norms, work conduct remained at the top of the list of indicators of adaptability. For the penitentiary bureaucracy, classifications were not a source of explanation of criminality, but rather a way of measuring potential for social discipline. Classifications, used initially as tools of representation to render the indistinct mass of offenders into clear, distinct, and analyzable units, functioned in the punitive system as instruments to produce definitions of reintegration to modern Argentine society.

part three

Argentines on the Couch

Chapter Five

FROM THE PSYCHIATRIC HOSPITAL TO THE STREET

Enrique Pichon Rivière and the Diffusion of Psychoanalysis in Argentina

Hugo Vezzetti

In 1958, Enrique Pichon Rivière, one of the founding members of the Argentine Psychoanalytic Association, carried out an experiment under the name "Operación Rosario." With a group of collaborators Pichon tried to turn the whole city of Rosario (one of the largest cities in the country) into an "operative group" (meaning a group practice aimed at achieving specific goals) and attempted to use certain notions of psychoanalysis to understand, and change, patterns of social behavior. His main purpose was to induce a new learning by means of social reeducation on a microscale that could be extended to the entire society in order to reform attitudes, roles, and self-understanding. Pichon and his disciples have enthroned the Rosario Operation as a kind of mythical birth of community performances inspired in a new social discipline that combined Freudian ideas with a social psychology approach. Although it is impossible to evaluate the real impact of this intervention on the life of the city, since the only sources available are those produced by the organizers, the experience reflected a shift from the private therapeutic to a public and popular psychoanalysis conceived and practiced directly over society. The expansion of psychoanalytically inspired discourse and practices in Argentina during the 1950s and 1960s was part of a widespread movement whose impact may be readily observed today, from the growing presence of psychological issues in the mass media to the extensive inclusion of psychoanalysis in the program in psychology at the University of Buenos Aires and elsewhere.

For nearly thirty years, Enrique Pichon Rivière played a central role in Argentine psychoanalytic, psychiatric, and psychological circles. In the early 1940s, while still working as a psychiatrist at the Hospicio de las Mercedes, Pichon participated in the creation of the Argentine Psychoanalytic Association (APA, hereafter). He played a central role in the theoretical development and mass diffusion of psychoanalysis in Argentina by innovatively combining elements of psychoanalytic theory with social psychology centered on working with groups. In this respect, it can be said that Pichon disseminated psychoanalysis beyond its usual practice in the private consulting room.

During the 1960s Pichon shifted his attention from the insane to ordinary people, taking psychoanalysis from the couch to the street and using it to analyze the problems of everyday life. He also developed and popularized his own version of a psychoanalytically inspired social psychology based on what he called "operative groups." In doing so, he played a prominent role in diffusing psychoanalysis in Argentine society and culture. His work and his teaching were grounded in the context of rapid changes that took place in Argentine society and culture after the fall of Juan Perón's regime in 1955. Pichon was sensitive to those social and cultural changes.

The idea of social and cultural "modernization," moving from a traditional to a mass urban society, was a main component of a climate of reformism that characterized the period. Notably, modernization was not only related to the social and economic changes taking place—in particular the process of industrialization and migration from the country to the big cities—but also with deep cultural changes in society's attitudes and values as well. Within this context, fundamental changes and reforms took place in different areas and, in particular, in public institutions. At the University of

Buenos Aires two new academic programs, one in psychology one in sociology, were introduced in 1957. The first group of psychologists began to develop their practices in the early sixties, most of them within the public system of psychiatric assistance. The process of reform also swept through the public psychiatric system, giving origin to a program of mental health that led to new forms of psychiatric and psychotherapeutic treatments in general hospitals, as an alternative to hospitalization in the old-style asylum.

There is no consensus on whether a distinctly "Argentine" psycho-analytic school developed in the 1940s and 1950s. If such a school existed, it would not have been characterized so much by the orig-inality of its theoretical development as by its concern with social issues. In those years, for instance, Pichon wrote a weekly column on the psychology of everyday life for *Primera Plana*, a political and cultural magazine that had a great influence on the new Argentine journalism and was an important agent promoting cultural mod-ernization in themes such as women and changes in the family. In this context, not only did Pichon's work appeal to society at large, but also it was able to influence different segments of Argentine society. He exercised a strong influence in the development of Argentine psychiatry and psychology and was influential among the new generation of professionals searching for a different approach to problems of mental health. By means of his teaching and through group practices he was able to redefine psychoanalysis's conceptual apparatus. He also contributed to developing a particular sensitiv-ity to the social dimension of psychiatric disorders. Furthermore, he contributed to the implantation of psychological notions and views in Argentine culture. As a result of Pichon's work, psychol-ogy came to be perceived as a form of knowledge capable of pro-viding a new understanding of aspects of individual and social life.

Enrique Pichon Rivière was born in Geneva in 1907 to a French family temporarily settled there (see figures 20 and 21). Enrique's mother was his father Alfonse's second wife, and the sister of his deceased first wife. Although Enrique was the only child born to this second marriage, he grew up unaware that his "brothers" were in fact his half-brothers and his cousins. It is conceivable that this first "family secret" provided Pichon with a personal motivation for his lifelong research on family dynamics. He regarded the family as a network of drives and bonds as well as a knot of communication usually muddled by misunderstandings. His family moved to Argentina when he was a child, settling in the Chaco, a rural region near the tropics in the middle of the rain forest. Not only were they immigrants, but now they lived far from any major city and from the life habits they had been accustomed to in Europe. "My vocation for the human sciences arises from the attempt to solve the shadows of a conflict between two cultures," said Pichon upon recalling his childhood. His early years were dominated by a clash between the European, French intellectual tradition of his parents and the impact of his new way of life in rural Argentina. This new way of life included the learning of Guaraní Indian legends and myths. Pichon characterizes this opposition between the scientific and the mythic ways of understanding as the origin of his singular encounter with Freudian discourse, a work that combines the aims of scientific knowledge with the contents of dreams and fantasy. At the same time, he found in this duality a source of his permanent purpose of joining intellectual and rational views with notions emerging from popular culture and customs.[1]

By and large, these divided interests between psychiatry and medicine, on the one hand, and art and politics, on the other hand, characterized Pichon as a singular figure within the first psychoanalytic group in Buenos Aires. Pichon attended medical school in Rosario, but had to quit when he became ill. Afterward he migrated to Buenos Aires and completed his medical studies there. At the same time, he engaged in a bohemian lifestyle enriched by close contacts with such people as the writer Roberto Arlt, with whom he roomed.[2] Pichon wrote in cultural and literary magazines and for a short time worked as a journalist at *Crítica*, Buenos Aires's most popular newspaper of that time.[3] During this period he developed a deep interest in surrealism and modern art, an interest that would accompany him throughout his career. In the 1940s he became interested in and published several articles on Isidore Ducasse (1846–1870), also known as "Conde de Lautréamont," a French-

Figure 21. Enrique Pichon Rivière (1907–1977)
was known for his work on group therapy and for
his attempts at taking psychoanalysis "to the
streets." Courtesy Archivo de la Asociación
Psicoanalítica Argentina.

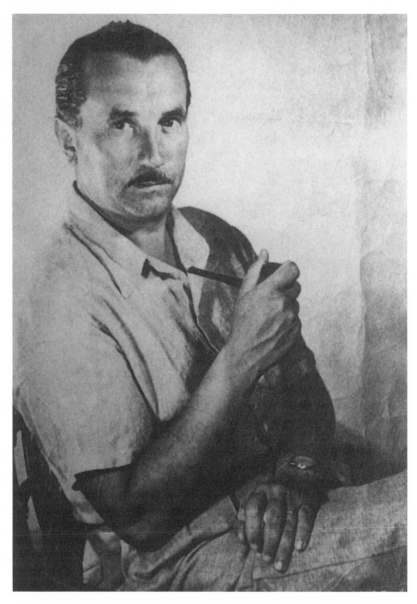

Figure 22. Enrique Pichon Rivière, from Jorge
Balán's *Cuéntame tu vida: Una biografía colectiva del
psicoanálisis en la Argentina* (Buenos Aires: Planeta,
1991). Reprinted with permission by Jorge Balán.

Uruguayan poet whose work would be influential among the surrealists. Pichon wrote simultaneously in *Ciclo*, a literary magazine, and in the *Revista de Psicoanálisis*, the new journal of the APA.[4] From the beginning, then, Pichon showed an atypical profile as a medical psychoanalyst widely connected with cultural, intellectual, and political life. While studying medicine, he initiated his first contacts with psychiatry at the Asylum of Torres, a public institution for mentally handicapped children in a rural area in the Province of Buenos Aires. After he graduated from medical school in 1936, he entered the Hospicio de las Mercedes as a physician, where he remained for more than fifteen years.

The Early Diffusion of Psychoanalysis

Pichon's efforts to link popular and literary culture to medicine and psychoanalysis is embodied in the creation in 1942 of the Argentine Psychoanalytic Association. The APA was the initiative of a small circle of physicians, who were deeply interested in Freud's works from a medical and therapeutic point of view. Within this group, Enrique Pichon Rivière played a central role in establishing extensive links with both the medical field and with the general public. As a result of his earlier training and practice as a psychiatrist, Pichon stressed the importance of psychoanalysis as a foundational element for a new psychiatry. Overall, his innovative influence on psychiatry pointed to two different directions. On the one hand, he produced a significant amount of writing on psychopathology. There he dealt with the classical forms of insanity (epilepsy, chronic delirium, schizophrenia, and melancholy), revising them from a psychoanalytic point of view. On the other hand, principally through his practice, Pichon developed a critical view of the psychiatric asylum. His primary concern was to transform the usual psychiatric practices that tended to isolate the mentally disturbed patient from the rest of society. Despite the change of name, mental hospitals were, in Pichon's view, similar to the old madhouses, which needed to be urgently reformed. He was particularly interested in the relationship between madness and social groups.

In addition to his psychiatric career and his work in spreading psychoanalytic knowledge through medical circles, Pichon also played an important role in the diffusion of Freudian-inspired treatments in psychiatry. He worked as a psychiatrist at the consulting room of the Liga Argentina de Higiene Mental (see the following chapter for details). Finding inspiration in the international movement of mental hygiene, the Liga was one of the first places where patients with psychiatric problems could be treated on an outpatient basis in Buenos Aires.

Pichon also played a decisive role in the origin of the Francisco Muñoz Foundation. This organization provided financial support for the *Revista Argentina de Psicoanálisis*, the first and most successful journal in Spanish devoted exclusively to psychoanalysis. It also provided funds for fellowships and loans for foreign students who traveled to Buenos Aires from all over Latin America to obtain psychoanalytic training. The foundation was named after Francisco Muñoz, a Spanish immigrant who had succeeded in business as the owner of one of the largest and most popular tailor shops in Buenos Aires. Muñoz had decided to sponsor the newborn association because he was a personal witness to the benefits of psychoanalytic therapy. The manager of his firm, a close personal friend, suffered from agoraphobia and, as a result, was bedridden and unable to leave home and work. Pichon was hired by Muñoz to conduct therapeutic sessions at the patient's home and was able to achieve a remarkable success.[5] Muñoz's decisive support for psychoanalysis, then, had arisen from his concern for his friend and the gratitude he felt for his cure. This exemplifies a singular trait in Argentina's reception of psychoanalysis: its early acceptance by nonmedical, ordinary people not associated with any particular intellectual or artistic circle. In this particular case the progress of psychoanalysis was supported by a businessman who was outside the cultural elite. In other countries the early cultural and social diffusion of psychoanalysis almost completely depended on the active intervention of socially prominent intellectuals. In Argentina support for psychoanalysis often came from nonelite social sectors.

Some "popular" discussions on psychoanalysis in magazines and publications for the general public in Buenos Aires had preceded the foundation of the APA by nearly two decades. In 1930, for instance, *Crítica* (which temporarily changed its name to *Jornada*) published a section presented as "psychoanalytic consulting," where readers were invited to submit their dreams. Not only did this section, signed by "Freudiano," offer interpretations of these dreams, but it also provided different notes, brief definitions and advice on psychological issues.[6] A few years later a popular series of books on psychoanalysis titled *Freud al alcance de todos* (Freud for everyone) was authored by a certain "Dr. Gómez Nerea." The collection was published by Tor, a large, popular publisher. The author behind the pen name was not actually a doctor but a Peruvian avant-garde writer and poet, Alberto Hidalgo. The collection, which sold many thousands of volumes between 1935 and the late 1940s, consisted of ten small books with such titles as "Freud and the Sex Problem," "Freud and Maniac Acts," "Freud and Sexual Hygiene," and "Freud and the Mystery of Dreams."[7] The fact that Freud's name was included in the title of each volume shows that he was already well-known as the creator of psychoanalysis and enjoyed wide recognition among the general public.

Stefan Zweig's widely read biography of Freud, published also by Tor in 1933, contributed greatly to strengthening the impact of psychoanalytic ideas outside the medical field, even beyond the realms of academia and "high culture." Zweig was a Austrian-born German writer who achieved distinction in several genres. His interest in psychology and in the teachings of Sigmund Freud led to his most characteristic work, the subtle portrayal of imaginary and historical characters. Zweig's biography of Freud offered a picture of Freud as an intellectual and moral figure of his time, who dealt with problems that were important to ordinary people and who illuminated the cultural changes of modern society so that they could be better understood and managed. Zweig's biography of Freud was translated into several languages around the world. It can be argued that Zweig's ideas were much more influential in the dissemination of psychoanalysis among the general public than the actions of the psychoanalytic establishment.

Psychoanalysis had an impact on both the medical and psychiatric circles as well. Another central figure among the APA's founding members, who later became an active diffuser of psychoanalysis, was Arnaldo Rascovsky. He came to psychoanalysis with vast previous experience in pediatrics accumulated at the Children's Hospital of Buenos Aires. After beginning in the pediatric clinic, he subsequently oriented his work toward psychosomatic medicine. Psychosomatic disorders are conditions in which psychological stresses adversely affect physiological (somatic) functioning to the point of distress. These disorders may include hypertension, gastrointestinal disturbances, migraine and tension headaches, dermatitis, and ulcers. In general, then, the early links between psychoanalysis and the general medical field in Argentina show the psychoanalysts' firm commitment to problems such as mental hygiene, pediatrics, and psychosomatic medicine, which were relevant to society at large and, furthermore, were considered important public issues. Those were the same topics that had been discussed in popular newspapers and magazines at least since the 1930s, for instance in *Viva cien años* (Live one hundred years), a "popular magazine of health" published in Buenos Aires from 1934 to 1949. This magazine routinely published on topics related to the family, child rearing, the prevention of mental diseases, and the integration of physical and psychic dimensions in the treatment of somatic disease. Consequently, it tended to offer a real program of medicine for everybody, a program that included a good deal of practical and popular psychology. Moreover, the magazine also offered the advice of an anonymous "psychoanalyst" who responded to letters submitted mainly by female readers.[8]

"Argentine" psychoanalysis from the 1940s to the 1950s was thus characterized by its large-scale social diffusion. Pichon and Rascovsky played a central role in the dissemination of the discipline and in the general popular orientation of the discipline through their well-established positions in the medical profession as well as in other nonspecialist social circles. Both Rascovsky and Pichon came from middle-class, immigrant backgrounds, German-Jewish and French, respectively, and both had moved from the provinces to the big city of Buenos Aires. They led the early stages of implantation and diffusion of psychoanalysis, despite the fact that, in the years before the foundation of the APA, they could not claim the legitimate position of "analyst" according to the International Psychoanalytic Association regulations. That "title" and criteria was supplied by Angel Garma, a Spanish-born doctor who had received his psychoanalytic training in Berlin in the early 1930s and subsequently emigrated to Buenos Aires to escape the Spanish Civil War. From the point of view of the rules of the international organization of psychoanalysis, then, Garma was the most important figure of the founding group, which also included Celes Cárcamo and Marie Langer. Pichon and Rascovsky carried out their training analysis with Garma in the late 1930s. However, it could be argued that, with respect to the objective of establishing and developing wide links with the medical and cultural fields and, especially, combining medical issues with social and public concerns, the central figures of the group were Pichon and Rascovsky, both innovative in their fields and ready to take on the enterprise of psychoanalysis with energy and dedication.

It is important to stress here the role of immigration in the birth of Argentine psychoanalysis as a main factor in the reception and diffusion of Freudian ideas and practices in Buenos Aires society. There was a common ground between the first analytic group and society in general in that the composition of the group was entirely representative of the Argentine society as a whole. The APA's founding group, therefore, was a kind of "microcosm" of the community of Buenos Aires. Two of the members, the Spanish Angel Garma and the Austrian Jew Marie Langer, were recent foreign immigrants. Two others, Rascovsky and Pichon, were raised in Argentina by immigrant parents. Finally, Celes Cárcamo, a member of a traditional Argentine family, came from a conservative, Catholic background.[9]

In order to understand the importance of immigration, one should compare the Argentine reception of psychoanalysis with its reception in the United States. Nathan Hale, a prominent historian of psychoanalysis in the United States, claims that the dissemination of psychoanalysis throughout Western societies was the result of a "dual appeal," that is, of its simultaneous impact on physicians and laymen, scientists and humanists.[10] Briefly, psychoanalysis was received in America at the same time by physicians, many of whom worked in large institutions, and by writers and journalists, who were interested more in general public issues, such as sex and love, family troubles (especially child rearing), dreams and hidden aspects of personality, and violence and conflicts in society. Since the Freudian discipline is both a discursive body and a treatment for mental disease, this two-track reception was also a source of conflict regarding the uses and regulation of psychoanalysis as a therapeutic practice. In the United States, according to Hale, the psychoanalytic institution adopted the form of a medical and psychiatric profession beginning with the 1920s and, during the following decade, became a medical elite that established the training regulations. As a result, psychiatric residency was required from all candidates in psychoanalytic training.[11] Consequently, by the time of the arrival of immigrant analysts coming from Central Europe, psychoanalysis became a profitable profession in the United States, a part of the medical establishment, but with little connection to the humanities or the social sciences. In general, the incorporation of the newly arrived analysts, with few exceptions, reinforced the already rigid and hierarchical psychoanalytic system and the existing tendency toward the medicalization of psychoanalysis.

Similar to the case of the United States, psychoanalysis enjoyed a two-track reception in Argentina as well. Although the main project of the APA's founders was to receive medical recognition, the psychoanalytic links with cultural and social issues had remained a strong trait since the beginning. In this respect, Pichon's work and influence were increasingly important in spreading new ideas out of the professional circle, especially in the late 1950s and the early 1960s. But his actions in this direction had actually begun much earlier. For instance, in 1946 Pichon gave a radio speech, entitled "What Is Psychoanalysis?" broadcast by the Universidad de La Plata radio station.[12] His presentation emphasized the heroic vision of Freud as a revolutionary who had had to confront strong resistance, including his own inner resistance, in forging a new science. He suggested that there was an "integral conception of man" in Freud's discipline, which he conceived of as "biological and instinctual in its source, [and] social and cultural in its projections."[13]

Pichon, then, contributed to the diffusion of the Freudian discipline in several ways. He played a key role in the birth of the Muñoz Foundation and worked as a medical doctor at the consulting room at the Liga Argentina de Higiene Mental. Moreover, during the course of almost fifteen years, while working at the Hospicio de las Mercedes, he delivered a series of lectures on psychopathology from a psychoanalytic point of view. These lectures constituted a doorway to psychoanalysis for many young psychiatrists, some of whom would later join the APA psychoanalytic institute. Furthermore, in addition to his psychiatric work, which widened the Freudian impact on mental medicine, Pichon wrote several works on psychosomatic disease in order to engage psychoanalytical notions and procedures with a wide spectrum of medical practices. Even beyond this, he brought to the new psychoanalytic organization his experience as a writer and as a journalist and his association with literary circles.

However, the main target of Pichon's efforts in the diffusion of a psychoanalytically inspired teaching was his development of theory and practice for use with operative groups. This new approach extended its impact beyond the medical and therapeutic practices to bear on collective behavior. And although Pichon refers to this development as a shift from psychoanalysis to social psychology, it is possible to claim that in fact what he produced was an innovative merging of different disciplinary traditions.

Madness, the Family, and the Group

Pichon's interest in the psychology of groups began with his work with families of psychotic patients at the Hospicio de las Mercedes in the early 1940s. Pichon saw the family as the primary group and the ground from which individual symptoms arise. Consequently, he believed that treatment of the individual's mental troubles had to include family members. In this he was forced to confront the traditional psychiatric view that was focused on the isolated patient. He also went against the classic psychoanalytic view that ignored the family group as an important factor in the diagnosis and therapy of psychological disorders. In fact, Pichon's innovative point of view combined the dynamic psychoanalytic approach, centered on individual psychic conflict, with an approach that emphasized the frame of interactions in which the patient's troubles were located: the family. This inclination toward the group, which recognized specific dynamics and functions in the group's organization, did not come to him from his professional background, but rather from his early experience in team sports, especially soccer.

Pichon traced the origins of his interest in group work to his early family and social experiences. At the end of his life, in 1975, remembering his childhood and youth in the town of Goya, in the northeastern region of Argentina, he stated that, in the balance of his life's achievements, the foundation of a soccer club was just as important as his participation in the creation of Goya's Socialist Party. In general, recalling his early formative years, he locates the origin of his own group experiments in the typical "face-to-face" sociability of neighborhood relationships. However, he insisted on his early "passion" for sports in general, and for soccer in particular: "a beautiful sport, from which emerges a wide variety of conflicts." The soccer team offered him a model of interactive roles as a mobile, group structure that prevails over individual performance. In sports, then, as in other group situations that existed in a small village, Pichon discovered the "operative character" of groups.[14]

Given the importance of sports in his background, it was not strange that Pichon began his psychiatric practices at the Asilo de Torres by forming a soccer team in which he played alongside mentally deficient children. This was his first encounter with the asylum's environment of segregation. There, he began to experiment with group practices and developed the idea that mental troubles can be, if not defeated, at least repaired by means of associative interaction. Therefore, the most important remedy for mental disease was to be found in grouping and communication. A few years later, when working at the Hospicio de las Mercedes, he was driven by the same will of change that he had previously shown in the Asilo de Torres. In 1936 there were nearly 4,500 inmates in the men's asylum of Buenos Aires, the majority of the patients living in a complete state of *neglect*. One of Pichon's first initiatives was to form groups with nurses who were in daily contact with patients. The intended purpose of these groups was to give nurses practical training that would allow them to act as "leaders" for change, breaking down the rigid, stereotyped functions and practices of hospitalization and patient segregation.

There are some points worth noting about the operative groups. Their main goal was practical, that is, to achieve concrete results in collective behavior. This means that, in general, the group dynamic was not an objective in itself, but rather that it had to be integrated with an external goal defined as the group task. The task assigned could be anything, from winning a soccer game to improving psychiatric assistance to patients by providing better training for nurses, but the practical task had to exist as a point of reference for the group work. Later, in the early 1950s, Pichon was in charge of the Service for Adolescents at the Hospicio de las Mercedes. In a time of political tension, Pichon was denied a nursing staff due to his opposition, albeit mild, to the government of Juan Perón. Confronted with the lack of trained assistants, he resorted to group teaching, in which he included some patients, selected from among those who were in better mental condition. The nursing staff problem created the pressure to seek out a resolution, and in this experiment Pichon took another step in the direction of developing group operative practices.

Group practices also had to be sustained by a concrete living experience. In Pichon's view nurses (or recovered patients) were in a better position to function as group leaders than were medical students or even medical doctors, who did not have frequent contact with patients. At the beginning, the "operative" side of group activity aimed at what Pichon called "praxis," a pragmatic postulate that gave precedence to immediate, practical issues over theorization. The doing *(hacer)* is first and beforehand, which was a characteristic of Pichon's works. For instance, the work of the group of patients that acted as assistants was, at the same time, a way of learning new roles. Therefore, it is reasonable to claim that in the asylums he perfected his knowledge of the importance of leadership in changing collective behavior. From that time on to the creation of his School of Social Psychology in the 1960s, he persisted steadily in the vast project of training new leaders who could act as "social operators" in the reformation of society.

Somewhat later, in the 1950s, Pichon reached a more conceptual frame for his group practices through the Gestalt model. According to this model the starting point was not the individual, but rather the broader "field" in which the individual is included. The German word *Gestalt* is often rendered in psychology as "pattern" or "configuration." The Gestalt school's precepts, formulated as a reaction against the atomistic orientation of previous theories, emphasized that the whole is greater than its constituent parts. The Gestalt principles were later applied to motivation, social psychology, and personality, particularly by Kurt Lewin, a social psychologist known for his field theory of behavior, which holds that human behavior is a function of an individual's total psychological environment. He devoted the last years of his life, in the United States, to his research on *group dynamics*, believing that groups could change the individual behavior of their constituents.

In Pichon's view, behavior was always a social act, that is, interaction. In this respect, his thought on groups shows the visible influence of Kurt Lewin's social psychology. Briefly, Pichon began group practices as a primary tool for the treating of mental disorders. Afterward, shifting his attention from the treatment to the prevention of disease, he started to deal with the family group. In his psychiatric work he used to include the patient's family members and, in this direction, he stressed the importance of the family group in the individual's development. Finally, he was able to construct an innovative theory of the individual and the group that combined certain psychoanalytic concepts with notions of group dynamics originating from the social psychological tradition.

Psychoanalysis and Social Psychology

The family—the original group according to Pichon—occupied a central place in his group theory. His ideas were influenced by the theories of Melanie Klein and the "British school" of psychoanalysis, which was influential in the Argentine psychoanalytic establishment. Klein had made a deep revision of Freud's theory of the development of instincts. While Freud considered human instincts in terms of self-generating stages, centered on somatic sources (oral, anal, genital); Melanie Klein saw the instinctual life as formed from the beginning by internalization of early relations with the significant other.[15] According to Klein, there exists a rich "inner world" in the young child, which is the product of unconscious fantasies emerging from primary object relations and is filled with anxieties, in particular with paranoid and depressive anxiety. Paranoid anxiety refers to the child's projection of his or her hate and death wishes against the object: the mother, which consequently becomes threatening to the self's integrity. Depressive anxiety emerges from the child's fantasy that his or her hatred and aggression could harm or annihilate the "good" parts of the mother, and in this case the nucleus is the fear of losing the loved object.

Following Klein, Pichon translated the primary anxieties as "fear of attack" *(miedo al ataque)* and "fear of loss" *(miedo a la pérdida)* and proposed that they always formed a basic component, manifest or latent, in group dynamics. He suggested that behind the visible task of the group lay the demand of working through these anxieties so that group members would be able to manage collective action to accomplish certain goals. By contrast, Pichon shifted his views on psychopathology to his group theory, suggesting that all mental perturbation involved a *loss* (depressive nucleus). The "trauma of birth" was the first, original loss, and subsequently the different psychopathological states are basically attempts to manage and repair this loss. In a sense, it is possible to say that, according to Pichon's view, all groups are confronted with the interminable task of elaborating primary fantasies of loss and death. The group, then, is simultaneously the locus of evil and its remedy. Whereas at the level of the primary relation with the mother's body the group evokes the tragic fantasy of the confinement into the uterus and the traumatic separation of the birth, the group as a "team" is the support for the discriminative bond, the social link and the mobility of roles.

The other nucleus of Pichon's thoughts on groups is to be found in his interactive views of the relationship between the family group and a mentally ill family member. In this he made original use of

George Mead's theory of roles in order to uncover the *process* of "becoming" psychotic. Mead was an American philosopher prominent in both social psychology and the development of pragmatism. Mead's main contribution to social psychology was his attempt to show how the human self emerges in the process of social interaction. He stressed the importance of spoken language and used the model of games and sports to explain how the child can take the role of other persons and guide his or her behavior in terms of the effect this contemplated behavior will have on others.[16]

The patient, in Pichon's view, is the "spokesperson" *(portavoz)* of the anxieties and conflicts of his or her immediate group, that is, the family group. Symptoms reveal the latent structure of an unbearable situation of pain and disturbance that involves the whole group, of which he or she is "a spokesperson." Pichon claimed that the mentally ill played a role in a system of roles and positions that follow an unconscious family plot. He becomes a depository of the "bad" parts of the group, a kind of scapegoat, whose function allows the other members to rid themselves of their own states of distress, which, according to Pichon, are always collective. Therefore, this situation results in the family's break with the ill member who then tends to be segregated and confined as a way of projecting the evil out of the group. Given that to "cure" is to transform a system of roles, in Pichon's view not only does the ideal therapy need to include the whole family, but it should simultaneously be individual and social. It can be said that the operative group is conceived by Pichon as the opposite of the disturbed family group.

When Pichon was dismissed from his position at the Hospicio by the Perón government, he shifted his work to preventive intervention in the community by means of promoting group practices. In the late 1950s, he created in Buenos Aires the first of several schools he would found outside the structure of APA. Even if he had never left the official institution of psychoanalysis, his interest and his work increasingly pointed toward the public arena. His project was to form "social operators" who would be able to act directly in the community, facilitating an active adaptation of citizens to the changes taking place in Argentine society. His School of Social Psychology was opened mainly to a nonmedical audience, and there he developed group practices and training for a wide public. Pichon designed a general program of social reform that clearly went beyond the traditional framework of psychoanalysis, and even beyond the mental hygiene tradition of preventing psychic troubles. In Pichon's views, whereas the psychoanalyst treats individuals, the social therapist works with groups to produce a positive learning. Pichon himself regarded this stage of his trajectory as a "break" with Freudian orthodoxy so that he could achieve a real "democratization of psychoanalysis" inspired by social claims.[17]

Pichon's program materialized as a school for training social agents. For him, practical goals took precedence over theoretical concerns: "Social psychology is the science of interactions aiming at a planned social change." It is projected and conceived of as an operative "praxis," a synthesis of theory and practice.[18] Since the operative group was the central tool in this extensive program, it required a more technical definition. He proposed the operative group as an instrumental device that could be applied to many purposes, from teaching to curing, while also serving as a means of intervention in different collective organizations. The group setting included the functions of a "coordinator" and an "observer." The former was responsible for facilitating the group dynamic by means of verbal indications and interpretations. According to Pichon's view of the group, the coordinator's work pointed not only to the explicit dimension (the task) but also to the latent obstacles emerging from the basic anxieties, for instance, the fear of losing love. By "obstacle" he meant the stereotypic pattern that blocks group learning and communication that, in general, characterizes what Pichon calls a "situation of change."

For instance, he used the expression "fear of asphalt" to refer to the feelings and conflicts arising among rural migrants when they move to the city. This was a common situation among the popular classes of Buenos Aires. Basically, as long as the new migrant lost the rural habitat, which included attitudes and worldviews, he was confronted with unknown conditions that threatened his identity. In this case, in an operative group with migrants, the coordinator's functions, then, would basically tend to promote the interaction and mobility of roles and to bring to light these patterns that are the core of the "resistance to change."[19] The group observer had a less prominent position and played a nonparticipant role, recording the "material" emerging from the interactions, verbal and nonverbal, and reporting directly to the coordinator.

It is important to highlight what was new in Pichon's work. Previously, the reception of Freudianism was mainly characterized by the popularization of what was presented as a completely reshaped science of sex, love, and the emotional dimension of individual behavior. Psychoanalysis was associated with the meaning of dreams and the strength of instincts, especially the erotic ones. For the general public, psychoanalysis dealt with the secret "neurosis" that everybody carries around without fully acknowledging it—in short, the "deep self" that tended to be uncovered and presented as the true core of the individual.[20] The main character of this popular psychoanalysis was the child. Not only was psychoanalytic discourse presented in general as a psychology of the early stages of individual development, but, even more importantly, the meaning of adult behavior was to be found in the emotional features attributed to the "inner" infant existing inside each person.

Since Pichon's theory did not deal with the deep self but rather with human interactions and communication, his approach included a program of group training. The scheme he promoted implied a real shift from the individual sexual body to the social group body and from the primary emotional bonds to interactive roles. Pichon's point of view recognized a psychoanalytical inspiration regarding the latent level of the group, that is, the complex of unconscious feelings and thoughts that proceed without the awareness of the members. In his model, however, the more explicit forms of intervention refer to interaction, communication, and learning, which means that the view of the human agent as subject of attachments prevails over the figure of the instinctive child. Finally, in Pichon's program, psychoanalytic concepts were revised in their meaning and scope by his innovative intersection of models arising from the social sciences (especially group psychology) and the wide field of public preventive mental hygiene.

The expansion of psychoanalytically inspired discourse and practices in those years became evident in the extensive inclusion of psychoanalysis in the new program of psychology at the University of Buenos Aires. José Bleger, who was a member of the APA and a disciple of Pichon, played a central role in these early days of the university's psychology program. In 1966 he published his *Psicohigiene y psicología institucional* (Psycho-hygiene and institutional psychology), where he proposed a broad-new project of applied psychology to be included in the general field of psychohygiene. It is not difficult to observe the influence of Pichon's ideas and objectives on the primary goals of psycho-hygiene that refer directly to the social functions of psychology and its practitioners. In Bleger's view the crisis of the applied dimension of psychology could only find a solution in the psychologists' full commitment to the "reformist" mood that promoted social change. Thus, for him, as for Pichon, the psychologist should be a new kind of professional able to act as an *agent of social change.*[21]

Of course, the use of the word "hygiene" showed the inspiration that Bleger had taken from public medicine. He had started his career by teaching mental hygiene. The general meaning of hygiene when applied to psychology was understood as a commitment to *public* matters as opposed to the *private* setting of the psychoanalyst's office. When Bleger gave examples of the kind of situations that could be considered typical problems for psychological practice, for instance, he mentioned ordinary conflicts such as tensions in a factory, raising children in the family, or the sexual guidance of teenagers. Briefly, for Bleger a broad model of hygiene provided the basic pattern for constructing a new psychological field, while the methods and concepts of psychoanalysis supplied the specific tools.[22] It is not difficult to comprehend, therefore, the importance of Pichon's ideas for the program of psychological training that José Bleger developed in the psychology programs in Buenos Aires and Rosario.

The Rosario Operation

According to Pichon, a second mythical birth of the "operative group" took place in the large industrial city, Rosario, a context distinct from that of his early use of groups in the mental asylum. This "refoundation" of the operative group in a large city created a new perspective, since the group horizon was the *public*, taking into consideration the sociopolitical dimension. The Rosario Operation of 1958 was an attempt to test and demonstrate the power and scope of operative groups as psychosocial tools capable of successful intervention in the human problems that arose in a metropolis. The operation was presented to a wide public as a model of "social research" that, while producing new knowledge about society, would also act practically "to solve" certain problems, which were conceived of as "some kinds of interactions that hinder the full development of human existence."[23] The new figure of "social psychologist" is here introduced as an "agent of social change."

The experiment was prepared in advance by Pichon's team in Buenos Aires and announced in Rosario, where it was conducted at the Department of Economics of the University of Rosario. The plan consisted of a sequence of group meetings open to a variety of participants without any kind of selection. The projected groups included not only students and professors of medicine, psychology, philosophy, literature, and economics but also nonacademic participants, as required by one of the basic postulates of Pichon's theory of groups. The presence of individuals from different backgrounds (boxers and homemakers, truck drivers and prostitutes, among others) would facilitate the reciprocal enrichment of the total group through the variability and mobility of roles. The more different the prior roles of the members the more rich the learning process in the group, which was conceived basically as the capacity of tolerating and adopting a variety of roles.

The scheme for the successive stages of the experiment offers a clear presentation of the setting. Pichon personally conducted the first phase, which consisted of the planned preparation of the team. Afterward, when Pichon's team was already in Rosario, the collective work began with an opening speech given by Pichon, the general director, presenting the general frame of the experiment to the participants. Immediately after Pichon's first speech, a working session of the "heterogeneous groups" took place. The groups were formed at random, mixing professionals of different disciplines, university graduates, students, and members without academic qualification. Each group included a coordinator and observer who were part of the trained team. It is not possible to know exactly how many people took part in the event. But in an article Pichon later coauthored with three of his disciples, he states there were fifteen groups, each with about 9 members. There were therefore approximately 135 participants. However, Fernando Ulloa, one of Pichon's followers who also participated in the experiment, believes that there were many more, about one thousand in all.[24] After the initial meeting of the full groups, a supervisory meeting was held, assembling all the coordinators and observers under Pichon's direction. A second session of the same groups was followed by a second supervisory meeting. This concluded the first "tour" of the operation. The second phase, building on the results obtained in these first meetings, began with another speech by Pichon and then continued with a session of "homogeneous groups," that is, groups assembled by profession or activity. There were a dozen groups recruited from medical doctors, psychologists, statisticians, boxers, painters, insurance clerks, and the like. After a third supervisory meeting the complete experiment reached a conclusion with the last of Pichon's general speeches. In each of his speeches, Pichon combined his general view about groups with the common issues that coordinators and observers had passed on from the group work.

According to the plan, the core of the proposed work was located in the transition from the first to the second speech of the general director, that is, between the end of the initial phase and the beginning of the second phase. During this stage of the experiment, the "public" became a "group" in a sense that stressed not only its interactive but also its self-governing dimension. What was important in the experiment was the practical, "operative" goal of an interactive learning that was different from traditional academic knowledge. At the same time, Pichon played a central role in the proceedings as the sole authority who controlled every thread of the experience. His strong leadership, however, posed a problem: How much of the collective work in this practical experience depended on Pichon's "charisma"? With respect to this issue, it was somewhat paradoxical to project an increasing horizontal popular participation by means of an "operation" that was mainly dependent on the person and leadership of a single individual, Pichon. In any case, one of the most important aspects of the operation was that it established a new interactive communication on a microsocial scale by putting in touch an aggregate of subjects who were previously unknown to each other. Thus, the personal, "private" aim of learning through the group action went hand in hand with the social projection toward the public space, that is, the realm of human claims and needs emerging within the big city. Although the "private" dimension of the operation was still close to the model of the therapeutic group, the group's location in a public place, the inclusion of nonprofessional groups, and the emphasis on social issues established strong links with larger projects of social reform. It can be argued that the paradigm of the operative group seeks to associate the imagined ideal family group with the utopia of a perfect society in a combination where every conflict would be solved by means of communication tools.

After the Rosario Operation Pichon and some members of his team remained involved by giving speeches and developing a social-psychological teaching to reinforce the group movement in Rosario. Although it is not possible to evaluate the real impact of the event of 1958 in changing the sociability of those who were engaged in the group performance, the model of the "Rosario experiment" helped to legitimize, at least in Buenos Aires, the School of Social Psychology and its activities. After Pichon's death in 1977, several schools were established throughout the country that imitated this model: outside the university and appealing to a nonacademic public. In these schools the group process is conceived of as a movement capable of changing the subjects involved and, at the same time and by extension, society at large. In accordance with this view the "operative" family was extended to the ideal of an integrated and communicative society, a democratic utopia. The formative process of an interactive tissue would proceed from the microsocial to the macrosocial. So this process goes hand in hand with the building of a network of flexible roles and with the capacity of what Pichon calls "metalearning" *(metaaprendizaje)*, that is, the capacity of "learning to learn" *(aprender a aprender)*.

Operación Rosario occurred in Argentina at a time of intellectual and political optimism that had been initiated by the fall of Perón's regime in 1955. Peronism was seen as much more than just a regime or a political identity: it seemed to crystallize a stage of cultural and political lag in the country. The reformist mainstream saw Peronism as a retardant element in society. Peronism was perceived by its opponents as a force opposed to modernization and as a source of intolerance, one of the main causes of Argentina's failure in political and social life. Pichon's work was therefore connected to the democratic expectations originating in Argentine society after the fall of Perón.

The Social Psychology of Everyday Life

Pichon's interest in the conflicts emerging in daily social life was central to his concern with the uses and developments of operative practices. Unfortunately, there are almost no records or publications on the experiments Pichon and his team carried out during the 1960s. It is only possible to explore some indirect references included in Pichon's own works or in notes taken by his students and collaborators. In 1967, nine years after the Rosario Operation, Pichon returned to that city with some of his disciples to give a series of lectures.[25] The first speech, given by Pichon himself, stated the general premises of an operative social psychology. He defined it as "the science of interrelation," which deals with immediate events, in the "here and now." According to him, social psychology brings to light the latent contents, that is the unconscious aspects of behavior, removing the obstacles that prevent learning and communication. Consequently, Pichon emphasized that this special "discipline" was different from the kinds of knowledge offered by a university. Given the close link between theory and

group psychologists he hire

e, research and action, those who wanted to be trained in erative tools would have to develop their learning directly by practical means. At the same time, the objectives of this operative discipline always pointed to intervene in attitudes expressing what Pichon call "resistance to change." For instance, Pichon presented in his speech an example of the kind of social situation that could be treated by the intervention of the social psychologist.

He used the case of a small town on the periphery of the metropolitan Buenos Aires area, where local residents had resisted the installation of a public water system. When the whole system of pipes was ready to be connected to the town's residences, the people had showed strong resistance. Even when an epidemic of gastroenteritis caused by the old system threatened the town, most of the residents preferred to keep using well water, demonstrating their "resistance to change." Pichon and his team were hired by the municipal government. His first action was to install the headquarters of his operation in the central bar of the town, thereby making his presence highly visible. Pichon's group then started working early in the morning distributing a questionnaire house to house. The results were picked up later the same morning. Local opinion was clear: 70 percent of the residents refused to voluntarily connect their houses to the new water system.

The Pichon group's investigation of local resistance discovered that one influential woman had swayed the whole community. Not only was she a kind of "healer" but also she was a local Peronist political leader and the principal abortionist in town. She acted, in Pichon's words, as the "leader of the resistance to change." The woman had convinced her neighbors that the water coming directly from the earth (for example, from the old wells) had some special qualities that would strengthen the body.

The questionnaire had been left in every house with the request that the entire family discuss each item as it was completed. Of course, in almost every family sharp conflicts arose between the conservatives and those who were interested in a new approach and were more willing to accept change. The survey itself provoked a high level of controversy, even a climate of violence, which threatened the experiment itself. As a result the entire group of social psychologists came close to being expelled from the town. At that point Pichon decided to directly involve the healer, the visible leader of the resistance, in solving the problem, and went to see her. He decided, strategically, to challenge the woman and encouraged her to participate in the experiment as an "honorary social worker." He was able to convince her of the importance of the role she could play in the community, if she would work together with Pichon's team to improve the living conditions of the people. Pichon also made her realize that her political ambitions could be better realized if she supported change. Remarkably, almost on the same day in which the operation began, Pichon was able to "convert" the woman to the modern "clean water" opinion.

However, there was another problem. Most of the people in town had refused the public water system because of the added expense they had incurred during the construction of private pumping installations. In a meeting with some of the town's leaders in the evening, Pichon was able to convince the municipal government to buy the used pumps and other equipment of the old system at a price that would cover the cost of the new connections, thus subsidizing the transition. Immediately, some of the neighbors began selling their devices and materials at the general store. By the next morning almost all the residents had gotten rid of their old water pumps and had begun to ask to be connected to the public water system. Finally, a general meeting was held in the town's social club during which the healer played an outstanding public role in supporting the new consensus. In conclusion, through an intensive intervention requiring a couple of days of full-time work, Pichon's group had succeeded in transforming attitudes and motivations. Pichon presented this experience as the first work toward a planned social change and, at the same time, as the best example of social psychology's ability to intervene and play an active role in everyday life.

Because of the lack of adequate records and publications, it is difficult to review in more detail the social work and practices carried out by Pichon and his disciples. It is known, however, that professors and students from the psychology program in Buenos Aires, especially those who worked with José Bleger and Fernando Ulloa, developed social practices inspired by his views. Bleger was a leftist intellectual and had been a member of the Argentine Communist Party until 1961, while Pichon, who did not have a partisan affiliation, was politically close to democratic socialism. In general, social work in the slums and poor neighborhoods in the metropolitan areas of Buenos Aires in the late 1960s converged with leftist political militancy. The goals of these groups working in marginal areas were to help people get organized so that they could stand up to the state (or even to fight the state through collective mobilization) demanding improvement of their living conditions or claiming access to utilities, such as electricity, public water, sewers, and public schools. Nevertheless, it is clear that the Pichonian group movement had its greatest influence not so much among the poor or the marginal neighborhoods as within the urban middle-class in Buenos Aires and other large cities. Group practices had spread to an ample spectrum of scholars and professionals and especially to students of psychology, sociology, and the arts. An extensive net of small circles and associations proliferated outside of the University of Buenos Aires. This movement accelerated after the military coup of 1966, fueling the diffusion of discourses and practices inspired by psychoanalysis and by group activities that, in some cases, utilized Pichon's techniques.

The operative group's technique, for instance, was used in Buenos Aires during these years as a teaching tool for a theater course focusing on topics such as the role of the director, the play, the actors, and the mise-en-scène.[26] In this case, the group task was to improve the learning of dramatic direction by means of group work. The convergence between the operative group and the theatrical situation found its ground in the "dramatic model" of roles and conflicts in the group. So, in the learning experience, the participants interacted and superposed their own personality traits on the play's plot and on the differences and oppositions among the characters.

It was at this time, during 1966 and 1967, that Pichon and Ana Quiroga (his wife at that time) published a series of notes in *Primera*

Plana.[27] This weekly magazine had been created in 1962 and was a visible sign of the "new times" in culture and society that had followed the fall of the Peronist regime.[28] The magazine was both a part and a result of the modernizing wave discussed earlier. Every week *Primera Plana* dealt with national political issues, giving ample space to the voices of the political and cultural protagonists and, at the same time, exploring everyday issues, such as changes in the family and the couple, the new roles of women in society, and the varied uses, individual and social, of psychoanalysis. It also offered an up-to-date review of recent productions in literature, cinema, and the arts. Furthermore, the magazine, directed by Jacobo Timerman, played an important role in the creation of what was known as the Latin American literary "boom." Meanwhile, following European and American models, *Primera Plana* showcased the promises of the 1960s: new French and Italian cinema, music from Europe and the United States, new fashion and lifestyles, and even the explorations of a fundamental revolution in morals and habits.

Psychoanalysis found a visible place in the magazine through interviews and notes. (See figure 22.) It is reasonable to claim that the new "psy" discourse was introduced as a tool of modernization, a process that had to include a reform of private habits, as was suggested by Pichon's insistence on the value of change. The magazine was conceived of and projected by Timerman as a central tool in promoting a general transformation of Argentine society.[29] The interest in "psy" discourse and practices was representative of the wide acceptance they had reached among the intellectual middle-class public, which constituted a significant part of the periodical's readers.

This was the context for Pichon and Quiroga's series on "psychology of everyday life." Some common traits in this series that communicated both *Primera Plana*'s general orientation and Pichon's approach to the problems of interaction and conflicts in social life are easily identifiable. The "psychology of everyday life" began by proposing a new view of themes that were a common part of everyday experience. Some of these subjects were picked up from newspaper headlines (floods, events of social violence, or the Soccer World Championship), while others were more general topics such

Figure 23. "Psychoanalysis does not exist" says Freud while lying on a couch in a cover of *Primera Plana.* This magazine was instrumental in the diffusion of a psychoanalytic culture in Argentina. Cover of *Primera Plana*, August, 1965. Courtesy of New York University in Buenos Aires' library.

as vacations, the body, love and the couple, and others. On the one hand, the articles were conceived from a journalist's point of view aiming at commenting on the relevant events, or even trying to anticipate what could be important for the public. On the other hand, the authors introduced a new social psychology, which revealed a Freudian inspiration, proposing a deeper look with the goal of revealing hidden, latent meanings. For instance, when a big flood afflicted part of the country, in 1966, one of the articles was dedicated to a general survey of psychological reactions to natural catastrophes. Pichon's theory on interaction and attachment provided the conceptual framework for shedding light on human behavior in an unexpected crisis. According to this view the flood or other crises that threatened normal living conditions led to denial of oncoming disaster. This denial was conceived by Pichon as a form of "resistance to change." In a second phase of reaction, fear shifted to panic, a potential source of dangerous, uncontrolled collective behavior. Here the reader was asked to see a group situation: even if the individual's reaction could be compared to a mental disorder (as a kind of paranoia), Pichon's approach focused on the collective experience and took into account the social phenomena, such as roles, leadership, rumors, and group fantasies.[30]

Similarly, other notes published in this series addressed the subjective conflicts that arose when migrants moved from the countryside to the big city, that is, to Buenos Aires. "Fear of asphalt" was the expression coined by Pichon to condense a complex spectrum of attitudes and feelings relating to personal and group identity and the primary sense of belonging *(pertenencia)*.[31] Pichon suggested that a sort of "ecological psychology" focused on the importance of places and the environment in forming the social subject. He did not accept the behaviorist view that the external milieu could be considered as merely a pole of stimulus that generated, through conditioning, answers and reactions. Pichon considered the habitat as an inner group formation, a frame encompassing the early bonds and primary roles linking the subject to the inner original family that was the result of the individual's early experiences. The migrant, argued Pichon, would try at the same time to cut loose some of his earlier attachments while also trying to preserve others so that he or she could successfully face any novel threat from the unknown world. In a sense, Pichon was able to propose a distinctive approach to the subjective troubles arising in the big city and even to sketch out a conceptual scheme for a social psychology of life in the metropolis.

Soccer, the most popular sport in Argentina, was also the subject matter of several articles. Some of them attempted to present a general overview of the group or team situation by means of explaining the network of interrelated roles that are the basis for a team's action during a game. The model of the sport group was an important component of George Mead's social psychology and had also had a decisive role in Pichon's emphasis on groups. Several articles dedicated to soccer dealt with events during the 1966 World Soccer Championship where the Argentine team was defeated by England. At the time the Argentine soccer team began its competition in the World Cup, a military coup took place in Argentina, establishing General Onganía's dictatorship.

Pichon and Quiroga found it convenient to write on the relationship between soccer and politics on that occasion. The reigning view was to consider soccer in its collective dimension as a generator of mass reactions and a reflector of public opinion. Again, Pichon's Freudian background is evident in the analysis of the latent content of social representations, beliefs, and feelings. Discussing the soccer team's performance along these lines, their article emphasized the dimension of fantasies that sustained a collective identification, including political ideals and images of the country. A mixed composition of wishes and fears impeded the nation's ability to face and accept defeat by the English, leading to the consequent collective denial. As a result, the widespread fantasy of a conspiracy against the Argentine team in the World Cup spread among the public, which in turn awakened hate and distrust toward the old imperialist metropolis, London. Finally, even if the national team had failed in its goals, they were received as "moral winners" at home. Maintaining this delusion that they had won a symbolic victory helped transpose the nation's hopes and desires onto the new military government.[32]

Pichon was dealing with notoriously tough political issues such as nationalism, national identity, and, in particular, the support and conformism awakened by the military coup. Although evaluating the impact of these kinds of articles proves difficult, one can argue that they were unusual among the press's treatment of current events. Equally important, they showed Pichon's purpose of going beyond the knowledge and consciousness of the ordinary public. It could then be argued that some of these views on daily collective life went beyond the purpose of applied psychology and combined reformist aims with an original form of intellectual intervention concerning some critical characteristics of urban Argentine society.

In conclusion, Pichon was the central figure in the emergence of a new "psy" culture that spread through Buenos Aires during the 1960s and later reached the principal Argentine cities. Nevertheless, his teaching and his work have to be considered in the general frame of the process of changes that, by these years, had given birth to a new culture and a new society. Not only did Pichon play an outstanding role in producing a deep renewal of psychoanalysis and psychiatry in his time, but also he contributed to the implantation of new psychological discourses and practices in Argentine society. On the one hand, he was a real "leader of change" (in Pichonian words) in promoting a nonorthodox version of psychoanalysis among a new generation of psychiatrists who sought to renovate the entire field of mental health public assistance. On the other hand, his ideas also had a decisive and crucial impact on the new professional group of psychologists who adopted some of his views. Moreover, his teaching and his professional example proposed a free "use" of psychoanalytic notions that became widely diffused throughout Argentine culture and, above all, that was borrowed by progressive intellectuals who tried to bring together philosophy and the social sciences.

During the 1960s psychoanalysis permeated Argentine society: it was both a modern kind of psychotherapy, an object of consumption for middle-class sectors, and a multifarious corpus of discourse that provided a sort of general and common knowledge for diverse uses. The 1960s were a time of change in beliefs and attitudes, and Pichon was certainly a man embedded in his time. But he also actively contributed to enlightening and shaping his society. Pichon's social psychology, which proposed a special mix of a psychoanalytically inspired thought with group dynamics, enjoyed a strong and multifaceted reception. This teaching, developed out of the university, succeeded in simultaneously influencing both professionals and the lay public alike.

Looking at Pichon from the perspective of mental health practices, one can conclude that Pichon's actions and the wave of reform during the sixties left the psychiatric field transformed. Even though Pichon himself did not hold an academic position, his work triggered a similar transformation in the field of psychology. Nevertheless, the most important influence of his work can be found in its immense cultural effects on society. Pichon extended the dynamics of modernization beyond the educated middle class. In carrying out this task he had to deal with popular subjects— soccer, migratory movements from the countryside to the city, the psychological effects of natural catastrophes—which primarily affected the lower strata of society. At the same time, he contributed steadily, although indirectly, to focusing public attention on popular subjects, teaching with his example, and opening new ways of considering the problems of the disadvantaged classes. Of course, Pichon's free version of psychoanalysis occasionally elicited some criticism from people more concerned with theoretical and doctrinal issues, but through his work and action a democratic shift took place in Argentine psychoanalysis, making it a permanent feature in contemporary Argentine society.

Chapter Six

PSYCHIATRISTS AND THE RECEPTION OF PSYCHOANALYSIS, 1910s–1970s

Mariano Plotkin

In 1927, Juan Ramón Beltrán, a medical doctor with a distinguished career in forensic psychiatry, was appointed by a criminal court to determine the mental competence of a man accused of committing several crimes. In his report to the judge, Beltrán concluded that the defendant was clearly a degenerate and an innate criminal in the Lombrosian sense, an atavistic remnant of previous evolutionary stages. The degeneration manifested itself in the individual's abundant "physical stigmas," including flat feet and unusually shaped ears and teeth. Oddly enough, however, after discussing the patient's sexual behavior, Beltrán ended his report by pointing out that "what makes this observation all the more interesting is the patient's sexual history. . . . This constitutes a serious argument in favor of the much-attacked Freudian thesis, which in this case we accept completely."[1] For Beltrán, therefore, the violent behavior of this criminal was the result of a combination of degeneration and pathological sexual drives. Beltrán was using two hardly compatible theoretical bodies: the theory of degeneration, and Sigmund Freud's psychoanalysis. The theory of degeneration remained, with nuances, a major current of thought in Argentine psychiatry until as late as the 1940s. This theory was based on the idea that mental and physical diseases were passed on from generation to generation, each time in a heavier and more destructive dose. In Argentina these ideas were combined with Cesare Lombroso's criminal anthropology that claimed that criminals and madmen were atavistic vestiges of previous stages of human development.

Psychoanalysis, created by the Viennese Sigmund Freud, by contrast, emphasized the importance of unconscious drives (particularly those of a sexual nature) in human behavior. Dream analysis as well as the interpretation of "slips"—unconscious acts such as saying one thing when one is trying to say something else— were considered by Freud as the "royal path" to access areas of the unconscious. Psychoanalysis focused on the development of the mind as opposed to somatic theories that concentrated on the body (particularly on the morphology of the brain as well as on certain external physical features), as the determinant of psychiatric conditions.

Beltrán's eclectic combination of psychoanalysis and degeneracy theory shows a particular pattern of early reception of psychoanalysis in Argentine psychiatric circles, a pattern that could be defined as "amalgamation." Psychoanalysis, like other psychiatric theories, was added to an existing theoretical and therapeutic arsenal that contained assumptions and practices, which, in many cases, were incompatible with each other. Moreover, this particular pattern of reception was not linear and progressive. The acceptance of new ideas was linked instead to broad cultural (and to some extent political) developments in Argentine society as well as to the professionalization of psychiatry in the country.

Although in Argentina the main paths of reception and diffusion of psychoanalysis developed mostly outside the psychiatric establishment, the introduction of psychoanalysis into some key areas of the Argentine public system of psychiatric assistance greatly contributed to the broad dissemination of psychoanalytic thought in society. The complex relationship between psychoanalysis and psychiatry developed from the beginning of the twentieth century and endured through the early 1980s. The reception of psychoanalysis took place in medical circles, and this, in turn, affected the constitution and development of the Argentine "psychoanalytic culture."[2]

Psychoanalysis and Psychiatry: An Uneasy Relationship

Psychiatric practice was born in Argentina under the influence of positivism[3], which since the 1880s had constituted the "official ideology" of Latin American intellectual elites. Positivism emphasized the centrality of empirical observation as the only valid form of knowledge and was not hospitable to such empirically "weak" theories as psychoanalysis. Freud's theory was considered a pan-sexualist theory that slipped into the nonscientific realm of things that were too practical and too mundane. Argentine doctors were instead extremely receptive to purely somatic theories that emphasized the "observable" dimension of the causes of mental diseases, such as degeneration theory.

In Argentina, the theory of degeneration had a particular connotation because it was associated with the phenomenon of large-scale immigration. The European immigrant, once perceived as the coveted seed for the civilization of the country, was by the 1910s seen as the origin of class or, more generally, social conflict and cultural malaise. Nationalist thinkers at the beginning of the century generally believed that uncontrolled immigration would degrade the national race by incorporating large numbers of European degenerates into society.[4] The image of the "crazy immigrant" became a stock character in Argentine popular culture and literature during the first decades of the twentieth century. Psychiatry, at the same time, became part of a larger medical apparatus set up by the state to discipline and improve the conditions of living of the new urban masses.

The theory of degeneration, particularly when it was applied to *degenerate* forensic psychiatry, could lead to diametrically different conclusions. In 1911, for instance, Francisco de Veyga, a reputed doctor who worked for the police department and who had been one of José Ingenieros's teachers, proposed the imprisonment for indefinite terms of all degenerates regardless of whether they had committed crimes. De Veyga rationalized that since degenerates were by definition impossible to rehabilitate, and since sooner or later they would necessarily engage in criminal activities because it was in their nature to do so, the state would do society a favor by isolating degenerates as soon as possible. Among the potential victims of de Veyga's proposed "great confinement" were the vagrants, homeless, homosexuals, and even lawyers who knowingly defended criminals, political "bosses," and stock market speculators.[5]

Only a few years later, however, a progressive judge well versed in the latest psychiatric theories of the times decided not to send a multiple murderer of young children to prison because the criminal showed clear stigmas of degeneration. The presence of such stigmas was, according to the judge, evidence that the criminal was not in control of his violent tendencies and was, therefore, not responsible for his acts. Instead, the judge sent him to a psychiatric ward.[6] Whereas for de Veyga degeneracy theory laid the foundation for a broad program of social control, for the judge in this case degeneration constituted a mitigating factor, similar to alienation, that should lead to a less punitive sentence.

Given the uncontested hegemony of somatic approaches to psychiatry, and in particular of the theory of degeneration, psychoanalysis, although it was known and discussed in medical circles, did not find an easy place for itself in the therapeutic arsenal of Argentine psychiatrists during the first decades of the twentieth century. Unlike their Brazilian colleagues who, since the 1910s, integrated psychoanalysis into their theoretical equipment, Argentine psychiatrists were reticent to accept the Freudian system until decades later. Brazilians saw psychoanalysis, understood as the science that dealt with the "wild aspects" of human nature, as an instrument for subduing what they perceived as the exotic and "savage" components of their own culture.[7] A few Brazilian psychiatrists who promoted the use of psychoanalysis visited Argentina in the 1910s and 1920s to lecture on the subject but, exceptions notwithstanding, failed to convince their Argentine colleagues about the virtues of psychoanalysis.

The Argentines' reticence toward psychoanalysis was due in part to the profound influence that French and Italian psychiatry exercised in the development of Argentine psychiatry. The Argentine elite looked at Europe, particularly at France, as a beacon of civilization, and Argentine medical doctors were no exception to that general rule. Only those professionals who could show some degree of success in Europe received recognition from the Argentine medical establishment. "From the intellectual point of view, we are French," declared Horacio Piñero, a psychiatrist and Professor of Psychology at the University of Buenos Aires, in a speech given at the Sorbonne in 1903.[8] French and, to a lesser extent, Italian and German were considered mandatory languages for Argentine physicians, and Argentine journals routinely published articles in those languages without providing translation. For different reasons neither the Italian nor the French psychiatric tradition was particularly receptive to psychoanalysis during the early years of the century.

In France, the deeply rooted neurological tradition, the influence of degeneracy theory, as well as a certain anti-German (and anti-Semitic) nationalist feelings conspired against the reception of psychoanalysis in psychiatric circles. However, Freudism was popular among some avant-garde artists and novelists. French psychiatrists characterized psychoanalysis as a pan-sexual theory lacking scientific foundations.[9] In Italy the prestige of Cesare Lombroso's criminal anthropology with its strong emphasis on heredity and degeneration, on the one hand, and the deep influence of the conservative Catholic Church that opposed psychoanalysis's open discussion on sexuality, on the other hand, made the reception of psychoanalysis difficult. Later, the emergence of Fascism, a totalitarian regime that considered psychoanalysis subversive, posed new limitations to the diffusion of Freudism in Italy.[10]

The reluctance of Argentine doctors to incorporate psychoanalysis into their therapeutic and theoretical tool kit does not mean that it was unknown or little discussed in Argentina. Although it occupied a growing place in debates among psychiatrists, psychoanalysis was still considered a "foreign theory," something that did not fit into the psychiatric tradition of the country but that, at the same time, could not be ignored by professionals who boasted of being *a la páge* of theoretical developments.

The first-known mention of psychoanalysis in a scientific forum in Argentina took place as early as 1910, when Germán Greve, a Chilean physician, read his paper "Sobre psicología y psicoterapia de ciertos estados angustiosos" (On the psychology and psychotherapy of certain states of anxiety) at a medical conference held in Buenos Aires.[11] Greve used psychoanalytic concepts, but acknowledged that he had some reservations about certain aspects of the Freudian system. Aware that he was breaking an accepted paradigm by introducing a new and controversial psychological theory, Greve tried to fit his approach into an already accepted tradition: the French school. He went out of his way to show the compatibilities between his particular interpretation of psychoanalysis and the presumptions of French psychiatry. By doing this, Greve began a tradition that would shape the early reception of psychoanalysis in Argentina. Freud would be accessed in French, mostly through secondhand commentators, both by sympathizers and detractors. This was true even after Antonio López Ballesteros's translation into Spanish of Freud's *Complete Works* became available in the early 1920s.

How Greve's colleagues received his paper is unknown, but by the late 1910s Argentine psychiatrists were discussing psychoanalysis, and by the 1920s a small but growing group of doctors began to incorporate psychoanalytic concepts in their work and began publishing papers on the discipline. Some even began to use psychoanalysis as a therapeutic technique. Nevertheless, their knowledge about psychoanalysis remained derivative and based on French sources. Fernando Gorriti, for instance, was a progressive psychiatrist who had been a cofounder of an open-door colony for mental patients in the Province of Buenos Aires. He published a book in 1930 on his experiences of dream analysis with a patient. Gorriti claimed he was able to cure a patient through the analysis of his dreams following the Freudian technique. He had analyzed as many as seventy-four dreams of that single patient. Like Greve twenty years before him, Gorriti, who did not cite his sources, still felt compelled to find compatibilities between psychoanalysis and the more universally accepted French school in order to legitimize his use of the Freudian technique. Gorriti even sent a copy of the volume to Freud who, needless to say, was pleased by it, since he was eager to disseminate psychoanalytic knowledge in what he considered exotic lands.[12]

Gorriti was not the only prominent Argentine doctor interested in Freudism. Others, including Alejandro Raitzin, a highly respected psychiatrist, and Gonzalo Bosch (see figure 23), one of the most prestigious psychiatrists in the country, showed interest for and curiosity in psychoanalysis at some point. However, these specialists accepted only those elements of psychoanalytic theory that were compatible with the findings of the French school. Similarly, those who opposed psychoanalysis did so basing their opinions on the criticism that French doctors made of Freudism: for them psychoanalysis was a doctrine of dubious morality with no scientific foundation. At one point, Raitzin acknowledged that his familiarity with psychoanalysis was limited to his reading of French commentators.[13]

The growing, but still incomplete, acceptance of psychoanalysis by Argentine psychiatrists must be viewed in the context of broader cultural developments in society. Particularly important was the crisis of the positivist paradigm that had dominated science and public discourse since the 1870s. Since the late 1910s, there had been a greater acceptance in Latin America than in the previous decades of European idealist philosophy that contradicted positivism. This was partly a reaction against what was then perceived as a threat—both cultural and political—posed by the growing Anglo-American power in the world and, particularly, by the expansive "materialist empire of the North" (that is, the United States). Some influential Latin American intellectuals started seeing positivism as a philosophy that legitimized materialism. From Uruguayan writer José Enrique Rodó's influential book *Ariel* published in 1900, to the "Ateneo de la Juventud" organized in Mexico by young intellectuals, an antipositivist/antimaterialist wave spread throughout Latin America. Years later, World War I would accelerate the crisis of positivism by demonstrating to Latin American intellectuals the destructive potential of the technological and scientific advances promoted by European civilization. In the previous decades scientific and technological

Figure 24. Dr. Gonzalo Bosch, in the front, wearing
white coat. At his right, wearing a black suit, is Pierre
Janet, the French psychologist, during the latter's visit to
Argentina (from Balán's *Cuéntame tu vida: Una biografía
colectiva del psicoanálisis en la Argentina* [Buenos Aires:
Planeta, 1991]). Courtesy of Jorge Balán.

development were perceived as good in themselves. The war showed their dark side and encouraged Latin American elites to search for other systems of thought that emphasized the spiritual dimension of reality. Furthermore, a growing nationalist feeling among intellectuals looking for the "true roots of the nationality" in the spiritual elements of the region's Spanish Catholic origins, also contributed to the crisis of positivism.

The crisis of positivism was felt in the medical profession as well and opened the door for the reception of alternative therapeutic theories. Positivist doctors had been obsessed with the somatic aspects of psychiatry. In the new cultural environment there was growing interest in the mind and the "spirit" as well as in the body. Throughout the 1920s the degeneracy paradigm began to lose the influence it previously had exercised, yet it continued to occupy a prominent place among psychiatric theories until the 1940s.[14] In this new context psychoanalysis, perceived by some as a "science of the spirit," found more receptive ears among local doctors. Moreover, from the 1920s, and particularly during the 1930s, new psychiatric therapies became available worldwide, including shock therapies and pharmacology. Now psychiatric treatments could offer some hope of improvement for mental patients. However, most of those therapies, although successful, were not grounded in firm theoretical foundations. As the German-born Argentine psychiatrist E. Eduardo Krapf pointed out in the late 1930s, "[There are] two completely new methods of treatment that changed the therapeutic aspect of psychiatry: the treatment of general paralysis by malaria [Wagner-Jauregg's method created in 1917] . . . , and the treatment of schizophrenia through insulin shock [Sakel's method introduced in 1934]. . . . Both methods were discovered as a result of lucky clinical observation, and both lack to this day adequate theoretical foundations."[15]

The weak theoretical foundation of those somatic therapies led some progressive psychiatrists to question the very foundations of classic psychiatric (and by extension medical) practice. They espoused a broader conception of medicine in which the psychological dimension of diseases could not be ignored any longer. From doctors who recommended "hearing" patients and the use of a more humane approach to their needs, to those who promoted specific psychotherapeutic techniques, there was a trend toward accepting the use of psychotherapy more generally, and toward the recognition that patients should be listened to. This new tendency became clear, for instance, in forensic psychiatry.

In 1941, Drs. J. Delpiano and E. López Bancalari were appointed by the court to determine the level of responsibility and mental competence of Rafael Ladrón de Guevara, who had confessed to killing his wife and four of his six children and then setting fire to his house. After committing these murders Ladrón de Guevara also killed Mr. Cuviello who had earlier tried to cheat him in a commercial operation. After the examination, the psychiatrists concluded that the defendant was responsible for his actions and should therefore be imprisoned. However, the psychiatric theories used by these doctors to reach their conclusion were as far from degeneration theory as they could possibly be. First of all, Delpiano and López Bancalari decided that it was important to *listen to* what the defendant had to say and also to try to reconstruct his early life in order to understand his criminal behavior. Ladrón's crimes, according to the psychiatrists, could be understood as a result of the fact that "in his unconscious there was a feeling of rebellion against the injustice of his suffering," which originated in the conflictive relationship he had with his wife. Delpiano and López Bancalari asserted that "his behavior [Ladrón's] becomes clear to us at the light of the Freudian theory." This behavior was the result of some kind of compulsion, which he could not totally control. This compulsion originated not in degeneration but rather in the patient's unconscious drives that could be discovered through listening and not through the observation of physical stigmas.

Ladrón's violent homicides had, according to these doctors, a history that had to be examined in order to *understand* what had happened. Of course there were many psychiatrists who remained loyal to old paradigms, but in general Argentine psychiatrists gradually abandoned a purely somatic approach to mental diseases and became more concerned with a global vision of mental patients. This vision would integrate the psychical dimension: the mind as well as the brain. Among the new psychiatric tendencies, psychoanalysis seemed to offer the strongest theoretical foundations. Some psychiatrists argued that psychoanalysis could even offer an explanation for the success of somatic therapies. Enrique Pichon Rivière, for instance (see chapter 5 of this volume), one of the pioneers in the use of electro-convulsive therapy (ECT) in Argentina and later a founding member of the Argentine Psychoanalytic Association and a "diffuser" of psychoanalysis, claimed that shock therapy worked in cases of melancholy because it fulfilled the patient's wish for punishment, therefore reducing the tension between the id and the superego.[16] Most psychiatrists, however, did not abandon their previous notions. Instead, they combined degeneracy theory with other recent theories including Freud's psychoanalysis.

The emergence of new treatments contributed to the acceleration of the professionalization of psychiatry. Psychoanalysis's relatively strong theoretical foundations contributed to its acceptance by progressive psychiatrists. Paradoxically, however, the incomplete characteristic of that professionalization, the fact that there were areas of the art of healing people not yet under the total control of doctors, opened other spaces for the reception of psychotherapy and, by extension, of psychoanalysis. Well into the 1930s, there were still some "gray areas" in the field of psychiatric assistance for which not only the medical monopoly was contested, but for which there was still room for collaboration between physicians and lay practitioners. One of these areas was defined precisely by psychotherapy. Although the use of psychotherapy was gradually becoming more acceptable within the medical profession, licensed doctors had not been able to establish their monopoly over its practice. There was, therefore, room for a popular reception of psychotherapeutic methods that not only did not compete with the doctors' medical use of it, but that was complementary to it.

In the 1920s James Mapelli, an Italian hypnotist and illusionist, arrived in Argentina. He combined his shows in theaters and music halls with a professional practice of his own version of psychotherapy, which he called *"psicoinervación,"* in an office he had been allowed to use in a public hospital. Although he did not have a medical degree, he became a member of the board of editors of many professional journals in Argentina and presented papers at medical conferences.[17] Similarly, Arminda Aberastury, the wife of Enrique Pichon Rivière, practiced child-psychoanalysis in an office given to her for that purpose at a public hospital where her husband worked as a psychiatrist. In spite of the fact that she did not have a college degree at that time, Aberastury published articles and book reviews in medical journals. Only in the 1950s did the government begin regulating the practice of psychotherapy (and of psychoanalysis in particular), authorizing medical doctors alone to perform it.

Beginning in the late 1920s the foundations of traditional psychiatry were revised by progressive sectors within the profession, resulting in the acceptance of new scientific theories by Argentine practitioners. One of these theories, the diffusion of which would facilitate the incorporation of psychoanalysis into psychiatry, was mental hygiene.

The Liga Argentina de Higiene Mental: Eugenics and Modernization

In 1927 Dr. Fernando Gorriti submitted a proposal for the creation of a Liga Social de Higiene Mental, inspired by the movement that had emerged in the United States under the leadership of former psychiatric patient Clifford Beers and the psychiatrist Adolf Meyer. In 1908 Clifford Beers had been a young Yale graduate who, after spending two years in a mental institution as a patient, wrote a book, *A Mind that Found Itself,* which was an account of his experiences and a plea for a more humane treatment of psychiatric patients. This book, published with the encouragement of Meyer and philosopher-psychologist William James, gave origin to the movement of mental hygiene. According to historian Nathan Hale, the original purpose of the movement in the United States was "to stimulate research for the causes of insanity and to arouse public demands for the improvement of mental hospitals. The movement became an important intermediary between specialists and the public and later, after 1918, a transmitter of diluted psychoanalytic ideas."[18] Institutions promoting mental hygiene inspired by this American model were soon created in different parts of the world, including Latin America.[19]

Gorriti's proposal was approved, and the Liga Argentina de Higiene Mental was constituted in December 1929 with the purpose of "the promotion of the prevention of mental disorders, the improvement of the conditions of assistance of psychopaths, and the development of mental hygiene in the areas of individual activity, schooling, and professional and social activities."[20] Its board of directors included some of the most prestigious members of the psychiatric guild. Moreover, the Liga also attracted a large number of nonmedical members, particularly lawyers and even some politicians. Theoretical differences notwithstanding, the members of the Liga agreed that the material conditions found in public psychiatric institutions in Argentina were unacceptable. Overcrowding and lack of minimal hygienic conditions were chronic problems that had forced the authorities to close the two mental hospitals on more than one occasion. As late as in 1956 the Hospital Nacional Neuropsiquiátrico de Mujeres (Psychiatric Women's Hospital, previously called Hospital Nacional de Alienadas and later Hospital Braulio Moyano) housed more than twice as many patients as beds it had available. At the Hospital Nacional Neuropsiquiátrico de Hombres (Psychiatric Men's Hospital, formerly called Hospicio de las Mercedes and later Hospital Nacional José T. Borda) the situation was not any better. Similarly, the rates of mortality in some mental hospitals were extremely high. In Colonia Cerdá for retarded children, for instance, a chilling 58.6 percent of the total of patients who left the hospital in 1957 had died under care.[21] Some members of the Liga, however, had already introduced improvements, such as outpatient services, in their own institutions.[22]

The Liga de Higiene Mental progressed relatively fast. It started receiving federal, municipal, and private funds, including the donation of public buildings.[23] In 1940 it operated an Instituto Neuropsiquiátrico (Neuropsychiatric Institute), which, under the direction of Ciampi, provided assistance to children with mental disorders. The Liga also established outpatient psychiatric services at the Neuropsiquiátrico and elsewhere, and created the first school of social workers in the country. During the 1930s and 1940s the Liga also established regional branches in various provinces of the country. Key to this expansion was the Liga's ability to attract public attention and support due in part to the prestige of its members, in particular Dr. Gonzalo Bosch. He was appointed director of the Hospicio de las Mercedes in 1934 and later, in 1944, he would be appointed to the chair of psychiatry at the University of Buenos Aires.

One of the central assumptions of the Liga and in general of the movement of mental hygiene was that mental disorders were preventable and, more importantly, curable. Many of the preventive policies proposed by the Liga followed the classic eugenic model, including the limitation and control of immigration and premarital blood testing. However, the idea of prevention itself and of curability helped to undermine the earlier hegemony of the degeneration paradigm that was an important component of understanding mental disorders until late in the 1940s. The idea that mental disorders could be cured implied an interest in exploring new areas of treatment and new therapeutic techniques. Moreover, reformers argued that the possibility of preventing mental diseases was dependent on early detection and treatment. Mild neuroses were therefore one of the focuses of the Liga's attention; thus, outpatient assistance and the use of psychotherapy were emphasized. Furthermore, if mild neuroses were worth treating, then a "gray area" was defined between alienation and "normality," blurring the distinction between the two. "The alienated [person] is not an 'alien' [ajeno]," claimed Bosch in 1941 during the inauguration of a show of artistic works done by patients of the Liga's mental institutions. "No one is absolutely sane," he went on to say.[24] Although Bosch did not practice psychoanalysis, he showed some interest for, and was ready to support the practice of, a discipline that concentrated its attention precisely on the fringes of normality. Moreover, the emphasis on environmental conditions would later invite new concerns about the role of family as a potential pathogenic agent, which was one of the foundations of the psychoanalytic approach.[25] The Liga opened a space within the psychiatric establishment for the acceptance of psychotherapy and psychoanalysis, a space that would fructify decades later, after the fall of the government of Juan Perón in 1955. Many analysts started their career at the Liga.

Another area of activity for the Liga was the education of the population through radio messages, conferences, and publications. The Liga emphasized the need to eliminate social prejudices against psychiatric patients. It published the *Revista Argentina de Higiene Mental* (*RAHM*, hereafter), a magazine for a popular diffusion of mental hygiene information and related issues aimed at a nonspecialized public. The Liga's explicit message in all these efforts was that the mental patient was just a sick person who deserved treatment. As a natural consequence of this notion and also as a general way of reducing the patient population at psychiatric hospitals, the Liga promoted the creation of psychiatric services in general hospitals. This would open an important door for the entrance of psychoanalysis into psychiatric practice decades later, in the 1960s.

The Liga's publications included the use of psychoanalytic concepts. This was in part the result of the increasing American influence on Argentine psychiatry, particularly from the 1940s onward. Gradually, English came to replace French and Italian as the second language of Argentine medical journals. American neopsychoanalysis, which de-emphasized the centrality of sexuality and stressed the role of culture instead, enjoyed a relatively wide reception in Argentine psychiatric circles. *RAHM* often published translations of articles that had previously appeared in American journals in which the influence of psychoanalysis was clear. Since *RAHM* and particularly the Liga's radio conferences reached a relatively large audience, broader sectors of the population became informed not only about mental disorders, their treatment, and prevention in general but also about psychoanalysis as one of those possible treatments.

In spite of its modernizing spirit, the Argentine Liga's reformist efforts had serious limitations. First, although it promoted a relatively broad notion of psychiatric assistance, the Liga movement emerged within the psychiatric establishment that was still committed to the asylum model. Bosch, the president of the Liga, was at the same time the director of the old Hospicio. Second, the Liga as an organization was patterned after the traditional model of philanthropic society, although relying heavily on state funds. It even had a society of ladies auxiliary. Thus, the Liga leadership viewed the improvement of the conditions of the mental patients as a philanthropic task, which could be carried out without a radical change in the structure of the system of psychiatric assistance.[26] However, the Liga did lay the foundations for the future incorporation of psychoanalysis into the public system of psychiatric assistance.

Psychoanalysis and Political Ideology

The Liga Argentina de Higiene Mental and the other progressive institutions concerned with psychiatric assistance that emerged in Argentina during the late 1920s and 1930s promoted the use of psychoanalysis in psychiatric circles with some degree of success. In general, doctors who became interested in psychoanalysis were those who were dissatisfied with traditional psychiatry and who sought a renovation of their discipline. Psychoanalysis was in general associated with modernity.[27] However, local doctors had a diverse understanding of psychoanalysis and, in many cases, filtered their understanding through political and social ideology.[28] A right-wing doctor such as Juan Ramón Beltrán, for instance, who was close to antidemocratic sectors of the Argentine military in the 1930s, considered that psychoanalysis, combined with Lombrosian criminal anthropology, could be used as a tool to enhance social control. In his view, psychoanalysis was valuable because it showed that, "The child, far from being something chaste, pure, morally spotless, is immoral, impure. Education, society, custom, the family, and so on will purify the child, will give him, with time, the necessary morality, will elevate his temperament and its natural tendencies."[29] Instead of constituting "neurogenic" elements as Freud had suggested, the agents of social control had for Beltrán a "purifying" effect that could be enlightened by the use of psychoanalytic knowledge.

This conservative interpretation of psychoanalysis, however, was not the only interpretation of the Freudian system existing in Argentina at that time. Other doctors, most of them close to the political and social left, offered a different reading of psychoanalysis. For psychiatrists like Gregorio Bermann, Jorge Thénon, and Emilio Pizarro Crespo, for instance (all three were either members or sympathizers of the Argentine Communist Party at some point), psychoanalysis could lay the foundation for an overdue renovation of psychiatry and for broader transformations of society as well. According to Pizarro Crespo, for instance, psychoanalysis was the battering ram to break the hegemony of the degeneracy paradigm. He wrote, "It is to the credit of the 'psychoanalytic school' the incalculable merit of having taken away for the first time the obsessive neurotic, hysteric and phobic disorders, from the shadowy realm of genetic fatalism . . . to which the current medical doctrines of 'heredity' and 'degeneration' had them condemned."[30] More generally, according to Pizarro Crespo, psychotherapy in general and psychoanalysis in particular would play a crucial role in the construction of a new, socialist society. Psychoanalysis could help to analyze and "dissect" some typical bourgeois "social" diseases, such as narcissism, which would be overcome with the establishment of a postbourgeois society.[31] Similarly, Bermann wanted to use psychoanalysis as an important tool for a broad program of social reforms.[32]

The fact that psychoanalysis received such widely different ideological readings in Argentina was not a unique phenomenon. In France, for instance, both leftist surrealist artists and some doctors members of the right-wing organization Action Française made ideological appropriations of psychoanalysis and tried to use it to support their own social and political agendas. More intriguing, however, is the fact that in Argentina conservative and leftist psychiatrists lived in what seemed to be a peaceful coexistence. Unlike their counterparts in other parts of the world, they published their antithetical points of view in the same journals and participated in the foundation of the same scientific institutions. Moreover, there did not seem to be debate among these promoters of obviously incompatible points of view.

In Argentina, politically conservative and politically progressive doctors with opposite interpretations of the nature of their discipline and of psychoanalysis in particular were able to coexist without inconvenience or discussion. It seemed as if all interpretations of psychiatry and of psychoanalysis could find a place within the psychiatric field. Beltrán, for instance, not only published in but was also a member of the board of editors of Bermann's (himself a fellow traveler of the Communist Party) openly leftist journal *Psicoterapia*, published in the city of Córdoba in 1936 and 1937. *Psicoterapia*, which promoted the use of psychotherapy and particularly of psychoanalysis among psychiatrists, was a deeply and openly politically committed publication.[33] If Beltrán was accepted on its board of editors, it was because political allegiances notwithstanding, he shared with Bermann an interest in promoting the use of psychoanalysis even though they understood the nature of their discipline very differently.

At the other end of the ideological spectrum, *Anales de Biotipología* (Annals of biotypology), a journal published by the openly philo-fascist institution Asociación de Biotipología, Eugenesia y Medicina Social (Association of Biotypology, Eugenics and Social Medicine, an organization sponsored by the Italian Embassy), routinely published articles by leftist doctors and intellectuals, including some prominent members of the Argentine Socialist Party. *Anales* published many articles promoting the use of psychoanalysis that were written in a similar tone and sometimes by the same people who wrote articles published in *Psicoterapia* and other leftist journals. Professional and scientific journals could have clear political affiliations, but those affiliations did not prevent them from interacting peacefully.

The situation was different in other countries, and it would also come to be different in Argentina a few years later. In Republican Spain, for instance, society was much more politically polarized than in Argentina, and politics permeated the scientific field. There, the validity of scientific theories in general was discussed in political terms. In Spain during the 1930s psychoanalysis was associated with the political and cultural left and was therefore rejected totally by conservative sectors. In the late 1920s the Spanish philosopher José Ortega y Gasset, by no means a radical leftist himself, had developed some reservations about psychoanalysis. However, he was almost forced to endorse it in the early 1930s for political reasons.

"One could almost say that I am anti-Freudian," wrote Ortega in "Vitalidad, alma, espíritu," "except for two reasons: the first, because that would situate me among mean-looking people [*gente de mala catadura*, meaning political reactionaries]; the second, a decisive reason, is that in this epoch when everybody is 'anti,' I aspire to *be* and not to *be against.*"[34] The value of the discipline for Ortega, therefore, was not determined by its possible scientific value, but rather by its political implications. Similarly, in 1935, Luís Jiménez de Asúa, a reputed Spanish lawyer and a professor of penal law at the University of Madrid, pointed out that his opinions on the value of the application of psychoanalysis to criminology were determined, above all, by the fact that he was "a lawyer sympathetic to socialism."[35] At that time psychoanalysis was generally perceived in Spain as an instrument for political and sexual liberation. That was not the case in Argentina, or at least not in the early 1930s. Toward the end of the decade the situation would change dramatically.

In 1942 a group of doctors led by Spanish émigré Angel Garma created the Argentine Psychoanalytic Association (APA, hereafter) as a branch of the International Psychoanalytic Association (see figures 24 and 25). Surprisingly only one of its founding members, Enrique Pichon Rivière, was a practicing psychiatrist. None of the psychiatrists who had been interested in psychoanalysis since the 1920s showed any interest in becoming a member of this newly created institution. Moreover, after the first few years of life of the institution, psychoanalysts affiliated to the APA refrained from participating in professional activities sponsored by the psychiatric establishment, while psychiatrists were neither invited nor interested in the scientific events organized by psychoanalysts. The bridge between psychiatry and psychoanalysis (that is, the specific theory based on Freud's ideas) established since the 1920s now vanished. The creation of a psychoanalytic association that represented orthodoxy and that enforced internationally imposed standards for psychoanalytic training constituted an important factor in the emergence of this gap between practitioners of the two disciplines. Psychoanalytic institutions forced doctors with many years of practice to start from scratch, an expensive and time-consuming psychoanalytic training. However, other factors were also important. In other countries such as Brazil, France, and the United States psychiatrists who had shown an interest in psychoanalysis before the creation of national psychoanalytic associations became members and leaders of the new institutions. This did not happen in Argentina. In order to explain the "forking paths" followed by the two disciplines in Argentina during the 1940s, one must look at the broader political and cultural contexts.

Polarization of Society and the Politicization of Science

In the 1930s and early 1940s Argentine society suffered a political transformation that would have important consequences in the intellectual milieu. This transformation was linked to a general breakdown of a sixty-year-old liberal consensus among the Argentine ruling class. Since the 1870s liberalism had constituted what Charles Hale calls a "unifying myth" for Latin Americans generally and for Argentines in particular. This consensus began to break up in the 1920s when it became clear (at least for some) that the economic "invisible hand" (the unimpeded rule of the free market) would not secure economic prosperity forever. This crisis of the liberal consensus was also linked to the crisis of positivism. Moreover, some intellectuals felt attracted by the extreme ideological alternatives ranging from communism to different forms of fascism that emerged in post–World War I Europe. Consequences of this crisis were a gradual radicalization of political positions and eventually the widely supported coup d'etat led by the fascist sympathizer General José F. Uriburu that overthrew President Hipólito Yrigoyen in 1930, thus ending a fifty-year period of institutional stability in Argentina. International and domestic events such as the Spanish Civil War (1936–1939), the emergence of Nazism, the radicalization of Fascism after 1925, World War II, and particularly Argentina's second military coup d'etat in 1943 and its consequence, and the emergence of Peronism in 1945 all contributed to deepening the politicization of Argentine society and to its ideological and political polarization. This politicization also permeated the nation's cultural realm.

Figure 25. Four of the founding members of the
Argentine Psychoanalytic Association. Clockwise
from left to right: Celes Cárcamo (seated); Angel
Garma, the APA's first president; Enrique Pichon
Rivière; and Arnaldo Rascovsky. Rascovsky and
Pichon were extremely active in the dissemination of
psychoanalysis in Argentina. Notice Freud's picture
hanging on the wall. Courtesy of Archivo de la
Asociación Psicoanalítica Argentina.

The radicalization of international and local politics forced Argentine intellectuals to take sides. Ideological differences that had been previously overlooked now became irreconcilable. This was explicitly recognized, for instance, by nationalist right-wing historian Julio Irazusta who, referring to the usual meetings of intellectuals at liberal writer Victoria Ocampo's home, said in his memoirs: "Eduardo Mallea, Pedro Henríquez Ureña, María de Maetzu, Cármen Gándara . . . and innumerable others [liberal intellectuals] who do not come to mind associated with us in an environment of civilized conviviality. . . . If this experiment ceased, it was partly due to the European War, which confounded their spirits and divided them into international factions."[36]

Two clear and unbridgeable political and cultural poles thus became defined in the Argentine cultural fabric: a "liberal" progressive one, and a "nationalist-Catholic" one. "Liberals" and "nationalists" created their own spaces of expression and debate that became ideologically self-contained. They nucleated themselves in institutions and publications created during the 1930s that openly expressed their ideological allegiances and had little space for representatives of the other ideological pole. The peaceful coexistence of the previous years became more difficult to sustain.

This ideological polarization also had an impact in scientific and professional communities. As Telma Reca, a renowned child psychiatrist, wrote to an officer of the Rockefeller Foundation in 1944, "The present [political] situation . . . exerts its influence upon all our activities."[37] In the particular case of psychiatry it provoked new alignments. Jorge Thénon and Gregorio Bermann, for instance, who in the previous decades had found their leftist sympathies compatible with a particular interpretation of Freudian thought, found in the new ideological context of the 1940s that they were forced to choose an allegiance. The Argentine Communist Party, following dictates coming from Moscow, openly denounced psychoanalysis as a bourgeois, idealistic doctrine, lacking scientific foundations.[38] Both Thénon and Bermann then opted to privilege their political loyalties over their intellectual passions and publicly rejected psychoanalysis. At the other end of the ideological spectrum, the fascist Asociación de Biotipología also became more

Figure 26. Five of the founding members and an
early associate. Clockwise from left to right: Marie
Langer, an Austrian-born analyst known for her
later involvement in leftist politics and feminism in
the 1970s; Angel Garma; Arnaldo Rascovsky;
Enrique Pichon Rivière; Celes Cárcamo; and Lucio
Rascovsky, brother of Arnaldo. Courtesy of Archivo
de la Asociación Psicoanalítica Argentina.

homogeneous ideologically by the late 1930s. Progressive authors who had previously contributed to *Anales de Biotipología* now disappeared from the journal's pages. Favorable references to psychoanalysis (now dismissed as a Jewish science by the right) also disappeared.

After the emergence of Peronism in 1945 the political polarization of Argentine society continued to deepen. The government of Juan Perón had traumatic effects on Argentine society. The importance of the Peronist experience in redefining not only political but also social and cultural identities cannot be overemphasized.[39] Peronism made it possible for the working class to become a crucial protagonist in Argentine politics. Perón gave the workers a new identity as a class. By contrast, the political factions that opposed him, ranging from socialists and communists to liberals and some conservatives, formed a heterogeneous coalition that defined itself solely in terms of its opposition to Perón and his politics.

From its beginnings Peronism was characterized by its opponents as a political aberration, as the essential "other," and as a pathology in Argentine history. Perón introduced changes in society that were difficult to swallow for the traditional ruling sectors. Moreover, Perón's totalitarian tendency (which became more evident during his second term in office, 1952–1955) closed the spaces of public debate. At the same time the regime encouraged the public worship of Perón and Evita. From schools to hospitals most public institutions bore the name of the ruling couple. School texts and syllabi were changed to reflect "Peronist values."[40] During the Peronist decade politics became charged with strong affective components evident on both sides, Peronist and anti-Peronist. Politics was lived as a passion. Families were broken up because some members were Peronist while others were anti-Peronist. Society became defined in terms of the Peronist/anti-Peronist antinomy; all other political ideologies were subsumed into this dichotomy.[41]

The tensions generated by the emergence of Peronism in 1945 deepened a tendency that had begun in the 1930s: the diversification of an intellectual life outside the university. In such a cultural environment psychoanalysis gradually came to be seen as one component of the cultural system that emerged in opposition to

Peronism. Although Perón did not openly persecute "cultural opponents," the propagandistic apparatus of the regime made clear its opposition to such "modern" intellectual currents as avant-garde art, existentialism, psychoanalysis, and the like, which were characterized as nonnational and nonpopular, and therefore as anti-Peronist, oligarchic ways of thinking. In the general environment of intellectual flatness promoted by Peronism, psychoanalysis was perceived as part of the system of "cultural resistance." Most psychoanalysts who were known for their liberal, anti-Peronist sympathies felt threatened by the Peronist regime, and some of them considered emigration. The fact that uniformed police officers were always present at APA meetings certainly contributed to these fears. Moreover, Dr. Ramón Carrillo, a neurosurgeon who served as Perón's minister of public health, did not miss an opportunity to make negative remarks about psychoanalysis. More importantly, during the Perón government, psychoanalysts were excluded from the public system of psychiatric assistance.

Whereas the crisis of positivist and somatic psychiatry of the 1920s had opened spaces for the reception of psychoanalysis in psychiatric circles, and for the coexistence of different interpretations of the discipline, the ideological and political crisis of the late 1930s and 1940s limited and eventually closed those spaces. Moreover, the existence of an institution that could enforce psychoanalytic orthodoxy after 1942 and whose claims of monopoly over the "right interpretation" of the Freudian word were legitimized by its being a branch of an international association, restricted even more the possibility of alternative interpretations of Freudism. Early members of APA were people identified with the liberal tradition that was now under assault. The APA founder, Spanish doctor Angel Garma, and others had given talks and participated actively at the Centro Republicano Español (Spanish Republican Center). (During the first years of his government, Perón was a strong supporter of the Franco dictatorship.) Members of APA and sympathizers of psychoanalysis would lecture regularly on psychoanalysis and related topics at the Colegio Libre de Estudios Superiores (CLES)—a kind of parallel private institution of higher education that openly opposed Peronism and that during the Perón regime hired many of the professors that had been fired from the university for political reasons. During the Perón regime, the CLES was harassed by the authorities and eventually was forced to stop its activities.

The divergence between psychoanalysis and psychiatry in the 1940s was thus related to broad political, cultural, and social developments taking place in society. This divergence would be at least partially reversed during the 1960s in the new environment that emerged after the fall of Perón in 1955, an environment defined by important changes that took place in the psychiatric field, in the psychoanalytic community, and in society at large.

The Emergence of Mental Health and the Creation of Psychiatric Services in General Hospitals

Juan Perón was overthrown by a military coup in 1955. At least at the beginning the new government enjoyed the support of all sectors of society that had previously opposed Perón, including progressive intellectuals. The new regime set for itself the task of founding a post-Peronist republic, in spite of the fact that virtually all the working class continued to be Peronist to the core. Although the military officers that replaced Perón soon discovered that they had far less political room to maneuver than they had expected, their explicit purpose was to de-Peronize the country following the model of de-Nazification carried out by the allied forces of occupation in Germany after World War II. The mere mention of the names of Perón or Eva, or the public display of Peronist symbols was criminalized. Perón, who left the country as a political exile, had to be referred to in the press as the "escaped tyrant."

Two important and convergent tendencies can be distinguished in the years after the fall of Perón. First, there was a strong revival of intellectual and cultural activity, which had been buried under Peronism and now reemerged modernized. Moreover, traditional institutions such as the university, badly damaged during the Peronist decade, recovered their lost prestige and became once again engines for cultural and scientific modernization. New programs in the social sciences, including a heavily psychoanalytical one in psychology, were created at the University of Buenos Aires and elsewhere. Intellectual currents such as French existentialism, Marxist philosophy, and also psychoanalysis became highly fashionable and broadly disseminated in society.

Second, the post-Peronist government, in spite of its authoritarian social and political policies, sought to foster the modernization of the economy and society more generally by promoting it from above. Among the areas that the authorities attempted to modernize was the public system of psychiatric assistance. More receptive than in the Peronist times to new currents of thought in different areas of human activity, the public health authorities embraced during the late 1950s the concept of "mental health," which displaced the traditional "mental hygiene."

Mental health was a concept developed after World War II in Great Britain and in the United States and that was promoted by the World Health Organization. It expanded on some of the notions disseminated by the mental hygiene movement but approached them from a different angle. The main idea behind it was that mental health could not be defined merely as the absence of psychiatric disorders, but rather had to be understood as a positive, integral aspect of the general welfare of the population. "Health is not only the absence of sickness, but a state of physical equilibrium and of mental and social welfare."[42] Mental health's purpose was to work not only with those who already suffered mental disorders but also (and fundamentally) with the "healthy" population, in order to promote health. This definition of mental health provoked the redefinition of the scope of psychiatry. Mental health was not seen as a mere medical issue any longer. If it was a general condition of people, then psychiatry was only one of the tools available to achieve it. Although the movement of mental hygiene had centered its attention in improving the conditions of the psychiatric institutions, mental health could only be meaningful outside the system of the asylum. Psychoanalysis, which already enjoyed broad popularity in Argentina, constituted one of the foundations of the new approach.[43] Consistent with the idea of promoting mental health, the government created an Instituto

Nacional de Salud Mental (National Institute for Mental Health; INSM, hereafter) in 1957. The INSM was an autarkic organism that centralized psychiatric assistance and efforts to prevent mental diseases. Many prominent psychoanalysts were appointed to top positions at the INSM.

The increasing incorporation of psychoanalysis into psychiatric practice was also made possible by important changes that took place within the psychoanalytic community. During the late 1950s, after the fall of Perón, a progressive and more socially conscious sector of psychoanalysts gathered around Enrique Pichon Rivière and his disciples José Bleger, Fernando Ulloa, David Liberman, and others gradually emerged within the APA. These psychoanalysts believed that the practice of psychoanalysis should not be confined to the analyst's private office and therefore promoted a more socialized use of the Freudian technique and theory. They wanted to take psychoanalysis to public hospitals and make it available to all sectors of society, and not only to the most affluent ones. Moreover, Pichon's and others' work on the use of psychoanalysis for the treatment of psychotic patients also promoted an approach between psychoanalysis and psychiatry. Given these developing tendencies within psychiatry and psychoanalysis, the conditions for a new convergence between the two disciplines did not originate in the traditional psychiatric hospitals, which were still very much oriented toward the practice of classic psychiatry and still in the hands of conservative professionals, but rather in the new institutions created by the INSM. Among them, the most important were the psychiatric services established in general hospitals during the late 1950s and 1960s, an old goal of the mental hygiene movement, which only materialized after the fall of Perón. The most influential of those services was the one headed since 1956 by Dr. Mauricio Goldenberg, a former member of the Liga Argentina de Higiene Mental, at the Hospital Gregorio Aráoz Alfaro in the industrial suburb of Lanús, in the Province of Buenos Aires.

Goldenberg introduced an interdisciplinary approach to psychiatry in which psychoanalysis gradually played an increasing role. He also occupied important official positions. In 1958 he served briefly as president of the INSM, and later, in the mid-1960s, he was a member of a municipal commission set up in Buenos Aires to overhaul the city's system of psychiatric assistance. During his tenure the city of Buenos Aires reached an agreement with the APA for the training in psychoanalysis of psychiatrists employed in the municipal mental health system.

Goldenberg was a personal friend of many psychoanalysts. From the beginning he started hiring young capable psychoanalysts in training at APA, most of whom were disciples of Pichon Rivière or members of his group. Moreover, Goldenberg also promoted the creation of interdisciplinary groups. His service was the first one to include psychologists, sociologists, anthropologists, and other social scientists.[44] Gradually, Goldenberg's service became a major center of psychiatric assistance, research, and teaching. Moreover, it became a model for other psychiatric services in general hospitals because it achieved a good level of integration with other services of the hospital. It provided advice and psychological assistance to patients treated for general medical conditions. The Gregorio Aráoz Alfaro was the first hospital in Argentina (and the most successful) in integrating psychiatry and psychology into general medicine. In 1964 alone Goldenberg's service assisted 14,222 patients, both as in-patient and out-patient.

Just as in the United States, the psychiatric services that had been established in general hospitals such as the Aráoz Alfaro played several key roles in the diffusion of psychoanalysis in society. First, they offered psychoanalytically oriented treatment to low-income patients who otherwise would not have had access to it. In Argentina public hospitals must provide free health care to anyone requesting it. The public hospitals (and the Aráoz Alfaro, located in an industrial suburb of Buenos Aires in particular) catered to a working-class clientele. The percentage of patients suffering from neuroses (mild forms of mental disorders that can be treated with psychotherapy) of the total of patients assisted at Goldenberg's service rose from 39.5 percent in 1960 to 54 percent in 1964.[45] Since most of the psychotherapy offered was psychoanalytically oriented the service not only made psychoanalytic practice but also a "psychoanalytic culture" available to broader sectors of society, including workers and lower-class homemakers.[46] In 1962, thirty-two out of the fifty doctors working at Goldenberg's service were in or had completed analytic training.[47] Second, the psychiatric services at general hospitals achieved an old goal of mental hygienists: they contributed to the elimination of the moral stigma usually associated with mental disorders. Psychiatric patients treated in general hospitals felt that they were regular patients. Third, by incorporating psychiatrists and psychologists into general hospitals, the services changed the culture of the hospital. Doctors started to pay more attention to the psychological dimension of somatic disorders. Clinicians began talking about psychosomatic diseases, those physical disorders caused by psychical traumas. Psychiatrists were seen as natural members of the hospital's staff, and their profession gained in acceptance and prestige.[48] Finally, a service such as Goldenberg's provided alternative spaces outside the traditional psychiatric hospital for the training of young psychiatrists with progressive ideas and social concerns.

The psychiatric services established in some general hospitals became a privileged space for the diffusion of a psychoanalytic way of thinking about psychiatric problems and human relationships. Psychoanalytically oriented psychological support was not provided on demand, but it was an integral part of the general medical assistance. Psychologists shared with clinical doctors the aura of authority provided by the hospital environment.

Although psychoanalysis became accepted by some progressive sectors of the psychiatric community, there was still a "hard nucleus" within the profession that was very much attached to classic psychiatry. Given the positive social evaluation that psychoanalysis enjoyed in Argentine society at that time, those doctors who rejected it were characterized as "reactionaries." They were powerful because they controlled the two public psychiatric hospitals in Buenos Aires (one for men, the other for women), which continued to be the backbone of the public system of psychiatric assistance. They also controlled the powerful chair of psychiatry of the University of Buenos Aires. Both institutions were connected since traditionally the holder of the university chair was often also the director of one of the psychiatric hospitals. In 1965 the chair in psychiatry became vacant, and Goldenberg applied for the position (he was then an associate professor). Horacio Etchegoyen, an APA psychoanalyst, was appointed a member of the search committee. Powerful doctors linked to the psychiatric establishment fought back and finally succeeded in having Etchegoyen (who was obviously sympathetic to Goldenberg), removed from the jury on the grounds that he had presented a pornographic paper at APA. Of course, Etchegoyen's paper was not pornographic. As is the case with most psychoanalytic works, it contained open references to sexuality. The charge of pornography was an excuse used by conservative doctors to exclude him (and thus Goldenberg) from prominent positions in the psychiatric system. Without Etchegoyen, who was finally fired from his teaching position at the University of Mendoza as a result of the pressure put by his political enemies in Buenos Aires, Goldenberg was turned down and a psychiatrist of the old school was finally appointed to the chair post.[49]

During the 1960s and 1970s Argentina went through a long process of political instability and radicalization characterized by the appearance of left-wing guerrilla groups and the implementation of harshly repressive policies by the state. In those years violence became a central feature of Argentine political culture. Society became deeply politicized, and psychiatrists and psychoanalysts were no exception. In 1971 a group of leftist psychoanalysts split from the Argentine Psychoanalytic Association because they considered it to be too conservative. The rebels wanted to put psychoanalysis at the service of revolution. For this purpose they joined a group of equally radicalized psychiatrists. Some leftist activists saw psychoanalysis—or at least a politicized version of it that emphasized its "liberating aspects"—as a tool for revolution.[50]

Paradoxically, some of the most daring experiments carried out in the public system of psychiatric assistance, including the introduction of highly controversial "therapeutic communities," took place under the repressive military regimes that ruled Argentina between 1966 and 1973.[51] However, precisely because of the country's instability (nine presidents ruled Argentina between 1955 and 1973), no long-term plan in any aspect of the national life could be carried out successfully. The budget assigned to the area of public health continued to be small (in spite of episodic and spasmodic increases). With ups and downs, the most progressive sectors of the psychiatric establishment continued to be receptive to psychoanalysis in a general context in which Freudism was becoming a central component of the urban culture of the country, including for leftist activists.

After the period of political and social chaos that followed a short second government by Juan Perón (1973–1974), who died in 1974 leaving his wife Isabel as president (she was the vice president), in 1976 Argentina suffered yet another military coup that submerged the country in a situation of unprecedented violence. With the excuse of fighting leftist guerrillas, the generals who took power in 1976 unleashed a murderous terror on the population. Between 1976 and 1983 almost thirty thousand Argentines disappeared at the hands of the repressive Armed Forces. Well educated in the so-called National Security Doctrine, the generals were suspicious of anything that looked vaguely subversive. The social sciences, in particular sociology, anthropology, and psychology as well as the progressive experiments carried out at public psychiatric hospitals that included in most cases the use of psychoanalysis, were among their first targets. According to one general, Marx and Freud were "intellectual criminals." The fact that most of the doctors who performed those experiments (such as therapeutic communities) were also leftist sympathizers further complicated their position in the eyes of the generals. In the year of the coup a naval officer claimed, "Centers of mental health assistance had been turned into centers of subversive indoctrination. . . . [There, the Armed Forces found] Presses devoted to the preparation of pornographic [*sic*] material, sexual promiscuity among psychiatric patients encouraged by a propaganda that justified it through a kind of liberation from psychiatric depression."[52] Similarly, a magazine unofficially sponsored by the government intelligence service quoted a source saying that "from the beginning of the war against subversion, among the information evaluated was the relationship of psychoanalysis to terrorism. . . . It has been proved that many subversives were enlisted in the active fight after spending time on the analyst's couch."[53]

Although not particularly concerned with the private practice of psychoanalysis, the military regime considered any socialized practice of psychoanalysis subversive. Politically committed analysts—including a sitting president of the Asociación de Psicólogos de Buenos Aires (Association of Psychologists of Buenos Aires)—were arrested, tortured, driven to exile, and in some cases killed or "disappeared." Dr. Eduardo Pavlovsky, for instance, a well-known leftist psychoanalyst who was also an internationally known playwright, had provoked the rage of the military with one of his plays, *Señor Galíndez*, which denounced illegal tortures. Moreover, Pavlovsky was also a human-rights activist. He had to escape through the window of his consulting room during a session of group psychotherapy when armed men wearing masks forced their way into his office with the purpose of kidnapping him. It was no secret that his death would have pleased more than one military officer. Similarly, Dr. Marie Langer, a Viennese-born analyst who had been a founding member of the APA and who later became a leftist activist, went into exile when she learned through a patient that her name had appeared in a death list of the military. Dr. Goldenberg also had to go into exile, and his successor in Lanús, Valentin Baremblit, was dismissed and later arrested and tortured. Politically active analysts and psychiatrists, particularly those who treated leftist political activists, were forced to change offices periodically in order to avoid detection and arrest. As therapists of political militants they had access (unwillingly) to crucial information that could be valuable for the military. As one psychoanalyst recalls, "They [some militants we were treating] really needed to talk and they did so in excess. . . . I ended up knowing too much at times!"[54] In some extreme cases analysts even saw patients in public parks or in restaurants without knowing their true identity, in order to protect themselves and the patient. "What an ironic situation . . . for security reasons, neither of us [patient and therapist] learned each other's name, even though I knew very intimate details about their lives."[55]

The psychoanalytic establishment incarnated by the APA, however, and the conservative sectors of the psychoanalytic community were pretty much left alone. In fact, some conservative members of APA were routinely featured in the government-controlled media. One senior APA analyst went on the record saying that terrorism (meaning leftist militancy) was a mental disease in the same category as psychosis, neurosis, tobacco addiction, or drug addiction.[56] As long as psychoanalysis was confined to the analyst's couch, the military did not see it as a threat in spite of the rhetoric used by some of the most reactionary generals. In fact, psychoanalysis was such a central component of Argentine culture that the children of some of the generals were themselves psychoanalysis-practicing psychologists. What was not admissible was the "social" use of psychoanalysis for progressive experiments that were considered subversive. The military eliminated again the connection between psychoanalysis and psychiatry, as well as the use of psychoanalysis in public hospitals.

With the return of democracy in 1983 the forces that had been repressed for seven years emerged again. Small wonder that when democracy was finally reestablished the recovery of the tradition of convergence between psychiatry and psychoanalysis became a central goal for progressive psychiatrists and psychoanalysts who were appointed to key positions in the public mental health system. Although public funds continued to be scarce and conditions in psychiatric hospitals deficient, today, psychoanalysis has a pervasive presence even among those sectors linked to the traditional mental hospitals that had traditionally opposed it. Today, nevertheless, psychoanalysts are facing another challenge: the effects of an economic crisis and the spread of alternative short therapies, New Age practices, and drug therapy. People want fast results and have less money available for long-term therapies. Yet, the culture of psychoanalysis is deeply rooted in Argentine society. From a therapeutic technique, psychoanalysis has become in Argentina a system of beliefs.

Since the late 1950s psychoanalysis has become a central component of the Argentine urban culture. This centrality originated in the concurrence of a number of important social, political, and cultural factors and was the result of a complex historical development. Unlike in the United States, in Argentina psychoanalysis was not absorbed by the psychiatric establishment. It can be said that the dissemination of psychoanalysis in Argentina took place outside, and at the fringes of, psychiatry.

However, one important space for the diffusion of psychoanalysis in Argentina was its gradual acceptance by sectors of the psychiatric community perceived as progressive. This acceptance was not a linear process and was very much influenced by broader developments in Argentine society. Moreover, it did not take place, at least initially, in the traditional and powerful institutions that were at the center of the public system of psychiatric assistance (for example, the large psychiatric hospitals), but rather in psychiatric services established in general hospitals. This relative eccentricity of psychoanalysis in psychiatry, nonetheless, contributed to the public acceptation of Freudism, since treatments in general hospitals (even psychiatric treatment) did not carry the moral "stigma" that confinement in a psychiatric asylum did. Therefore, it can be argued that in Argentina the incorporation of psychoanalysis into psychiatry contributed to the "cultural" diffusion of psychoanalysis precisely because it took place at the margins of the psychiatric establishment.

Epilogue

MENTAL HEALTH AND
THE ARGENTINE CRISIS

Mariano Plotkin

On a hot summer evening of March 2002, a political scientist friend of mine and I attended a meeting of one of the many popular neighborhood assemblies that had proliferated in Buenos Aires since a political and social crisis of unheard of proportions had exploded in Argentina in December 2001. Like other similar assemblies, this one met on one of the street corners of the city. Neighbors gathered there to express publicly their grievances and points of views about the problems that affected the country. At the beginning the assemblies, meeting almost in every neighborhood, attracted small crowds; by the time I attended this particular one (towards the end of the summer), however, they were already declining. There were only twenty or twenty-five people on that Tuesday night on the corner of Raúl Scalabrini Ortiz street and Córdoba Avenue (a middle class neighborhood). After a series of improvised speeches given by neighbors on themes ranging from proposals for neighborhood-based collective purchases of food and other basic products to predictable diatribes against politicians and the International Monetary Fund, one of the informal leaders of the assembly handed out leaflets about the activities carried out by the group.

This "Boletín de la Asamblea Vecinal" is a crude four-page long photocopy containing three sections. The first one, titled "¿Por qué caceroleamos?" ("why we bang our saucepans?," a reference to the typical form of protest of the popular assemblies) encourages people to attend the gatherings, promising that new forms of democratic participation will emerge from them. The second section is a testimonial from one of the neighborhood participants explaining how attending the meetings had changed his life. The third part is an ironical "story" about what the government had done to the people. What immediately grabbed my attention, however, was a short note about one quarter of a page long that offered "free group psychotherapeutic assistance" The "ad" reads:

> We, the members of the health commission [of the assembly], are seriously taking into consideration the severe suffering that many of our neighbors are undergoing as a result of the current crisis. Many people suffer from anguish, anxiety, fear, desperation, psychosomatic diseases, and sleeping problems. These disorders, besides generating suffering, turn people even more vulnerable to the problems that we Argentines have to live through today. For those who need it we offer for a limited period of time free group therapeutic assistance. The group will be coordinated by a team of mental health specialists and will operate at the *Fundación Redes Internacional de Salud Mental.*

Similar signs offering psychoanalytically oriented psychotherapeutic assistance for free or for a very low price (about 2 dollars a session at the current rate of exchange) have proliferated in buses, subways and metropolitan trains. In a typical porteño fashion psychotherapy is offered as a privileged tool to confront, if not the causes, at least some of the consequences of the crisis.

Argentina has suffered four years of continuous economic depression. Within the last year the Argentine economy actually shrank by more than 15%. There is a record external debt, skyrocketing levels of unemployment, poverty, and hunger, as well as acts of corruption carried out with impunity by government officials. One senator (who is also a well known union leader) went on the record saying that all the problems of the country could be solved if "we"—meaning all politicians including, of course and principally, himself—, stopped robbing for two years. The crisis finally exploded politically in the second half of December of 2001, when the people took to the streets banging saucepans as a form of protest and demanding the resignation of the government. In fact, the straw that broke the camel's back had been a decree issued by the government in early December that froze all bank accounts. There were widespread acts of vandalism and episodes of violent political protest which were met by brutal police repression that left over twenty people dead and numerous others seriously injured on the nights of December 20th and 21st.[1] As a result of these events President Fernando de la Rua, who by that time had no political support whatsoever, not even from his own party, resigned and in an act of desperation left the governmental palace in a helicopter that took off from the roof. After appointing an interim president who served just one day, an ad-hoc congressional assembly appointed a caretaker president who also resigned within a few days, giving way to still another interim president. Finally, the legislative assembly elected Eduardo Duhalde, the former governor of the powerful province of Buenos Aires as the new president, giving him the mandate to call for elections by December 2003.[2] In the short lapse of ten days Argentina had had a record five different heads of state.

Immediately after taking power Mr. Duhalde announced that people would recover their savings, now frozen in banks, in the original currency in which they made their deposits (meaning U.S. dollars or Argentine pesos). However, it soon became clear that this would not be possible. Only a few days after the initial announcement the government devalued the local currency. In February it announced that all bank deposits originally made in U.S. dollars would be converted to pesos at an exchange rate much below market value. The government also decided that the already very devalued deposits would be converted into long-term certificates of deposit. In other words, the government informed the public that its money would be returned in a much devalued currency and that this could not happen before five or even ten years had passed. Since then many other economic plans have been proposed, sometimes at a rate of two or three alternatives in a single day. Most of these schemes were soon abandoned, while some others are still under discussion, including the forcible conversion of all frozen accounts into government bonds. The problem is that since the Argentine state is in default on its debt, it is obvious that any bond issued by the government would have little value in the market. In the meantime, the government has been desperately trying to reach an agreement with the International Monetary Fund.

In the middle of the crisis, which included the country's default on its external debt, a severe devaluation of the currency, and the concomitant appearance of two-digit inflation, people started organizing themselves in neighborhood assemblies like the one I attended. The assemblies were spaces where people, who felt betrayed by their elected officials, could freely express their complaints and seek solutions at the local level. The *cacerlolazos*, banging of saucepans (cacerolas), became a symbol of those assemblies. Added to the economic and social crisis, a crisis of representation also developed. People lost confidence in the politicians who were supposed to represent them, in the federal judges and in the state in general. Many politicians, legislators and judges (including a few justices of the Supreme Court) now cannot walk in the streets of Buenos Aires and other major cities without fear of being abused and in some cases physically assaulted by people who recognize them. The most unpopular politicians also suffered *escraches*. The *escrache* is a form of protest that emerged in the last few years. It originated in the frustration that some people feel with the judicial system's failure to punish former repressors who were active during the dictatorship. It vaguely resembles the *charivaries* of early modern France and consists in short, but very visible and noisy demonstrations carried out by a group of activists at the door of the building where the person to be *escrachada* lives. The demonstration is usually combined with graffities signaling the home of the person *escrachada*. The slogan of the *cacerolazos* is "que se vayan todos," which could be roughly translated as "all of them must leave." "Them," of course, refers to politicians and judges. The economic crisis that the country is suffering now, probably the worst ever in its history, has affected almost all social sectors. The related political crisis is adding to feelings of insecurity. People who used to feel secure in their jobs and who had enjoyed relatively high levels of income found themselves from one day to the next with neither security nor salaries. The depth of the crisis seems to confirm Paul Samuelson's pessimism. More than twenty years ago the American Nobel laureate in Economics said that he recognized four economic systems: capitalism, communism, Japan (a country with very few natural resources where, nonetheless, everything seemed to work at that time) and Argentina (a country endowed with lots of natural resources, where nothing seems to work properly). He also said that he had explanations for the first two of the systems enumerated, but had nothing to say about the latter two.

Mental health professionals have not been exempted from the consequences of this crisis. Formerly well off psychiatrists, psychoanalysts and psychologists are now seeking alternative sources of income. Luis, for instance, a psychologist in his mid-forties, can be found on Saturday afternoons sitting at one of the several "club de trueque" (clubs of exchange) that have mushroomed in the city during the last few years. These clubs are spaces where people can exchange goods and services without using official money. In an economy where money is such a scarce commodity, the clubs constitute real lifesavers for people from many different social backgrounds. Luis is there to exchange "hours of psychoanalytic therapy" for the goods and services he needs. In fact, each barter club has established a system of vouchers which can be exchanged for other goods and services. The appearance of this informal "money" shows the profoundity of the monetary crisis facing Argentina. In some cases vouchers issued by one club are accepted by other clubs, thus becoming a kind of quasi-money. Recently, the police discovered the existence of counterfeit vouchers in the market. Each participant in the clubs sets a price in vouchers for his/her goods and services. I asked Luis how many vouchers his hours of therapy were worth. "I set them at 50 vouchers," he replied, "but I may change the price according to demand." Participating in a "club del trueque" is a way of surviving but is also a manner of showing solidarity for people in need.

In terms of the demand for psychological and psychiatric assistance, the crisis gave origin to a paradoxical situation. While more people are demanding mental health services, at the same time, more psychologists and psychoanalysts are left with very few patients and even less income. "I don't set my fees any longer," says Carlos, a fifty five year old psychoanalyst and one of the few ones I know who still has enough patients to fill ten hour working days, five days a week, "when a new patient shows up I just ask how much he or she can pay without jeopardizing his/her basic needs, and I accommodate to that. The old patients pay what they can, how they can (meaning in currency or in government bonds), and when they can." Similarly, Marta, a 63 year-old psychologist who also practices psychoanalysis says "I have patients who now cannot pay but, what do you want me to do? They need me and I can not just let them go. I tell them that they can pay whenever they can or, otherwise, we just set a symbolic fee of one peso (less than 30 cents at the current rate of exchange) per session of therapy. In any case," continues Marta, "the chain of payment is now broken and I also only pay my bills when I can." Abel, a prestigious psychologist with over thirty five years of practice behind him, is even less fortunate. At the present time he only has five patients. "Only a few years ago I used to have a waiting list" Abel remembers with nostalgia. This situation in which psychotherapists accommodate their fees to their patients' possibilities is indeed a truly new phenomenon in a country where in the "good old times" therapists, who traditionally took their summer vacations during the month of February, would charge their patients for the whole month of January regardless whether they would take vacations during that month or not (remember that January and February are the summer months in the southern hemisphere). This situation was particularly painful for patients who were lawyers since in Argentina the courts take a January recess, and therefore lawyers can only take their summer vacations during that month.

The fact that psychologists and psychoanalysts are suffering from a lack of patients—a situation that has been even treated iron-ically by popular humorists[3]—however, is not just the direct result of the crisis. There are other dimensions to it that are also related to the crisis but in a less direct fashion. While fewer people are lying on the psychoanalyst's couch[4], the demand for psychiatric services in public hospitals increased by 30% within the last year. Since the 1960s, as discussed in chapter 6, Argentina has seen a growing tra-dition of general public hospitals providing free psychoanalytically oriented psychiatric care to the public. However, in these days the typical patient of the public hospitals differs from the traditional clientele. Many of the people who now go to the hospitals seeking free psychiatric assistance are members of the "new poor class," former middle class people who, as a result of the current crisis, have recently lost their jobs and are now forced to seek free public assistance. "There is a social class," says Dr. Eduardo Grande, a psy-chiatrist in a public hospital, "who did not previously use to come to the hospital, people who have lost their jobs and their "pre-pagas" (the Argentine version of HMOs). This middle class has slowly displaced the poor who cannot come to the public hospital any longer because they cannot even pay for the public transport that would bring them here."[5] This is a generalized problem that forces doctors working in public hospitals: to provide poor patients with the total course of medication they prescribe for the full length of the treatment because they (the doctors) know that those who made it to the hospital (who are usually in very serious condition) are unlikely to come back for follow ups. The most common dis-orders the "new poor people" suffer from are those linked to states of anguish and depression. A paradoxical situation emerged in the last few years. Although the total sales of general prescription med-ications decreased by 50% due to higher prices and reduced cov-erage by the "pre-pagas," the sales of psychiatric medication increased by almost 4%.[6] In particular, antidepressant sales increased by 13% during the year 2001. It seems that as a result of the crisis people who have had to give up on the use of regular med-ication are still demanding psychiatric drugs.

Obviously, the inability to pay for long psychoanalytic therapies takes many people to the public hospitals where shorter free therapies—which are still more or less based on psychoanalytic theory—are available. Nonetheless, as many psychoanalysts now recognize, there are other factors, beyond economic constrains, that explain the decline in the demand for traditional psychoanalysis. The crisis brought with it a new feeling of urgency. The new kind of problems that people have to face and the anxieties these problems provoke cannot be dealt with by long therapies that address the deep dimensions of the unconscious. Many psychiatrists agree that people now want faster solutions to their problems. This is why many public hospitals also offer group therapy for newly unemployed people, therapies that focus precisely on the problems of identity provoked by unemployment. This feeling of urgency also explains the increase in the consumption of psychiatric drugs in a country where there still exists a strong prejudice against somatic-based psychiatric treatments.[7] Argentina is a country where large number of psychiatric services at public hospitals are run by psychoanalysts followers of the doctrines of Jacques Lacan. These analysts focus on the symbolic aspects of the unconscious and consider that psychiatric medication can only provide temporary relief to psychiatric symptoms. In fact, according to Lacanian psychoanalysts, this kind of medication is only useful as a tool to create the conditions that allow psychotic (and therefore non analyzable patients) to be temporarily turned into psychoanalytic patients. The belief is that medication treats symptoms while only psychoanalysis can provide a cure, since it operates on the structure of the patient's unconscious. Psychoanalytically oriented psychiatrists and therapists, however, are realizing that now Prozac is gradually replacing Lacanian psychoanalysis as a therapy of choice for patients, at least for those who go to hospitals and other public institutions. This change in the therapeutic mood closes a circle that opened forty years ago.

Until relatively recent times psychiatrists working in public hospitals had been educated in the classic somatic psychiatric tradition and had been reluctant to introduce psychodynamic techniques. One of the few exceptions to this pattern was the psychopathological service led during the 1960s by Dr. Mauricio

Goldenberg at the Gregorio Aráoz Alfaro Hospital in Lanús. In the 1970s and 80s, the situation started changing, particularly after 1984 when psychoanalytically trained psychologists were authorized by the democratic government to practice psychotherapy. In a few years psychologists started filling important positions at public hospitals and introducing there Lacan's psychoanalysis with its strong emphasis on the symbolic dimension of the unconscious. While classic somatic psychiatry based on the administration of electro-convulsive therapies (ECT) and other shock therapies had been associated with the repressive practices of the military governments, psychoanalysis has occupied in the social imagination the place of a non-repressive, liberating alternative to it. Any intervention on the body (as opposed to on the mind) of psychiatric patients was perceived as one step short of torture. Therefore it is not surprising that after the restoration of democracy in 1983 psychoanalysts started occupying important positions in the public system of provision of psychiatric assistance.[8] This situation, of course generated deep tensions between analysts and professionals coming from other theoretical traditions. These tensions are sometimes evident in different wards within the same hospital. While the men's ward of the Hospital Piñero, for instance, is run mostly by psychiatrists with a strong interest in neuroscience and therefore with little interest for psychoanalysis, the women's ward is in the hand of Lacanian analysts with no interest whatsoever in neuroscience.[9]

In spite of the diffusion of psychoanalysis in public hospitals, however, it seems that now the tide is turning back to a renovated somatic psychiatry no longer based on the administration of shock therapy, but rather in the administration of last generation psychopharmaceutical medication. The new generation of young psychiatrists interested in neuroscience do not see themselves as the heirs of the old generation of classic psychiatrists, but rather as the avantgarde of the modernization of their discipline. In fact, they complain that Lacanian analysts are extremely rigid and dogmatic because they reject any alternative theory. In the view of the neuroscientists the Lacanian analysts represent the reactionary sectors within the field of mental health.

This revival of a renovated somatic psychiatry, however, is not matched by a similar displacement of psychoanalysis from the central place it still occupies in Argentine urban culture. In Argentina people still boast about going to a shrink, but often feel ashamed of taking anti-depressive pills. In the mind of the educated middle class the proliferation of psycho pharmaceutical medication is associated with American imperialism and materialism which contrasts with Argentina's supposedly more philosophical and spiritual orientation. Thus, the diffusion of the different editions of the *Diagnostic and Statistical Manual of Mental Disorders* produced by the American Psychiatric Association, known as DSM III and DSM IV (standardized manuals for the diagnosis and treatment of mental disorders) is seen as evidence of penetration of the interests of American pharmaceutical companies in the Argentine psychiatric field. In the last few years psychoanalysis has occupied a much more central place in the social imagination than as a therapeutic technique. While at the clinical level psychoanalysis has had to compete not only with psychiatric medication, but also with shorter and cheaper self-help techniques and new age inspired practices; psychoanalytic terms have permeated everyday speech, and psychoanalytic concepts and notions still inform people's understanding of reality.

The crisis has clearly affected mental health providers, particularly psychoanalysts, but what do they have to say about the crisis? A quick look at the Argentine media during the last year or so reveals two things. First, psychoanalysts are sought after by the media to provide explanations about what is going on. They are very often featured in newspapers, and in radio and TV shows. Some psychoanalysts have written popular articles and books on the crisis. Second, it is now obvious that psychoanalysts *as psychoanalysts* have very few interesting things to say about the current state of affairs when they try to discuss reality from the psychoanalytic point of view. This lack of insight on the part of analysts, however, has not always been the case.

Since the 1960s psychoanalysis has been much more than a psychological theory or a therapeutic method in Argentina. It can be argued that for important sectors of the Argentine population (mainly the urban, educated middle class) psychoanalysis has constituted one of the "filters of intelligibility" through which various aspects of reality have been "read" and interpreted. Moreover, psychoanalysis has provided a language for describing reality that has permeated nearly every social sector. In particular, during the politically, socially and culturally convoluted decades of 1960 and 1970, socially committed psychoanalysts, as well as philosophers and social scientists in general used concepts originating in psychoanalytic theory as interpretive tools to analyze broader social and political issues.[10] Following Sherry Turkle's study of the development of psychoanalysis in France, it can be said that since the 1960s a true "psychoanalytic culture" has developed in Argentina.[11]

I have already discussed the reasons for the success of psychoanalysis as a cultural phenomenon in Argentina elsewhere.[12] To put it simply, since the late 1950s and early 1960s there has been a convergence of factors that facilitated the diffusion of psychoanalysis. Particularly in the 1960s, psychoanalysis became associated with modernity and with personal freedom. It generated private spaces that were perceived as non-repressive and progressive responses to a highly repressive political environment. At the same time, psychoanalysis was seen as a central element of cultural modernity. It provided a language legitimized by its supposedly scientific nature that was deemed appropriate for the discussion of the anxieties provoked by the fast social modernization and political instability Argentina experienced following the fall of the government of Juan Perón in 1955. Furthermore, an active group of "diffusers" of psychoanalytic thought and language (highly visible analysts, pediatricians, popular magazines, etc.) contributed to the dissemination of the Freudian system of thought.

There was, however, another level of diffusion of the psychoanalytic thought that had an enormous influence among college students and progressive intellectuals in general. During the 1960s it had become clear to Argentine leftist intellectuals that the analytic instruments provided by the canonical versions of Marxism promoted by the Communist Party were simply not adequate to understand the complexities of Argentine's social and political reality. This happened in a moment when the left hegemonized the field of cultural production in Latin America in general and in Argentina in particular. Confronted with this realization progressive Argentine intellectuals sought new analytic instruments in the social sciences and, particularly, in psychoanalysis. The use of psychoanalysis as an instrument of social analysis was tied to the influence that French philosophy and in particular the ideas of Jean-Paul Sartre had in Argentine intellectual circles. According to Sartre, only psychoanalysis could provide Marxism with its missing dimension: a theory of subjectivity.[13] Many intellectuals engaged psychoanalysis, both as a therapy and as a theoretical system after reading Sartre's work. Later in the sixties, the diffusion of the writings of French structuralist Marxist philosopher Louis Althusser was instrumental in the Argentine reception of the psychoanalytic theory of French analyst Jacques Lacan. According to Althusser, only Lacan provided the "correct" and revolutionary interpretation of Freud's psychoanalysis. In the 1960s and 1970s progressive Argentine intellectuals, including a few politically committed psychoanalysts, used philosophically informed versions of psychoanalytic theory as analytic tools to understand and describe broad aspects of the social and political reality.

Of course, Argentines were not the only ones to use psychoanalytic theory as an instrument for social analysis. Freud himself had made incursions into sociological discussion in some of his late writings such as *Totem and Taboo, Civilization and its Discontent, The Future of an Illusion* or *Group Psychology and the Analysis of the Ego,* among others. Moreover, philosophers such as Herbert Marcuse, Erich Fromm, and Sartre, all used elements of psychoanalytic theory to analyze certain aspects of contemporary society. The popularization of political readings of Freudism took place in Argentina and elsewhere mostly during the 1960s when politics tended to be psychologized; the "personal" became "political" and the "political" became "personal." This "psychologization of politics," nonetheless, did not necessarily lead the political left to psychoanalysis. In the United States, for instance, only those intellectual sectors of the left influenced by the works of Marcuse or Fromm became interested in psychoanalysis. Generally speaking, the left embraced a humanistic psychology that had been born as an optimistic alternative to (essentially pessimistic) psychoanalysis, which had become the core of mainstream psychiatry in the U.S. since World War II. In Argentina the situation was rather different. There, the new left was born of a traumatic soul-searching. Argentine leftist intellectuals were more interested in preparing the conditions for revolution and in understanding why and how they always seemed to be caught on the wrong side of history (they had opposed the government of Juan Perón who had mastered the support of the working class), than in focusing on such immediate goals as civil rights or stopping the Vietnam War. In Argentina psychoanalysis was a more suitable tool than humanistic psychology for self-understanding at a time when the left, given the political conditions of the country, had very few reasons to feel optimistic.[14]

In the 1960s, years that are usually characterized as the "golden age" of Argentine psychoanalysis, when the production of psychoanalytic thought was at the zenith of its vitality, psychoanalysts and social scientists made some important contributions to the understanding of broader problems using psychoanalytic concepts as analytic tools.[15] What has happened then in the "not-so-golden 2000s" when psychoanalysis has lost some of its power as a therapeutic method but still occupies a central place in the Argentine culture? Psychoanalytic concepts still permeate everyday speech and analysts are as visible as they can be. However, it seems that intellectuals are looking elsewhere for interpretive instruments. Perhaps we are seeing the end of the process that started in the 60s. We could characterize the present moment as one of trivialization of psychoanalytic thought. Freud himself had warned against the consequences of a vulgarization and banalization of his discipline. Freud also warned against the dangers of turning psychoanalysis into an all encompassing "vision of the world," a *Weltanschauung*.[16] During the 60s intellectuals and social scientists incorporated psychoanalysis into their interpretive toolbox. Today, with the popular dissemination of psychoanalysis as broad as it has ever been, it is the figure of the psychoanalyst him/herself more than psychoanalytic thought what has become emblematic of the place that psychoanalysis occupies in Argentine culture. Because everybody in Argentina thinks and speaks "psychoanalytically," it is natural then that psychoanalysts are sought by the media and by the public *as psychoanalysts*—not just as public intellectuals—to explain why things are the way they are, or to put it in other way, to "psychoanalyze reality." It seems that the fact that Buenos Aires has become the "world capital of psychoanalysis" has created the stereotype of the psychoanalyst as the person best equipped to understand an explain Argentine reality. This stereotype has crossed political and cultural frontiers. While intellectuals in the sixties added psychoanalysis to their conceptual artillery, today many psychoanalysts simply try to uncritically extend the use of psychoanalytic concepts to social and political analysis. The results of this banalization of psychoanalysis are highly disappointing and in some cases they are close to grotesque. Let us look at a couple of examples.

On January 24th 2002, the BBC World Service of London did a broadcast about the Argentine crisis. Most of the program consisted of interviews with prominent Argentine psychoanalysts. The analysts's contributions, however, were mostly limited to reductionist explanations of the origins of the crisis based on psychological generalizations heavily loaded with psychoanalytic jargon. Someone who was introduced as the secretary of the Argentine Psychoanalytic Association, for instance, explained that it is an essential aspect of Argentine character to oscillate between periods of supporting illusions and periods when reality becomes plain and conscious. She also added that there are moments when Argentines act with violence. "The dictatorial period was a war between terrorists and the military government, leaving 30,000 missing people as a result. When a traumatic situation is too hard to cope with, denial is one of the defense mechanisms, and when people are forbidden to talk and express themselves, to go to the street, then denial happens." According to this analyst, the denial that originated in the traumatic experience of the military government explains why people took so long to realize that the government policies were leading the country to disaster. People supported the illusion of prosperity during the Menem government because they were denying reality. Of course, reality in more complex than this, and many of the people who did support the Menem government had very good reasons to do so. During that period (which coincided with the decade of 1990) the distance between the very rich and the very poor increased dramatically in Argentina. Many powerful sectors of society grew more powerful and wealthier than ever before as a result of Menem's policies. This analyst is using psychoanalytic concepts that could be adequate to analyze individual neuroses, such as "denial" or "defense mechanism," to explain a complex social situation.

Perhaps more articulate but not necessarily more convincing than his colleague quoted above, was another senior analyst interviewed on the same BBC program. According to him the origin of the current crisis has to be traced to the Argentines' sense of guilt. "This unconscious feeling of guilt in our society is very deeply tied in with the still unprocessed aspects of the military government, the repression, the murders. I think this left many people feeling guilty and this feeling has much to do with the very late reactions of our society to the way it was being damaged by the people who were supposed to lead us to a better road." The traumatic effects of the military dictatorship on the population are undeniable.[17] Moreover, it is also true that those effects remain largely unprocessed by Argentine society. However, we should remember that during the first half of the 20th century much of Europe was ruled by dictators who were at least as brutal as those who ruled Argentina in the 1970s, if not much more (if there is a way of measuring brutality at that level). The "traumas" generated by those rulers (including two world wars and the Holocaust) and the concomitant feeling of collective guilt of the populations involved have been widely analyzed. Those feelings, however, did not provoke the kind of political and economic crisis that Argentines suffer now. The experience of the last Argentine dictatorship did leave psychological scars, not to mention the physical scars that some Argentines still bear, but other more immediate factors have contributed to triggering the crisis.

It has been almost twenty years since democracy was restored in the country. There is a whole new generation of Argentines who have come of age under the democratic system and who do not believe they have any reason to feel guilty. Moreover, while concepts like "unconscious feelings of guilt" may be useful to analyze individual neuroses, its usefulness for understanding social behavior is more than doubtful. Needless to say, these broad and at the same time shallow generalizations do not explain the origins or the nature of the crisis. Its causes are doubtlessly much more complex and multi-faceted than a social behavior provoked by the social trauma originating in a military dictatorship that ended two decades ago. Coming to terms with the dictatorship is a task still pending for Argentine society, but even if through a process of working with social memory Argentines manage to come to terms with their recent past, only part of the problem would be solved.[18]

Psychoanalysts, nonetheless, are not the only ones who emphasize the supposedly psychical origins of the crisis. Philosopher Alejandro Rozitchner, for instance, thinks that what is at the root of the crisis is that Argentines feel particularly attracted to disaster. There is a satisfaction with failure. Argentines feel happy when everything goes wrong. "We are a sado-masochistic country that can only feel joy in suffering."[19]

Attributing social crises to some essential dimension of the Argentines' collective psyche has been part of a long and utterly fruitless tradition in the history of the country. The origins of this tradition can be traced to the 19th century, but it became particularly popular in the 1930s.[20] Argentines, like any other people do not have a single, easily identifiable "collective soul (or psyche)" that is at the root of all their problems, and which would help to explain both failures and success of a nation. Of course there are some cultural patterns that can be identified, analyzed and interpreted. These cultural patterns, however, should be themselves subjected to historical analysis and, above all, "problematized" rather than used as the foundation of explanatory theories.

Less trivial, but not less obvious, is the discovery made by many analysts that external factors have to be taken very seriously when carrying out psychotherapy.[21] In fact, there is a demand from some of the more "socially committed" analysts to integrating the external reality into psychoanalytic practice.[22] This demand is not new, of course. Social psychiatry has a relatively long tradition in

Argentina. Since the 1950s there have been psychiatrists who claimed that social factors have to be taken into consideration in establishing the etiology of mental disorders. Among them was Enrique Pichon Rivière, whose life and works are discussed in this volume. Moreover, one of the complaints of the politically and socially active analysts of the sixties and seventies was that orthodox psychoanalysis promoted by the Argentine Psychoanalytic Association failed to consider the importance of external (i.e., social, political and economic) factors in the origin of neuroses. This was one of the main demands of the radicalized groups called *Plataforma* and *Documento* which split from the Argentine Psychoanalytic Association in the early 1970s.[23] Today, it seems that a good portion of the typical analytic session is spent discussing social and economic problems. External reality is now more than ever "contaminating" the analytic setting.

While some psychoanalysts insist on tracing the origin of the current social and economic problems to psychical factors, others try to generalize categories originating in psychoanalysis to describe political or social issues. Psychologist Lucía Martinto de Paschero, for instance, claims that the corrupt Argentine state suffers from a pathology of its super ego. There are individuals who never feel guilty no matter how horrible the acts they commit, because their super ego is not working properly. "The current situation forces one to extend these concepts to the space of the state where the system of corruption has been installed."[24]

It seems clear to me that neither the approach taken by the psychoanalysts interviewed by the BBC World Service, that is to say looking for the psychological origin of the crisis, nor the one taken by Martinto de Paschero, generalizing psychoanalytic concepts to describe social or political situations, adds much to an understanding of the crisis. In general, it seems that the psychoanalysts' analytic abilities reach a limit when they (the psychoanalytst) try to transfer concepts originating in psychoanalysis to the analysis of specific social situations. Not surprisingly, analysts are more successful in providing instruments for understanding the consequences of the crisis at the subjective level than in analyzing its origins and nature.

A case in point is the book *Dolor país*, authored by well known Paris trained psychoanalyst Silvia Bleichmar. The title of the book makes reference to the *riesgo país*, an economic index that measures the rate of interest that a country has to pay in order to borrow money in the international market. This index had obsessed Argentines until it skyrocketed to almost surrealistic heights after the country officially entered into default.[25] *Dolor país* is a slim volume published by an obscure publisher. Nonetheless, the book sold out three successive editions in less than one month. This surprised everyone, including Bleichmar herself, since the Argentine publishing business has been at a virtual stop since late 2001.[26]

Together with a sophisticated discussion of the subjective consequences of the economic and political crisis in terms of the disarticulation of people's subjectivity and identity that it has provoked, Bleichmar introduces an analysis of the causes of the crisis that is largely unconvincing. According to her, the problems Argentina is suffering now are the result of the uncritical application of murderous neo-liberal policies (which she compares to the Holocaust) by corrupt politicians in collusion with the International Monetary Fund: At the basis of the problem are, according to Bleichmar, "the corrupt governments that we have tolerated."[27] Why these politicians were elected by popular vote and in many cases re-elected several times, is something that Bleichmar does not discuss. I think that part of the success of Bleichmar's book originated precisely in that she places the guilt elsewhere. If according to Rozitchner it is our flirting with disaster that brought disaster, in Bleichmar's version the causes of the disaster can be attributed to corrupt politicians, callous international financial institutions and neo-liberal policies whose "banality of evil" (glossing Hannah Arendt's notion) is comparable, according to Bleichmar, to that of the nazis.[28] "No one can be blamed," says Bleichmar "for believing what the people in government told him/her."[29] Obviously, Bleichmar is very pessimistic about her fellow citizens' critical capacities. It is true that many people accepted what they were told, but it is also true that most of those who did so profited enormously from the policies that they now criticize.

Why do Argentine analysts seem unable to provide sound insights into the crisis? Perhaps this question itself is inadequate. Why should we expect psychoanalysts to shed light on a very complex social, political and economic situation, something that economists and political scientists are struggling to explain with very little success? The fact that psychoanalysts are so much in demand by the media to contribute their knowledge towards an understanding of the crisis says more about certain aspects of Argentine culture than about psychoanalysis and psychoanalysts. As I pointed out earlier in this chapter, since the 1960s psychoanalysis has provided a framework of intelligibility to many Argentines, for whom psychoanalysis still functions as a lens that filters reality. The central place that psychoanalysis occupies in the Argentine culture, and its consequent trivialization, has led to psychoanalysts being asked to provide answers that they are not especially equipped to provide. It seems that in Argentina psychoanalysts are expected to be able to talk about almost everything from the psychoanalytic point of view. Some psychoanalysts, however, refuse to psychoanalyze society. As Germán García, a prominent Argentine analyst follower of the doctrines of Jacques Lacan, told a journalist who insisted on asking him for a "psychoanalytic" interpretation of the crisis: "it is difficult to talk about collective anguish and it is not good that a psychoanalyst start saying too many generic things about collective situations."[30] García also pointed out that the study of collective anguish and panic is the realm of sociology more than that of psychology. Freud himself, even in his works usually considered as the most sociologically oriented, warned against establishing too close analogies between the psychological and the social spheres. In *The Future of an Illusion*, for instance, he wrote:

> But we should be very cautious and not forget that, after all, we are only dealing with analogies and that it is dangerous, not only with men, but also with concepts, to tear them from the sphere in which they have originated and been evolved. Moreover, the diagnosis of communal neuroses is faced with a special difficulty. In an individual neurosis we take as our starting point the

contrast that distinguishes the patient from his environment, which is assumed to be "normal." For a group all of whose members are affected by one and the same disorder no such background could exist.[31]

Some of Argentina's most lucid intellectuals are also psychoanalysts and psychologists, and they have made important contributions to the analysis of the current reality, but in general they have not made these contributions *as psychoanalysts*. In other words, their analysis may or may not be informed by parts of psychoanalytic theory, but when they are at their best, they do not attempt to generalizing without conceptual mediations concepts and notions originating in psychoanalysis into their analysis of social, political and economic issues. They are not "psychoanalyzing society." The most lucid of those intellectuals who in the 1960s approached psychoanalysis in search of interpretive instruments were also reluctant to do so. They used concepts and notions originating in psychoanalysis to inform and enrich their social analysis. The problem is that "psychoanalyzing society" is exactly what the media demands from psychoanalysts now and only a few of them seem to be able to resist the temptation.

Glossary

Agoraphobia: An exaggerated, inexplicable, and illogical fear of open spaces.

Anthropometry: The systematic collection and correlation of measurements of the human body, such as the length or size of the skull, ears, nose, and so forth. In the nineteenth century, anthropometric data were applied, often subjectively, by social scientists attempting to support theories associating biological race with levels of cultural and intellectual development. For instance, the Italian psychiatrist and sociologist Cesare Lombroso, seeking physical evidence of the so-called criminal type, used the methods of anthropometry to examine and categorize prison inmates.

Antipsychiatric Movement: Psychiatric and political movement of radical opposition to the standard treatments in psychiatry, such as hospitalization and electroshock. Its main figures were Ronald Laing and David Cooper in England, Franco Basaglia in Italy, and Thomas Szasz in the United States.

Bleger, José (1922–1972): Argentine psychoanalyst and a member of the Communist Party. Disciple of Enrique Pichon Rivière, he was influential as a professor of psychology at the University of Buenos Aires.

Born Criminal: A category of criminal type developed by Italian criminologist Cesare Lombroso in the nineteenth century based on Lombroso's belief that criminality was innate and that certain physical signs—often called "stigmata"—could be used to distinguish criminals from noncriminals.

Cárcamo, Celes (1903–1990): Argentine psychoanalyst and one of the founding members of the Argentine Psychoanalytic Association.

Chronical Delirium: A mental disturbance characterized by confusion, disordered speech, and hallucinations.

Criminal Anthropology: A branch of anthropology developed in the nineteenth century with a focus on the criminal as a human type, as an individual formed by a particular family background and social environment. This was a reaction against the older view that the focus of criminology should be on the crime.

Degeneration: A theory developed in the nineteenth century that maintained that humankind and even entire societies potentially suffered from either or both mental degeneration and physical degeneration, that is, deterioration of the mind (and one's morals) and of the body. People who were viewed as suffering from this pathological condition were called "degenerates." The counterpart to this condition was "regeneration," that is, the view that with the elimination of degenerates, society would be regenerated.

Dementia: A psychiatric term that in the nineteenth century meant madness.

Depressive Anxiety: In Melanie Klein's theory the second phase in child development is the depressive position. This phase is marked by the infant's recognition of the ambivalence of his feelings toward objects. The anxiety of this position is depressive, being related to fear of the potential harm that could be done to loved objects by the infant's own destructive impulses.

Dream Analysis: In Freud's view, the events of a dream (the manifest content) are produced by the so-called dreamwork, whose task is to give disguised expression to unconscious desires (the latent content). A central therapeutic technique employed in psychoanalysis is the interpretation of a patient's dreams, in the effort to understand the workings of his or her unconscious mind.

Ego: In psychoanalytic theory, that portion of the human personality that is experienced as the "self" or "I" and is in contact with the external world through perception.

Epilepsy: Sudden and recurrent disturbances in mental function, state of consciousness, sensory activity, or movements of the body, caused by paroxysmal malfunction of cerebral nerve cells.

Eugenics: The study of human improvement by genetic means.

Evolutionary Theory: The theory in biology postulating that the various types of animals and plants have their origin in other preexisting types and that the distinguishable differences are due to modifications in successive generations.

Field Theory: Kurt Lewin's theory that proposed that human behavior should be seen as part of a continuum, with individual variations from the norm being a function of tensions between perceptions of the self and of the environment.

Freud, Sigmund (1856–1939): The founder of psychoanalysis, at once a theory of the human psyche, a therapy for the relief of its ills, and an optic for the interpretation of culture and society.

Garma, Angel (1904–1993): Psychiatrist and psychoanalyst. Born in Spain, he emigrated to Buenos Aires in the 1930s and was one of the founding members of the Argentine Psychoanalytic Association.

Gestalt Psychology: Twentieth-century school of psychology that provided the foundation for the modern study of perception. Its precepts, formulated as a reaction against the atomistic orientation of previous theories, emphasized that the whole of anything is greater than its parts.

Hermaphrodite: Having both male and female characteristics (today often called intersexuality).

Hysteria: A type of psychiatric disorder in which a wide variety of sensory, motor, or psychic disturbances may occur. The term is derived from the Greek *hystera*, meaning "uterus," and reflects the ancient notion that hysteria was a specifically female disorder resulting from disturbances in uterine functions.

Id: In Freudian psychoanalytic theory, one of the three agencies of the human personality, along with the ego and superego. The oldest of these psychic realms in development, it contains the psychic content related to the primitive instincts of the body, notably sex and aggression, as well as all psychic material that is inherited and present at birth.

Ingenieros, José (1877–1925): Argentine psychiatrist, psychologist, and philosopher. A prominent figure of his time, he was one of the introducers of positivism in Argentina.

Instinct: In the behavioral sciences, an involuntary response to an external stimulus, resulting in a predictable and relatively fixed behavior pattern. The word instinct has been used also as an English translation for the German *Trieb* used by Freud especially in his studies of sex and aggression.

James, William (1842–1910): American philosopher and psychologist, a leader of the philosophical movement of pragmatism and of the psychological movement of functionalism.

Klein, Melanie, née Reizes (1882–1960): Austrian-born British psychoanalyst known for her work with young children, in which observations of free play provided insights into the child's unconscious fantasy life.

Langer, Marie (1910–1987): Austrian-born Argentine psychoanalyst who migrated to Argentina in the 1940s. She was a member of the early group that created the Argentine Psychoanalytic Association. She developed an important work in psychosomatic medicine, especially on feminine sexuality and reproductive disorders.

Legal Medicine: Also called medical jurisprudence, the science that deals with the relation and application of medical facts to legal problems. For instance, medical professionals giving legal evidence may appear before courts of law.

Lewin, Kurt (1890–1947): German-born American social psychologist known for his field theory of behavior, which holds that human behavior is a function of an individual's psychological environment.

Lombroso, Cesare (1836–1909): Italian criminologist and psychiatrist responsible for developing the idea of innate criminality.

Mead, George Herbert (1863–1931): American philosopher prominent in both social psychology and the development of pragmatism.

Melancholy: Chronic depression state that is marked by sadness, inactivity, and a reduced ability to enjoy life.

Meyer, Adolf (1866–1950): Influential American psychiatrist from 1900 to 1940, much of whose teaching has been incorporated into psychiatric theory and practice in the United States, Britain, and other English-speaking nations.

Morbid Heredity: In the nineteenth century a reference to unhealthy and harmful characteristics and conditions inherited from one's ancestors.

Neo-Lamarckism: Doctrines derived from Lamarck's theories that proposed the inheritance of acquired characteristics.

Neuroses: Mental disorder that causes a sense of distress and deficit in functioning. In the psychoanalytical view, neuroses arise from intrapsychic conflict (conflict between different drives, impulses, and motives held within various components of the mind).

Object Relations: Melanie Klein's object-relations theory related ego
development to the experience of various drive objects,
physical objects that were associated with psychic drives. In
the early states of development, Klein found, a child relates
to parts rather than to complete objects—for example, to the
breast rather than to the mother.

Onanism: Masturbation.

Operative Group: Theory and technique of groups created by Enrique
Pichon Rivière in Buenos Aires. He used notions of psychoanalysis an social psychology to understand and change
social roles.

Panoptic Vision: In the nineteenth century, a reference to an all-seeing
vision, originating from the concept of the circular prison
with cells and inmates visible from a central point.

Paranoid Anxiety: The primitive phase of child development was termed
by Klein the paranoid-schizoid position; the anxiety in this
position is persecutory, threatening the annihilation of the
self.

Phrenology: A science developed in the early nineteenth century that held
that the shape and size of the cranium indicated the level of
a person's intellect and his or her character.

Positivism: A philosophical system elaborated by French philosopher
August Comte (1798–1857) in the nineteenth century that
primarily relied on positive facts and observable phenomena
as the foundation of knowledge, and that rejected meta-
physics and theism.

Projection: In psychoanalysis a form of defense in which unwanted feelings
are displaced onto another person, where they then appear
as a threat from the external world. A common form of
projection occurs when an individual, threatened by his own
angry feelings, accuses another of harboring hostile
thoughts.

Psychiatry: The branch of medicine that is concerned with the diagnosis,
treatment, and prevention of mental disorders.

Psychoanalysis: A highly influential method of treating mental disorders,
shaped by psychoanalytic theory, which emphasizes unconscious mental processes and is sometimes described as
"depth psychology."

Psychosomatic Disorder: Condition in which psychological stresses adversely
affect physiological (somatic) functioning to the point of
distress.

Rascovsky, Arnaldo (1907–1995): Argentine psychoanalyst. He was one of the founding members of the Argentine Psychoanalytic Association; his work dealt mainly with psychosomatic disorders and child analysis.

Schizophrenia: Any of a group of severe mental disorders that have in common such symptoms as hallucinations, delusions, blunted emotions, disordered thinking, and a withdrawal from reality.

Somaticism: Theories of disease relating to or affecting the body, especially the body as considered to be separate from the mind.

Slips: Freud and his followers proposed that dreams and slips of the tongue were really concealed examples of unconscious content too threatening to be confronted directly.

Stigma: A mark on the skin indicating, for example, a medical condition; also the shame or disgrace attached to something regarded as socially unacceptable.

Superego: In the psychoanalytic theory of Sigmund Freud, the latest developing of three agencies (with the id and ego) of the human personality. The superego is the ethical component of the personality and provides the moral standards by which the ego operates.

Therapeutic Communities: An alternative way for treating mental disorders based on social and group techniques.

Trauma of Birth: Otto Rank, Austrian psychoanalyst, suggested that the basis of anxiety neurosis is a psychological trauma occurring during the birth of the individual.

Unconscious: The complex of mental activities within an individual that proceed without his awareness. Sigmund Freud, the founder of psychoanalysis, stated that unconscious processes may affect a person's behavior even though she or he cannot report on them.

Working-through: In the psychoanalytic cure, the psychic work by which the patient integrates the analyst's interpretation and overcomes/surpasses the resistance of the unconscious content.

Zweig, Stefan (1881–1942): German writer who achieved distinction in several genres—poetry, essays, short stories, and dramas—most notably in his interpretations of imaginary and historical characters.

Notes

Introduction

1. One is called Vulnerables and is a kind of "cultured" soap opera, the plot of which turns around the dramatization of group therapy. The other is called Todos al diván ("Everybody to the couch") and consists of "psychoanalytic interpretations" of a group of guests (usually local stars) given by a professional psychologist.

2. For a general discussion of the impact of positivism in Latin America, see Charles Hale, "Political and Social Ideas," in *Latin America: Economy and Society, 1870–1930*, ed. Leslie Bethell (Cambridge: Cambridge University Press, 1989), 240–72.

3. Nancy Leys Stepan, *"The Hour of Eugenics": Race, Gender and Nation in Latin America* (Ithaca, N.Y.: Cornell University Press, 1991), 3.

4. See, for instance, the widely read novel by Eugenio Cambaceres, *En la sangre* (1887), or by Julián Martel, *La bolsa* (1891). For a fascinating discussion of the development of naturalist-nationalist fiction in Argentina, see Gabriela Neuzeilles, *Ficciones somáticas: Naturalismo, nacionalismo y políticas médicas del cuerpo (Argentina 1880–1910)* (Buenos Aires: Beatriz Viterbo Editora, 2000).

5. Hugo Vezzetti, *La locura en la Argentina* (Buenos Aires: Folios, 1983).

6. See Eduardo Zimmermann, *Los liberales reformistas: La cuestión social en la Argentina, 1890–1916* (Buenos Aires: Editorial Sudamericana, 1995).

7. Augusto Ruíz Zevallos, *Psiquiatras y locos: Entre la modernización contra los Andes y el nuevo proyecto de modernidad. Perú: 1850–1930* (Lima: Instituto de Pasado y Presente, 1994), 16.

8. See, for instance, Stepan, *"The Hour of Eugenics"*; Thomas F. Glick, ed., *The Comparative Reception of Darwinism* (Austin: University of Texas Press, 1974); Thomas F. Glick, ed., *The Comparative Reception of Relativity* (Dordrecht: D. Reidel, 1987); and Thomas F. Glick, *Darwin y el darwinismo en el Uruguay y en América Latina* (Montevideo: Universidad de la República, 1989).

9. On the autonomy of the development of certain ideas in Argentine psychiatry, see Juan Carlos Stagnaro, "Acerca de la recepción e incorporación de ideas de la psiquiatría europea en Buenos Aires (1870–1890)," in *Psiquiatría, psicología y psicoanálisis. Historia y memoria*, ed. Julio César Ríos, Ricardo Ruiz, Juan Carlos Stagnaro, and Patricia Weissmann (Buenos Aires: Polemos, 2000), 32–40.

10. Howard Potter et al., "Problems Related to the Costs of Psychiatric and Psychoanalytic Training," *American Journal of Psychiatry* 1131 (May 1957): 1013–19, cited in Nathan Hale, *The Rise and Crisis of Psychoanalysis in the United States: Freud and the Americans, 1917–1985* (New York: Oxford University Press, 1995), 227.

11. For a discussion of the popular reception of psychoanalysis in Argentina, see Hugo Vezzetti, *Aventuras de Freud en el país de los argentinos: De José Ingenieros a Enrique Pichon Rivière* (Buenos Aires: Paidós, 1996); and Mariano Plotkin, "Tell Me Your Dreams: Psychoanalysis and Popular Culture in Buenos Aires, 1930–1950," *The Americas* 55, no. 4 (April 1999): 601–24.

12. Roy Porter and Mark S. Micale, "Introduction: Reflections on Psychiatry and Its Histories," in *Discovering the History of Psychiatry*, ed. Micale and Porter (Oxford: Oxford University Press, 1994), 3.

13. See, among many others, J. R. Whitwell, *Historical Notes on Psychiatry* (London: Lewis, 1936); Walter Bromberg, *The Mind of Man: The Story of Man's Conquest of Mental Illness* (New York: Harper, 1937); Noland Lewis, *A Short History of Psychiatric Achievements* (New York: W. W. Norton, 1941); and the more recent book by Franz Alexander and Sheldon Selesnick, *The History of Psychiatry: An Evaluation of Psychiatric Thought and Practice from Prehistoric Times to the Present* (New York: Harper & Row, 1966).

14. Michel Foucault, *Madness and Civilization: A History of Insanity in the Age of Reason* (New York: Random House, 1965); originally published in French as *Histoire de la folie a l'age classique* (Paris: Plon, 1961); Erving Goffman, *Asylums: Essays on the Social Situation of Mental Patients and Other Inmates* (New York: Anchor, 1961). Also very influential was Thomas Szasz, *The Myth of Mental Illness: Foundations of a Theory of Personal Conduct* (New York: Harper, 1961).

15. To mention just one recent example of a book influenced by Foucault, see Elizabeth Lunbeck, *The Psychiatric Persuasion: Knowledge, Gender and Power in Modern America* (Princeton, N.J.: Princeton University Press, 1995).

16. See, for instance, Joel Braslow, *Mental Ills and Bodily Cures: Psychiatric Treatment in the First Half of the Twentieth Century* (Berkeley and Los

Angeles: University of California Press, 1997); and in a more militant
anti-Freudian and anti-Foucaultian vein, Edward Shorter, *A Short
History of Psychiatry: From the Era of the Asylum to the Age of Prozac*
(New York: John Wiley and Sons, 1997).

17. This is Shorter's argument. Shorter, *Short History of Psychiatry*.

18. Porter and Micale, "Introduction."

19. This line of psychoanalytic historiography was inaugurated by Freud
himself. See Sigmund Freud, *On the History of the Psychoanalytic
Movement*, vol. 14 of *The Standard Edition of the Complete Psychological
Works of Sigmund Freud*, ed. James Strachey (London: Hogarth, 1981).
It was continued by Freud's disciple and biographer, Ernest Jones. See
his monumental *The Life and Works of Sigmund Freud*, 3 vols. (New
York: Basic Books, 1953). Also Philip Rieff, *Freud: The Mind of a
Moralist* (New York: Viking, 1959); and, more recently but in the same
tradition, Peter Gay, *Freud: A Mind of Our Time* (New York: W. W.
Norton, 1988).

20. John Forrester, "'A Whole Climate of Opinion': Rewriting the
History of Psychoanalysis," in *Discovering*, ed. Micale and Porter, 175.

21. Among the "anti-Freudian" studies that nonetheless keep Freud at the
center of the analysis and that are worth mentioning: Jeffrey M.
Masson, *The Assault on Truth: Freud's Suppression of the Seduction Theory*
(New York: Viking Penguin, 1985). More bitter criticism of Freud is
presented by Peter Swales, "Freud, Mina Barnays, and the Conquest
of Rome: New Light on the Origins of Psychoanalysis," *The New
American Review* (spring–summer 1982). An important attempt at de-
mythifying the role of Freud but still keeping him at the center of the
analysis is offered in Frank Sulloway, *Freud: Biologist of the Mind* (New
York: Basic Books, 1979). For a recent discussion, see Michael Roth,
ed., *Freud: Conflict and Culture* (New York: Alfred A. Knopf, 1998).

22. In this line, see Carl Schorske, *Fin-de-Siècle Vienna* (New York:
Vintage Books, 1981), chap. 4; and William McGrath, *Freud's
Discovery of Psychoanalysis* (Ithaca, N.Y.: Cornell University Press,
1986).

23. See, for instance, the classic work by Henri Ellemberger, *The
Discovery of the Unconscious* (New York: Basic Books, 1970).

24. For the history of psychoanalysis in France, see Elisabeth Roudinesco,
La bataille de cent ans: L'histoire de la psychanalyse en France 2 vols.
(Paris: Seuil, 1986). The second volume of this outstanding work has
been translated into English as *Jacques Lacan & Co: A History of
Psychoanalysis in France, 1925–1985* (London: Free Association Books,

1990). Sherry Turkle, *Psychoanalytic Politics: Jacques Lacan and Freud's French Revolution*, 2d ed. (London: Free Association Press, 1992). For the United States, see Nathan Hale, *Freud and the Americans*, 2 vols. (New York: Oxford University Press, 1995); and John Burnham, *Psychoanalysis and American Medicine, 1894–1918: Medicine, Science and Culture* (New York: International Universities Press, 1967). For Russia, see Alexander Etkind, *Eros of the Impossible: The History of Psychoanalysis in Russia* (Boulder, Colo.: Westview Press, 1997). For a comparative perspective, see Edith Kurzweil, *The Freudians: A Comparative Perspective* (New Haven, Conn.: Yale University Press, 1989), and the much less compelling by Roland Jaccard, ed., *Histoire de la psychanalyse*, 2 vols. (Paris: Hachette, 1982).

25. The notion of psychoanalytic culture is borrowed from Turkle, *Psychoanalytic Politics*.

26. To cite a few examples, see, for instance, Humberto Roselli, *Historia de la psiquiatría en Colombia* (Bogotá: Editorial Horizonte, 1968); Darcy de Mendoca Uchoa, *Organizaçao da psiquiatria no Brasil* (Sao Paulo: n.p., 1981); Julio Lardes González, *Historia de la psiquiatría universal y argentina: Visión sinóptica* (Buenos Aires: Promedicina, 1991); Emilio Valdizán, *Locos de la colonia*, 2d ed. (Lima: Instituto Nacional de Cultura, 1988); Javier Mariátegui, ed., *La psiquiatría en América Latina* (Buenos Aires: Losada, 1989); Heronides Coelho Filho, *A psiquiatria no pais de açucar* (Recife: Rodovalho, 1954); Oscar Valdivia Ponce, *Panorama de la psiquiatría en Peru* (Lima: Editorial de la Universidad, 1989–1991); Osvaldo Loudet and Elías Loudet, *Historia de la psiquiatría argentina* (Buenos Aires: Troquel, 1971); A. Guerrino, *La psiquiatría argentina* (Buenos Aires: Cuatro, 1982); and more recently, E. Balbo, "Argentine Alienism from 1852–1918," *History of Psychiatry* 2, no. 6 (June 1991). See also, Renato Alarcón, *Identidad de la psiquiatría latinoamericana: Voces y exploraciones en torno a una ciencia solidaria* (Mexico: Siglo XXI, 1990).

27. See, for instance, Ruíz Zevallos, *Psiquiatras y locos*; Jurandir Freire Costa, *História na psiquiatria no Brasil: Um corte ideológico* (Rio de Janeiro: Campus, 1980); and Vezzetti, *La locura*. Recent works on the history of science in Latin America include Marcos Cueto, *Excelencia científica en la periferia: Actividades científicas e investigación biomédica en el Peru, 1890–1950* (Lima: GRADE, 1989); Juan José Saldana, ed., *Historia social de las ciencias en América Latina* (Mexico: UNAM, 1996); and Juan José Saldana, ed., *Cross Cultural Diffusion of Science: Latin America* (Mexico: Sociedad Latinoamericana de Historia de las Ciencias y la Tecnología, 1988), among others.

28. Loudet and Loudet, *Historia de la psiquiatría*; Guerrino, *La psiquiatría*.

29. Vezzetti, *La locura.*

30. See Germán L. García, *La entrada del psicoanálisis en la Argentina: Obstáculos y perspectivas* (Buenos Aires: Catálogos, 1978). García's is a militant book written by a follower of the psychoanalytic doctrines of Jacques Lacan against the "official history" of psychoanalysis presented by the orthodox psychoanalytic institution incarnated by the Argentine Psychoanalytic Association. However, it is based on serious research and is the first book to discuss the early reception of psychoanalysis in Argentina. Books written in a more neutral tone include Hugo Vezzetti (ed.), *Freud en Buenos Aires, 1910–1939,* 2d ed. (Buenos Aires: Universidad de Quilmes, 1996). The book consists of a selection of documents preceded by a thorough introduction by Vezzetti; and Vezzetti, *Aventuras de Freud.* A collective biography of the Argentine Psychoanalytic Association can be found in Jorge Balán, *Cuéntame tu vida: Una biografía colectiva del psicoanálisis en la Argentina* (Buenos Aires: Planeta, 1991). See also Mariano Plotkin, *Freud in the Pampas: The Formation of a Psychoanalytic Culture in Argentina (1910–1983)* (Stanford, Calif.: Stanford University Press, 2001). "Official histories" of Argentine psychoanalysis produced by members of the Argentine Psychoanalytic Association include Arminda Aberastury, Marcelino Aberastury, and Fidias Cesio, *Historia, enseñanza y ejercicio legal del psicoanálisis* (Buenos Aires: Omega, 1967); and Jorge Mom, Gilda Foks, and Juan Carlos Suárez, *Asociación Psicoanalítica Argentina, 1942–1982* (Buenos Aires: APA, 1982).

Chapter 1

I am grateful to Mariano Plotkin, Lyman Johnson, Lila Caimari, Jonathan Ablard, and Kristin Ruggiero for comments. Thanks also to Charles Forcey Jr. for his reading of an earlier version of this chapter.

1. José Ingenieros, "Patología de los funciones psicosexuales: Nueva clasificación genética," *Archivos de Psiquiatría y Criminología* 9 (1910): 3–80, 35–36.

2. Ibid., 35. Although Ingenieros seemed to be influenced by Freud in his interpretation of psychopathology and in the incorporation of confessional (or "talk" therapy), he in fact explicitly distanced himself from the Freudian school.

3. Ibid.

4. Doctors and criminologists feminized hysterical men, deeming them "unfit" for the manly arts of war. Noted Argentine psychiatrist Francisco de Veyga, for example, studied hysterical men in his position as army doctor. See also a 1908 review of a French article on hysteria

in the army, in which the author suggested "carefully watching individuals who present stigmas" and especially avoiding alcoholism and venereal disease among armed troops. Review of Jorge Conor, "El histerismo en el ejército," *Archivos de Psiquiatría y Criminología* 7 (1908): 507.

5. As early as 1848, a medical student at the University of Buenos Aires published his medical thesis on "Hysteria considered as a nervous disease." José Lucena, "El histerismo considerado como un enfermedad nerviosa" (Medical thesis, Universidad de Buenos Aires, 1848).

6. On the legitimation of the psychiatric profession through hysteria studies in France, see Jan Goldstein, *Console and Classify: The French Psychiatric Profession in the Nineteenth Century* (Cambridge: Cambridge University Press, 1987), chap. 9.

7. The social and cultural meanings of hysteria have for some time been a topic of interest to historians. Yet in their various approaches, scholars have differed over how to "read" hysteria. They have argued about the exact power relationships between doctor and patient, the role of women as medical patients in the performance and definition of the condition, and even over whether hysteria "really" existed as a disease. Historians of medicine in Europe and the United States who have explored the social and cultural meanings of hysteria include Goldstein, *Console and Classify*; Elizabeth Lunbeck, *The Psychiatric Persuasion: Knowledge, Gender, and Power in Modern America* (Princeton, N.J.: Princeton University Press, 1994); and Elaine Showalter, *The Female Malady: Women, Madness, and English Culture, 1830–1980* (New York: Pantheon Books, 1985). For historiographical overview of "hysteria studies," see Sander Gilman et al., eds., *Hysteria beyond Freud* (Berkeley and Los Angeles: University of California Press, 1993); and Marc Micale, *Approaching Hysteria: Disease and Its Interpretations* (Princeton, N.J.: Princeton University Press, 1995).

8. Feature-length articles, case studies, and theoretical reviews on hysteria appeared frequently. See the articles cited here as well as published literature reviews such as "La nueva histeria," *Archivos de Psiquiatría y Criminología* 9 (1910): 620–26; review of J. Ferrand, "El concepto antiguo y moderno de la histeria," by L. Trepsat, *Archivos de Psiquiatría y Criminología* 12 (1913): 236–37. See also Daniel Matusevich, "José Ingenieros y sus escritos sobre la sexualidad en el nacimiento de la prensa psiquiatría argentina," *Temas de Historia de la Psiquiatría Argentina* 3 (winter 1997): 3–21, 4–8.

9. The most extensive Argentine study of hysteria in this period is José Ingenieros's *Histeria y sugestión* (1904) (Buenos Aires: L. J. Rosso, 1919). For other studies of hysteria in criminological publications, see Joaquín J. Durquet, "Paraplegia histérica: Curación por sugestión," *Archivos de Psiquiatría* 4 (1905): 306–18; Joaquín J. Durquet, "Manía ambulatoria

epiléptica y monoplegia histérica," *Archivos de Psiquiatría y Criminología* 5 (1906): 341; and "La nueva histeria," 620–26.

10. On turn-of-the-century Argentina, see Carlos Waisman, *Reversal of Development in Argentina: Postwar Counterrevolutionary Policies and their Structural Consequences* (Princeton, N.J.: Princeton University Press, 1987); David Rock, ed., *Argentina in the Twentieth Century* (London: Duckworth, 1975); David Rock, "Intellectual Precursors of Conservative Nationalism in Argentina, 1900–1927," *Hispanic American Historical Review* 67, no. 2 (1987): 271–300; David Rock, "Radical Populism and the Conservative Elite," in *Argentina in the Twentieth Century*, ed. David Rock. Carl Solberg discusses the immigrant story in Argentina in *Immigration and Nationalism: Argentina and Chile, 1890–1914* (Austin: University of Texas Press, 1970). And Sandra McGee Deutsch has examined the roots and rise of right-wing antidemocratic movements in response to demonstrations of both radicalism and liberalism after 1900. See Sandra McGee Deutsch, *Counterrevolution in Argentina, 1900–1932: The Argentine Patriotic League* (Lincoln: University of Nebraska Press, 1986).

11. For a typical, optimistic assessment, see Reginald Lloyd, ed., *Impresiones de la República Argentina en el siglo viente: Su historia, gente, comercio, industria y riqueza* (London: Lloyd's Publishing Co., 1911).

12. Rock, *Argentina*, 172.

13. Eduardo Wilde, medical doctor, well-known member of the influential "generation of 1880," described the encompassing character of late-nineteenth-century positivism: "Those were times of continuous dispute over opinions, reputations, and ideas. We all agreed on only one thing—that we were ultraliberals and revolutionists in art and in politics. It was imperative to reform beliefs, to institute socialism (liberal, intelligent, enlightened socialism), and to reorganize the republic—even more, to reorganize America, and to make out of all this a great nation." Wilde quoted in Romero, *History of Argentine Political Thought*, 185.

14. On the history of science in Argentina, see Miguel de Asúa and José Babini, eds., *La ciencia en Argentina: Perspectives históricas* (Buenos Aires: America Latina, 1993); José Babini, *Historia de la ciencia argentina* (Mexico City: FCE, 1949); Hugo Biagini, *El movimiento positivista argentino* (Buenos Aires: Belgrano, 1995); and Marcelo Montserrat, *Ciencia, historia, y sociedad en la Argentina del siglo XIX* (Buenos Aires: America Latina, 1993).

15. Due to space constraints, I can only give a brief summary here of the influential European theories and approaches applied by Argentine

psychiatrists. For further explanation of these theories, see Kristin Ruggiero's chapter in this volume. See also Julia E. Rodriguez, "Encoding the Criminal: Criminology and the Science of 'Social Defense' in Modernizing Argentina" (Unpublished Ph.D. thesis, Columbia University, 2000), chaps. 1 and 2.

16. The appearance of Charles Darwin's works in Spanish in 1877 helped to popularize evolutionary thought among Argentine intellectuals by the turn of the century. *The Archivos* favorably reviewed books by Darwin and his disciple Herbert Spencer. In a 1902 *Archivos* article, one author wrote, "To those who doubt Darwinist theories we can say: study, think, then strip yourself of all sectarian or religious concerns and arrive at the conclusions that the amazing talent of Darwin did, establishing the theory of evolution as base and principal of the modern human sciences." Benuzzi, review, "Herencia patología," *Archivos de Psiquiatría y Criminología* 1 (1902): 437.

17. From Savitz's "Introduction" in *Criminal Man, According to the Classification of Cesare Lombroso*, by Gina Lombroso-Ferrero (New York: Putnam, 1911), Introduction by Cesare Lombroso; reprint, new Introduction by Leonard D. Savitz (Montclair, N.J.: Patterson Smith, 1972), XI.

18. On the history of Argentine psychology, see Hugo Vezzetti, ed., *El nacimiento de la psicología en la Argentina: pensamiento psicológico y positivismo* (Buenos Aires: Puntosur, 1988); Hugo Vezzetti, *La locura en la Argentina* (Buenos Aires: Folios Ediciones, 1983).

19. Argentine psychiatrists favored Charcot's symptomological approach for years after the Freudian theory of sexual causes of hysteria was widely accepted. On the late-nineteenth-century paradigm shift in hysteria studies in European theory, see K. Codell Carter, "Germ Theory, Hysteria, and Freud's Early Work in Psychopathology," *Medical History* 24 (1980): 259–74.

20. According to Mariano Plotkin, the typical psychiatric examination included a search for physical signs of "degeneracy," at least until the 1940s. Mariano Ben Plotkin, "Freud, Politics, and the Porteños: The Reception of Psychoanalysis in Buenos Aires, 1910–1943," *Hispanic American Historical Review* 77, no. 1 (1997): 5. See also Eduardo A. Balbo, "El Manicomio en el alienismo argentino," *Asclepio* 40, no. 2 (1988): 151–62; Eduardo A. Balbo, "Argentine Alienism from 1852–1918," *History of Psychiatry* 2 (1991): 180–92, esp. 183.

21. Osvaldo Loudet and Osvaldo Elías Loudet, *Historia de la psiquiatría argentina* (Buenos Aires: Troquel, 1971), 59. Also see Jonathan Ablard's contribution to this volume.

22. On the early history of psychiatry, see Loudet and Loudet, *Historia de la psiquiatría argentina*; Vezzetti, La locura.

23. Beginning in the late 1890s, two strands of feminism, liberal and socialist, joined the public debate on legal reforms. The liberal feminists generally focused on the rights of married women and equality of the sexes. The socialist feminists introduced concerns for working women and their children. Both strands of feminism challenged assumptions of male superiority in the law and in the public consciousness. For example, while liberal feminists lobbied for equal individual and property rights for women, socialist feminists pointed out the sexual double standard. José Ingenieros and many other progressive scientists tended to sympathize with socialist feminism after 1900. They supported the agenda forwarding women's education, public health, and welfare reform, but avoided the question of suffrage and political rights.

24. Of course, the reality of sex roles was much more complicated. In this section, I am referring to gender ideology, not the actual lived experience of turn-of-the-century Argentine men and women. For recent historical studies of domestic life, see Fernando Devoto and Marta Madero, eds., *Historia de la Vida Privada en la Argentina* (Buenos Aires: Taurus, 1999). On women and their legal status in Argentina, see Asunción Lavrin, *Women, Feminism and Social Change in Argentina, Chile, and Uruguay, 1890–1940* (Lincoln: University of Nebraska Press, 1995); Donna Guy, *Sex and Danger in Buenos Aires: Prostitution, Family and Nation in Argentina* (Lincoln: University of Nebraska Press, 1990).

25. In putting forward a reformist, at times maternalist agenda, feminists themselves were disturbed by the seemingly anomalous and disturbing exhibitions of uncontrolled sexuality. This point of view fit the mainstream feminist movement's stance, protecting motherhood being the one area in which they were considered superior and indispensable. On maternalism in Argentina, see Lavrin, *Women, Feminism*, chap. 3; Donna Guy, "Mothers Alive and Dead: Multiple Concepts of Mothering in Buenos Aires," in *Sex and Sexuality in Latin America*, ed. Daniel Balderson and Donna Guy (New York: New York University Press, 1997), 155–72. For some examples of early medical discussions of scientific maternity, see "Higiene y Educación de la Primera Infancia" and "Consejos a las madres antes del nacimiento del niño," both in *Anales del Círculo Médico Argentino* 2, no. 3 (March 1, 1879): 364–69; "Estadística de la Maternidad del Hospital General de Mujeres," *Anales del Círculo Médico Argentino* 2, no. 6 (September 1, 1879): 450–55.

26. See, for instance, E. Del Valle Iberlucea, "Fundamentos científicos del divorcio," *Archivos de Psiquiatría y Criminología* 1 (1902): 392–485;

Barthou, "Sobre el divorcio," *Archivos de Psiquiatría y Criminología* 2
(1903): 374; Enrique Revilla, "La disolución del matrimonio por
locura de los cónyuges," *Archivos de Psiquiatría y Criminología* 2 (1903):
1–11. For an in-depth discussion of changes in civil law regarding
marriage, see Lavrin, *Women, Feminism,* 227–56.

27. "La cuestión del divorcio no es solo de interes para los matrimonias
en que la vida en comun es imposible: Interesa de igual modo a sus
familias, amigos, relaciones, y por repercusión de las costumbres a la
sociedad entera." Barthou, "Sobre el divorcio," 374.

28. As early as 1895, one physician had offered the view that, "When in
the presence of a hysterical woman, [the physician] should never
neglect to examine her genital apparatus, because we see with increasing frequency that there exists the productive source of hysteria"
(Cayetano Sobre-Casas, "La histeria en la ginecología," UBA medical
thesis, 1895, 40–41).

29. The impact of medical theories of hysteria on legal discourse remains
to be done. In preliminary research, I have found that concepts of
hysteria elaborated by psychiatrists in this period provided legal theorists with a handle by which they could categorize women in terms of
their relationship in civil and criminal law. For example, matrimonial
and divorce cases referred to hysteria, and lawyers often used hysteria
as an explanation for female criminal behavior. After the turn of the
century, they increasingly relied on psychiatrists and criminologists to
testify as "expert witnesses" in trials. Based as it was on "scientific
evidence," this testimony acquired a growing legitimacy in the eyes of
state officials. It also signaled a larger acceptance—although not
consistently or unanimously—of the categories of analysis applied to
men's and women's "nature." Moreover, scientific views on hysteria
and other forms of mental and bodily disturbance began to appear in
legislative accounts. Scientists introduced new proposed laws and
regulations, as well as interventions in the civic code, based on the
assumed significance of hysteria in marital and other relations. I
intend to explore these themes further in a forthcoming article.

30. Ricardo Schatz, "Contribution to the Study of Hysterical Paralysis,"
UBA medical thesis, 1891, 34.

31. Diógenes Decoud, "Estudio del hipnotismo," *Anales del Círculo Médico
Argentino* 11, no. 1 (January 1888): 4–27, 5.

32. Ibid.

33. Anciano Valdez, "Enseñanza de la neuropatología," *Archivos de
Psiquiatría y Criminología* 8 (1909): 711.

34. Ingenieros, *Histeria y sugestión,* 34.

35. So read an advertisement for Ingenieros's book, which was distributed as an insert in the journal *Semana Médica* in September 1904.

36. Ingenieros, *Histeria y sugestión*, 17.

37. Ibid., 40.

38. There was a racial dimension to this view as well. For instance, in one case, the author first described his patient and her antecedents, marking her racially as Jewish. In addition to pointing out her Jewish/Russian origins, he suggested that due to "simple ethnic motives" the doctors could assume that she suffered from "neuropathy or degenerative heredity." He pointed out that "in these past years attention has been called to the alarming frequency of neurosis and psychosis among the Jews. Also . . . class dimension . . . by mentioning work as the cause of her condition. Working in a clothes shop, F. W. began to hiccup after being seated next to a co-worker with a similar hiccup." Despite the "regular hygienic conditions" of the workshop, F. W. fell under the spell of hysteria. Augarde, "Un caso de hipo histérico," *Archivos de psiquiatría, criminología, y ciencias afines* 2 (1903): 488–91. See also Gilman, "The Image of the Hysteric," in Gilman et al., ed., *Hysteria Beyond Freud*.

39. Ingenieros, *Histeria y sugestión*, 98.

40. Ingenieros recommended a two-part treatment: for hysteria, laxatives and warm-water therapy; for the laughing fits, suggestive therapy and hypnosis. After a few months of therapy with successful results, doctors trained her mother to continue limited treatments at home. Ingenieros reported the patient cured one year later. Ibid.

41. It is important to point out that photographs were rare in this medical journal. When they did appear, they tended to focus on sexual conditions, such as the sexualized disorder of hysteria. Pictorial evidence of men's medical conditions were even more rare and tended to focus on grotesque or highly unusual conditions, such as a 1901 article on two cases of genital deformity in men. See "Dos casos raros de teratología," *Semana Médica*, June 6, 1901, 338–39.

42. It is important to remember that illustrations of any kind were rare in the Archivos. Occasionally, graphs or charts would appear, but representations of the body were especially uncommon. Moreover, when the editors chose to unveil a subject's body, it was (in these years at least) without exception that of a female.

43. He wrote, "There exist generalized tremors throughout her body that express an emotion or are under the impression of an exterior or psychic act" (Joaquín J. Durquet, "Paraplegia histérica," 306–18).

44. Ibid., 611.

45. Durquet applied that approach in a separate study in 1906. Durquet, "Manía ambulatoria epiléptica y monoplegia histérica," 341.

46. On the use of illustrations of the hysteric to instruct both doctor and patient, see Sander Gilman, "The Image of the Hysteric," in *Hysteria beyond Freud*, ed. Sander Gilman et al., 345–452.

47. Nicolás Vaschide, "La psiofisiología de impulso sexual," *Archivos de Psiquiatría y Criminología* 5 (1906): 417–27.

48. Bernardo Etchepare, "Desequilibrio Mental, morfinomanía, e histeria," *Archivos de Psiquiatría y Criminología* 11 (1912): 717–23.

49. Ibid., 718.

50. Despite all her supposedly problematic behavior, this particular patient was reported to show no signs of morphological anomalies. Etchepare wrote, "The examination of the patient's body does not show anything anormal. Her skull is regular, same as her face." Ibid., 722).

51. Ingenieros, *Histeria y sugestión*, 81–82.

52. Ibid., 71, 75.

53. Ibid., 8–9.

54. Rodriguez, "Encoding the Criminal," chap. 3; Ricardo D. Salvatore, "Criminology, Prison Reform, and the Buenos Aires Working Class," *Journal of Interdisciplinary History* 23, no. 2 (1992): 279–99.

55. For example, while men were thought to suffer hysteria in smaller numbers, those instances were usually seen in the context of failed military performance. Thus psychiatrists saw male hysteria in its social context, yet they appeared to simultaneously feminize the less frequently seen but equally disturbing male hysteric. Very few scholars have examined male hysteria; for two studies of the phenomenon in Germany, see Paul Lerner, "Psychiatry and Casualties of War in Germany, 1914–1918," *Journal of Contemporary History* 35 (January 2000); and Paul Lerner, "Hysterical Cures: Hypnosis, Gender and Performance in World War I and Weimar Germany," *History Workshop Journal* 45 (March 1998): 79–101.

Chapter 2

1. Archivo General de la Nación, Tribunal Criminal (AGN, TC) 2,C,46,1888, case against Luis Castruccio for poisoning of Alberto Bouchot Constantin.

2. Ibid.

3. Manuel Obarrio, "De los seguros sobre la vida," Revista de Derecho, Historia y Letras (DHL) 1 (1898): 489–504, 491–93.

4. Case against Castruccio.

5. Ibid.

6. Ibid.

7. Ibid.

8. Ibid.

9. Ibid.

10. On the Castro Rodríguez case, see José María Ramos Mejía, Florentino Ortega, and Marcelino Aravena, "El asesino de Olavarría: Su estado mental al cometer el crimen y despues de él. Responsibilidad. Interesante estudio médicolegal," *Revista Jurídica* (hereafter RJ)5 (1888): 428–52.

11. Luís María Drago, *Los hombres de presa* (Buenos Aires: Cultura Argentina, 1921), 29; Pedro Gori, "La ortodoxia antropológica en el derecho penal," RJ 15 (1898–1899): 73–78, 78.

12. Gina Lombroso, "Instituciones americanas: La Penitenciaria Nacional de Buenos Aires," *Archivos de Psiquiatría, Criminología y Ciencias Afines* (hereafter APCCA) 7 (1908): 236.

13. Case against Castruccio.

14. Ibid.

15. On the history of how masturbation, or onanism, came to be considered a sin, see Robert P. Neuman, "What Was the Sin of Onan? The Problem of Masturbation in Patriarchal Culture," *Psychocultural Review* 3, no. 1 (1979): 59–72. On masturbation in the late nineteenth century, see Robert P. Neuman, "The Priests of the Body and Masturbatory Insanity in the Late Nineteenth Century," *The Psychohistory Review* 6 (1978): 21–32.

16. Drago, *Hombres de presa*, 115.

17. Case against Castruccio; "Siguen los crimenes," RJ 5 (1888): 386–88.

18. J. Pérez, *Nueva medicina doméstica* (Buenos Aires: Revista, 1854), 169–70.

19. Víctor Mercante, *La crisis de la pubertad y sus consecuencias pedagógicas* (Buenos Aires: Cabaut, 1918), 187.

20. Drago, *Hombres de presa*, 115–16.

21. C. D. Benitez, "Erotismo contemplativo con impotencia sexual psíquica," APCCA 1 (1902): 235–39.

22. Lucas Ayarragaray, "Obsesión sexual: La mirada masturbadora. Estudio clínico," APCCA 1 (1902): 273–75. See also the case recorded by José Ingenieros, "Fetichista con hermafrodismo psíquico activo y alucinaciones eróticas del olfato," APCCA 1 (1902): 616–21, 619, where masturbation reportedly caused weakened nerve centers.

23. A. Morales Pérez, "Las horquillas en la masturbación femenina," APCCA 1 (1902): 428–30.

24. Lucas Ayarragaray, "Las obsesiones: Un caso de ereutofobia (obsesion de enrojecer)," APCCA 2 (1903): 423–27, 426.

25. Rafael Huertas García-Alejo, *Locura y degeneración: Psiquiatría y sociedad en el positivismo francés* (Madrid: Consejo Superior de Investigaciones Científicas, 1991), 34–36, 38; and Rafael Huertas García-Alejo, *El delincuente y su patología: Medicina, crimen y sociedad en el positivismo argentino* (Madrid: Consejo Superior de Investigaciones Científicas, 1991), 18.

26. Huertas, *Locura y degeneración*, 20.

27. Ibid., 34–36.

28. Eduardo Wilde, *Obras*, Part One, *Científicas*, vol. 3 (Buenos Aires: Plus Ultra, 1965), 272.

29. Huertas, *Delincuente y su patología*, 52–53, 58.

30. Ibid., 18, 20, 24–26.

31. José Nicolás Matienzo, "Sentencia," RJ 5 (1888): 304–9, 305.

32. Case against Castruccio.

33. Ibid.; Drago, *Hombres de presa*, 172.

34. Case against Castruccio.

35. Ibid.

36. Ibid.

37. This is a reference to Francois Leuret (1797–1851), author of works on hygiene in Paris.

38. Case against Castruccio.

39. Ibid. The French jurist referred to is Prosper Lucas (1805–1885), author of the classic work on heredity.

40. Ibid. The jurist referred to is Joaquin Francisco Pacheco (1808–1865), a Spanish expert on Spanish penal law.

41. Ibid.

42. Ibid.

43. Ibid.

44. Ibid.

45. Ibid.

46. Luís Reyna Almandos, *Dactiloscopia argentina: Su historia é influencia en la legislación* (La Plata: J. Sesé, 1909), 20.

47. José Ingenieros, "El envenenador Luis Castruccio," APCCA 8 (1909): 5–29, 5, 13.

48. Ibid., 22, 25, 29.

49. Enrique B. Prack, "Escuela antropológica criminal," RJ 8 (1891): 254–64, 255–58.

50. Wilde, Científicas, 247.

51. Rodolfo Benuzzi, "Sobre criminología," APCCA 1 (1902): 437–39, 439.

52. Lucas Ayarragaray, La imaginación y las pasiones como causas de enfermedades (Buenos Aires: thesis, Faculty of Medicine, 1887), 9.

53. José Ingenieros, "Sobre enfermedades simuladas. Notas médico-sociológicas," DHL 4, no. 12 (1902): 376–88, 380–81.

Chapter 3

1. Archivo del Poder Judicial de la Nación (hereafter APJN), "Elba M.," legajo 14592, fol. 564, no. 4689 (1921). All names and identifying features have been changed to protect the anonymity of patients.

2. Eduardo José Cárdenas, Ricardo Grimson, and José Atilio Alvarez, *El juicio de insania y la internación psiquiátrica* (Buenos Aires: Astrea, 1985), 111. "Sabido es que por normas administrativas internas, rutinas aceptadas y sobre todo por una incomprehensible tolerancia judicial, el principio básico que Vélez Sársfield estableció en el art. 482 del Código Civil fue sistemáticamente vulnerado en nuestro país. Que el enfermo no podrá ser trasladado a una 'casa de demente' sin autorización judicial fue letra muerta hasta fines de 1983."

3. Roy Porter, "Madness and its Institutions," in *Medicine in Society: Historical Essays*, ed. Andrew Weir (New York: Cambridge University Press, 1992), 277.

4. The principal archival source is the APJN. All the documents concern insanity proceedings on patients at the two public hospitals in Buenos Aires. Names have been changed to protect the privacy of patients and their families.

5. For the United States, see Elizabeth Lunbeck, *The Psychiatric Persuasion: Knowledge, Gender, and Power in Modern America* (Princeton, N.J.: Princeton University Press, 1994); David J. Rothman, *Conscience and Convenience: The Asylum and its Alternatives in Progressive America* (Boston: Little, Brown and Company, 1980). For France, see Ian Dowbiggin, *Inheriting Madness: Professionalization and Psychiatric Knowledge in Nineteenth-Century France* (Berkeley and Los Angeles: University of California Press, 1991).

6. Hugo Vezzetti, *La locura en la Argentina* (Buenos Aires: Paidós, 1985); see also Eduardo Balbo, "Argentinian Alienism from 1852–1918." See notes 6 and 10. *History of Psychiatry* 2:6, no. 2 (June 1991): 181–92. For

similar treatment on sexuality, see Jorge Salessi, *Médicos, maleantes y maricas: Higiene, criminología y homosexualidad en la construcción de la nación Argentina (Buenos Aires: 1871–1914)* (Rosario, Argentina: Beatriz Viterbo Editora, 1995); and Donna Guy, *Sex and Danger in Buenos Aires: Prostitution, Family, and Nation in Argentina* (Lincoln: University of Nebraska Press, 1991).

7. Joel Migdal, *Strong Societies and Weak States: State-Society Relations and State Capabilities in the Third World* (Princeton, N.J.: Princeton University Press, 1988), 18.

8. On the problem of enforcement of labor legislation in Argentina, see Asunción Lavrin, *Women, Feminism, and Social Change in Argentina, Chile, and Uruguay, 1890–1940* (Lincoln: University of Nebraska Press, 1995), 83; and Joel Horowitz, *Argentine Unions, the State and the Rise of Perón, 1930–1945* (Institute of International Studies, University of California, Berkeley, 1990), 35. Mariano Plotkin, *Mañana es San Perón: Propaganda, rituales políticos y educación en el régimen Peronista (1946–1955)* (Buenos Aires: Ariel Historia Argentina, 1993), 216–18.

9. Ernest Allen Crider, "Modernization and Human Welfare: The Asistencia Pública and Buenos Aires, 1888–1914" (Ph.D. diss., Ohio State University, 1988), 229–30.

10. Vezzetti, *La locura*; Balbo, "Argentinean Alienism."

11. Balbo, "Argentinian Alienism"; Vezzetti, *La locura*.

12. José Ingenieros, *La locura en la Argentina* (Buenos Aires: Agencia General de Librería y Publicaciones, 1920), 197–212. Luís Meyer, "Los comienzos del hospicio de las Mercedes," *Acta Psiquiátrica y Psicológica de América Látina* 33 (1987): 338–39. Mario Sbarbi, "Reseña histórica del Hospicio de las Mercedes," *Acta Neuropsiquiátrica Argentina* 6 (1960): 420–22. Balbo, "Argentinian Alienism."

13. Domingo Cabred, "Discurso inaugural de la Colonia Nacional de Alienados," *Revista de Derecho, Historia y Letras* 1, no. 3 (1899): 610–22; José Ingenieros, "Los asilos para alienados en la Argentina," *Revista de Criminología, Psiquiatría y Medicina-Legal* 8 (1920): 145.

14. The Province of Buenos Aires had the country's first provincial hospital since 1884. See Eduardo A. Balbo, "El Hospital Neuropsiquiátrico 'Melchor Romero' durante los años 1884–1918," in *Ciencia, vida y espacio en Iberoamérica: trabajos del Programa Movilizador del C.S.I.C.*, "Relaciones científicas y culturales entre España y América," ed. José Luís Peset (Madrid: Consejo Superior de Investigaciones Científicas, 1989), 53–75.

15. Moisés Malamud, *Domingo Cabred* (Buenos Aires: Ediciones Culturales Argentinas, 1972).

16. H. S. Ferns, Ezequiel Gallo, and Melville Watkins, "The Prairies and the Pampas: A Review Colloquium," *Business History Review* 67 (summer 1993): 279–99. See also José C. Moya, Cousins and Strangers: *Spanish Immigrants in Buenos Aires, 1850–1930* (Berkeley and Los Angeles: University of California Press, 1997). In 1914, the population of Buenos Aires was 51 percent foreign born.

17. Exequias Bringas Núñez, "Inmigración y locura (Algunos datos para la profilaxis de las enfermedades mentales en la República Argentina)," *Boletín del Asilo de Alienados en Oliva* 10, nos. 42–43 (May–December 1942): 168. Vezzetti, La locura, 185–232.

18. Vezzetti shows that the trend was already under way in the second half of the nineteenth century (Vezzetti, *La locura*, 59). See also "La hospitalización de Alienados en el País constituye un serio problema de solución inmediato," *La Nación*, January 26, 1934.

19. Sadly this state of affairs continued unabated to the present. On conditions in Argentina's hospitals in the late 1950s, see Sylvia Bermann, "Análisis de algunos datos de estadística psiquiátrica," *Acta Neuropsiquiátrica* 5 (1959): 150–60. Literature on current conditions and the medical and legal rights of patients is extensive. See Hugo Vezzetti, "Secuestrados en los manicomios," *Pagina12*, March 5, 1998; Leila Guerriero, "La Nave de los Locos," *Revista La Nación* 1430, December 1, 1996, 85–92; Isabel Ares, "Recorrido por el Borda," *Gaceta Psicológica* 66 (July 1985): 9–10

20. "Hospicio de las Mercedes: Memoria correspondiente al años 1910–1911," *Memoria del Ministerio de Relaciones Exteriores y Culto correspondiente al años 1910–11* (Buenos Aires: Ministerio de Relaciones Exteriores y Culto, 1912): 469; "Hospicio de las Mercedes: Memoria correspondiente al año 1917," *Memoria del Ministerio de Relaciones Exteriores y Culto correspondiente al años 1917–18* (Buenos Aires: Ministerio de Relaciones Exteriores y Culto, 1919): 980.

21. Sociedad de Beneficencia de la Capital, *Memoria del año 1902* (Buenos Aires: Imprenta y Encuadernación del Asilo de Huerfanos, 1903); Sociedad de Beneficencia de la Capital, *Memoría del año 1933* (Buenos Aires: Sociedad de Beneficencia de la Capital, 1934); and Sociedad de Beneficencia de la Capital, *Memoria del año 1943* (Buenos Aires: Sociedad de Beneficencia de la Capital, 1944).

22. Cynthia Jeffress Little, "The Society of Beneficence in Buenos Aires, 1823–1900," (Ph.D. diss., Temple University, 1980), 231. "During the colonial period and until 1871, Argentina had no body of law regulating commitment procedures."

23. "Título X, De los dementes e inhabilitados, Arts.140–152bis," in *Código*

Civil de la República Argentina y Legislación Complementaria (Buenos Aires: Abeledo-Perrot, 1976), 42–44.

24. "Servicio de Observación de Alienados," *Archivo de Psiquiatría y Criminología* 9 (March–April 1910): 254–56.

25. Ibid., 42. "Se declaran dementes los individuos de uno y otro sexo que se hallen en estado habitual de manía, demencia o imbecilidad, aunque tengan intervalos lúcidos, o la manía sea parcial." In 1968, the military government of General Juan Carlos Onganía narrowed these broad and vague criteria for determining mental competence under Law 17,711. The revised Article 141 judged mental competence in terms of one's ability to manage one's person and affairs. It read, "Persons will be declared incompetent by insanity who because of mental illness are not able to direct their person or administer their personal property."

26. Ibid., 42, Article 144: "Los que pueden pedir la declaración de demencia son: 1. El esposo o esposa no divorciados; 2. Los parientes del demente; 3. El Ministro de Menores; 4. El respectivo cónsul, si el demente fuese extranjero; 5. Cualquiera persona del pueblo, cuando el demente sea furioso, o incomode a sus vecinos."

27. Ibid., 43, Articles 147–52.

28. Ibid., "Titulo XIII, De la curatela, Capitulo I, Curatela a los incapaces mayores de edad, art. 482," in *Código Civil de la República Argentina*, 103. "El demente no será privado de su libertad personal sino en los casos en que sea de temer que, usando ella, se dañe a sí mismo o dañe a otros. No podrá tampoco ser trasladado a una casa de dementes sin autorización judicial."

29. Although this work looks only at public hospitals, there is a body of evidence that indicates that patients in private clinics were in fact likely to receive even fewer legal protections. See Clodomiro Cordero, *La Internación Pre-Judicial de Presuntos Dementes* (Buenos Aires: n.p., 1940), 3–13. For a case of accusation of wrongful confinement in a private hospital, see "Un Millonario Secuestrado en un Sanatorio," *Crítica* (April 22, 1928); "La hospitalización privada de alienados," *La Nación*, February 10, 1934.

30. For the problem of delays and other pitfalls in the United States, see Peter McCandless, *Moonlight, Magnolias and Madness: Insanity in South Carolina from the Colonial Period to the Progressive Era* (Chapel Hill: University of North Carolina Press, 1996), 264. "Until the early 1900s, the rules required that the regents personally examine the patients prior to dismissal. But the regents normally met only once a month, and sometimes they did not examine all or any of the patients the physicians recommended for discharge. Months might pass between the physicians recommendation and the actual time of release."

31. APJN, "Insania," "Josefina D.," legajo 19981, no. 20,373, fol. 44 (1937).

32. APJN, "Insania," "Carolina M." legajo 38678 (1943); APJN, "Insania," "Silvia O.," legajo 19981, no. 20,621 (1937).

33. APJN, "Insania," "José P.," legajo 10248, fol. 183 (1925).

34. APJN, "Insania," "Ivan G.," legajo 14235, fol. 91 (1911).

35. APJN, "Insania," "Samuel J.," legajo 20008 (1934).

36. APJN, "Insania," "Carlos Luís B.," legajo 19978 (1932). Hospicio de las Mercedes to Judge Francisco Quesada, October 21, 1932. "Como hasta la fecha no se ha tenido conocimiento de resolución alguna en favor de la libertad de B. y persistiendo su mejoría, reitero a V.S., el pedido que hacía en la citada nota."

37. APJN, "Insania," "Paulina C.," legajo 19999 (1933).

38. APJN, "Insania," "Jaime M.," legajo 20023, no. 13914, fol. 25 (1931). This subject was confined at the Hospicio's rural facility in the Province of Buenos Aires. In order to be inspected by court doctors, he had to be transferred to the Hospicio.

39. APJN, "Insania," "Francisco N.," legajo 22117, fol. 189 (1946).

40. Ministerio de Relaciones Exteriores y Culto, Memorias correspondiente al año 1913–14 (Buenos Aires: Talleres Gráficos de Selin Suarez, 1915): 505–6. At the time that Francisco wrote his letter, all public psychiatric hospitals were severely overcrowded. See Archivo General de la Nación-Sociedad de Beneficencia-Hospital Nacional de Alienadas, legajo 250, expediente 28.027, Edmundo M. to President Perón, October 31, 1947.

41. APJN, "Insania," "Elba M.," legajo 14592, fol. 564, no. 4689 (1921). For reference to this problem in the nineteenth century, see Little, "Society of Beneficence in Buenos Aires," 234. In October 1888, for example, the director of the Hospital Nacional de Alienadas reported that "husbands sometimes institutionalized their wives as a means to punish them or to wrest their inheritance."

42. D. Rosenhahn, "On Being Sane in Insane Places," Science 179 (1973): 250–58. Erving Goffman, Asylums: Essays on the Social Situation of Mental Patients and Other Inmates (New York: Anchor Books, 1961). Magazine articles from the 1920s to 1940s show patients in tattered clothing, dirty, and disheveled. See "No están todos los que son . . . una hora en el Hospicio de las Mercedes," Caras y Caretas 26, no. 1300 (September 1, 1923): n.p.; and Juan José Soiza Reilly, "Cuarenta mil locos en libertad: Una visita al Hospicio de las Mercedes," Caras y Caretas 37, no. 1864 (June 23, 1934): n.p. Until 1946, patients wore

uniforms with serial numbers on the shirt. Plotkin, *Mañana es San Perón*, 300.

43. Mariano Ben Plotkin, "Freud, Politics, and the Porteños: The Reception of Psychoanalysis in Buenos Aires, 1910–1943," *Hispanic American Historical Review* 77, no. 1 (February 1997): 49–50. "The theory of degeneration, created by French physician Benedict Augustin Morel in the nineteenth century, remained a major current of thought in Argentine psychiatry as late as the 1940s."

44. APJN, "Ivan G.," "Insania," legajo 14235, fol. 91 (1911). "A simple vista, se le observan algunos signos degenerativos, es de cabeza chica, tiene asimetria craneo." See also, APJN, "Enrique M.," "Insania," legajo 12409, fol. 59 (1908), which simply noted that the subject "presenta estigmas faciales degenerativas."

45. Osvaldo Loudet and Osvaldo Elías Loudet, *Historia de la psiquiatría argentina* (Buenos Aires: Troquel, 1971): 194–95.

46. On the issue of legal reform in Western Europe and the United States, see Peter McCandless, "Liberty and Lunacy: The Victorians and Wrongful Confinement," in *Madhouses, Mad-doctors, and Madmen: The Social History of Psychiatry in the Victorian Era*, ed. Andrew Scull (Philadelphia: University of Pennsylvania Press, 1981), 339–62; Richard W. Fox, "So Far Disordered in Mind": *Insanity in California, 1870–1930* (Berkeley and Los Angeles: University of California Press, 1978), 38; and Dowbiggin, *Inheriting Madness*, 93–115.

47. Loudet and Loudet, *Historia e la psiquiatría argentina*.

48. Ibid., 178.

49. Ibid., 179–80. In 1891, a medical thesis was accepted by the University of Buenos Aires on the topic of legislation for mental illness. As with Coni's proposal, the thesis reflects the failure of hospitals to follow civil code procedures. See Loudet and Loudet, *Historia de la psiquiatría argentina*, 185.

50. For the reforms of Piñero and Cabred, see Jonathan D. Ablard, "Madness in Buenos Aires: Psychiatry, Society, and the State in Argentina, 1890–1983" (Ph.D. diss., University of New Mexico, 2000), 92–136.

51. Ibid., 781–86.

52. Argentina. Congreso Nacional. *Diario de Sesiones de la Cámara de Diputados*: Año 1906 1, 11th sesión ordinaria (September 26, 1906), 1011. "Entre nosotros, la inspección y vigilancia, ejercida por una comisión de peritos, que es un resorte esencial de la protección directa del loco, falta en absoluto para los establecimientos públicos, para los

asilos privados y con mayor razón para las y los locos sueltos. Y sin embargo, esta misma inspección existe para los criminales."

53. Ibid. "Y como el loco sólo puede ser trasladado a un hospital especial por orden del juez . . . es evidente que los locos en cuya internación no se han llenado estas tramitaciones previas han sido ilegalmente internados."

54. Argentina. Congreso Nacional. *Diario de Sesiones de la Cámara de Diputados*: Año 1894 1, 26th sesión ordinaria (September 14, 1894), 788. "Situación excepcional, que denuncia la existencia de un problema gravísimo de nuestro sociabilidad, cual es, el de que los locos encerrados en nuestros manicomios, en una proporción que no bajará del 98 por ciento, se encuentran en condiciones ilegales: porque las disposiciones contenidas en los títulos X, XI y XIII del código civil, que a ellos se refieren, son letra muerta en el mayor número de casos, y en las principales medidas a que son sometido, como los de su sequestración en los asilos públicos y privados, y en la manera como se ejercita su curatela."

55. Ibid.

56. Argentina. Congreso Nacional. *Diario de Sesiones de la Cámara de Diputados* I, 26th sesión ordinaria (September 12, 1894), 752. Cantón observed that there were even fewer protections for the insane in Russia than in Argentina: "La inmensa mayoría de los dementes pueden ser secuestrados sin llenar requisito alguno, sin certificado médico, a pedido de cualquier persona interesada, con el único encargo por parte del director del manicomio de dar cuenta al gobernador de la localidad." The law had been drafted by Domingo Cabred, director of the men's Hospicio de las Mercedes.

57. In 1918, the women's hospital had a patient capacity of 800, but cared for more than 1,600 souls. See "Hospicio Nacional de Alienadas— Cargos contra su dirección," *La Unión*, July 23, 1918. A 1923 congressional investigation also found overcrowding, Diputados 6 (March 7, 1923), 349. On overcrowding in the 1930s, see Adolfo Lanús, "Veinticuatro horas de libertad en el manicomio," *Caras y Caretas* 33, no. 1647 (April 26, 1930). See also "La hospitalización de Alienados en el País constituye un serio problema de solución inmediato," *La Nación*, January 26, 1934. The HNA had a capacity of 1,600 but held 3,054 patients. The Hospicio, with 1,100 beds, held 1,990, but its satellite facility, with 1,200 beds, held 4,016.

58. Leopoldo Bard, "Proyecto de Ley sobre Legislación para los Establecimientos destinados a alienados," *Revista de Criminología, Psiquiatría y Medicina-Legal* 9, no. 52 (July–August 1922): 452–74.

59. Argentina. Congreso Nacional. *Diario de Sesiones de la Cámara de*

Diputados: Año 1926 VI, sesiones ordinarias, reunión 58 (September 29, 1926) (Buenos Aires: Imprenta y Encuadernación de la Cámara de Diputados, 1927), 432. "Me voy a limitar a decir a la Cámara, por el momento, que, de acuerdo con un informe semioficial, puedo asegurar que de 3,700 internados que hay en el hospicio de las Mercedes, el 80 por ciento, es decir, alrededor de 3,000 se encuentran allí sin que los jueces civiles sepan que están privadas de su libertad." Fonrouge's figures probably included patients at the Colonia Nacional de Alienados.

60. APJN, "Insania," legajo 19551, fol. 66. See also "Un Millonario Secuestrado en un Sanatorio."

61. Argentina. Congreso Nacional. *Diario de Sesiones de la Cámara de Diputados* VI, sesiones ordinarias, reunión 58 (September 29, 1926), 418. "Estos gocen de completa libertad de acción, sin el contolator eficaz y constante que debería ejercer el Departamento Nacional de Higiene."

62. Adolfo M. Sierra, "Entorno de tres proyectos legislativos sobre alienados," *La Nación*, December 29, 1926. Sierra also used the argument of medical confidentiality to oppose a proposal that doctors be obliged to report all drug addicts to the police.

63. Adolfo M. Sierra, "Problemas médicos actuales sobre tratamiento, profilaxis y eugénesis mentales," *Revista Argentina de Neurología, Psiquiatría y Medicina Legal* 4, no. 19 (January–February 1930): 34. "En efecto, la libertad de ingreso de alienados en sanatorios particulares no tienen en nuestros Códigos la menor restricción legal, lo cual contrasta con el formulismo que en las mismas circunstancias están sometidos en los manicomios oficiales."

64. Ibid., 34. "En el Hospicio y Colonia Nacional de Alienados existe un abogado, a sueldo, que ejerce a priori las funciones de curador de los alienados de estos establecimientos, siendo dicho letrado quien debe dar cuenta al juzgado correspondiente."

65. Maximo Agustín Cubas, "Los certificados médicos de alienación mental," *Boletín del Asilo de Alienados en Oliva* 3, no. 7 (March 1935): 35–45.

66. Such accusations were leveled against Hospicio director Alfredo Scárano after he was fired in 1930. See "Comprobaciones dolorosas," *La Nación*, August 20, 1931.

67. Although Cubas did not address the issue directly, clearly the intrusion of nonspecialists into this work impinged on the professional status and identity of Argentine psychiatrists.

68. Cubas, "Los certificados médicos." Cubas cited a recent case in which a patient arrived with physical wounds that the medical certificates did not mention. Cubas, "Los certificados médicos," 38–39.

69. Ibid., 38. "Y ocurre entonces que con harta frecuencia nos llegan individuos en estado de perfecta lucidez mental, que han padecido por ejemplo una confusion mental pasajera por intoxicación etílica o de otro origen y que ha hecho su proceso evolutivo durante su estadía en el calabozo que muchas veces se prolonga por un mes o más; [no tenemos, como es habitual, de tales enfermos, antecedentes hereditarios ni personales ni de la enfermedad actual; el policía que los acompaña, por lo general, nunca sabe nada]; el presunto insano, en quien ha desaparecido todo signo físico de intoxicación, niega toda consistencia a nuestras sospechas; pero como su alienación ha sido certificado por dos médicos, es necesario prolongar la observación por ver si surgen los signos delatores que la justifiquen; entretanto estamos privando de su libertad a un individuo mentalmente sano, que no constituye para la sociedad un peligro del que sea de nuestra incumbencia el protejerla."

70. Ibid., 39–40. Cubas then proceeds to outline the legal norms in various European countries.

71. Ibid., 35. Cubas alludes to a recent case at the HNA where doctors were charged with kidnapping. Unfortunately, the author does not provide precise details.

72. Conrado O. Ferrer, "Sobre las visitas a los alienados internados," *Boletín del Asilo de Alienados en Oliva* 6, nos. 19–22 (January–December 1938): 142. "Por falta de una ley de alienados, los enfermos mentales interados, se encuentran privados de su libertad con solo requisitos establecidos por la practica (dos certificados de alienacion mental, firmados por medicos ajenos a la casa y en los que se establezca la necesidad de hospitalización), pero que carecen de fuerza legal; asi que, nuestra internación actual, estaría consderada como un delito de secuestro arbitrario y los directores de los establecimientos, caerían bajo la sanción del Código Penal, en su artículo 141. Así los ha entendido en algunas ocasiones la Justicia."

73. The issue of professional protection survived at least until the 1960s, and probably later. See Bruno A. L. Fantoni, "Internación de Enfermos Mentales—Responsibilidad de los Directores," *Gaceta del Instituto Nacional de Salud Mental* 1, no. 1 (September 1963): n.p.

74. Ramón Carrillo, *Clasificación Sanitaria de los Enfermos Mentales: Relaciones entre Código Civil y Sanitario* (Buenos Aires: Talleres Gráficos del Ministro de Salud Pública de la Nación, n.d.), 11. "La situación jurídica de 'nuestros' enfermos mentales, los que tenemos internados oficialmente en los establecimientos del Ministerio, fué uno de los primeros problemas que me enfrenté como Ministro."

75. Ibid., 43. "En el Ministerio de Salud Pública tenemos establecimientos

en los que en conjunto están internados 15,000 alienados, admitidos gran parte de ellos sin la autorización del juez. Es decir, se ha planteado una situacion de hecho, al margen del Código Civil, pues éste exige la declaración judical previa a la internación del llamado demente. Nosotros no hemos podido iniciar todos los juicios correspondientes a los 15,000 internados porque son infinitamente mas los interados que las posiblidades de llevar adelante todos los juicios. En este último año, según creo, la Curaduría Oficial del Alienado, con gran esfuerzo y pocos recursos, ha seguido entre 1,000 y 1,200 juicios de insania en un vano afán de poner al día una tarea abandonada desde hace tantos años."

76. Ibid., 42–43.

77. Ibid., 49–50. "La interdiccion por enfermedad mental solo procede cuando la persona es mayor de 12 años y no puede actuar normalmente en la vida de relación ni conducirse a si mismo ni manejar sus negocios por padecer una afeccion de aquella indole."

78. Ibid., 50. "Porque lo que interesa a un juez es si el enfermo puede manejarse sus intereses, conducirse normalmente y realizar los actos comunes de la vida de relación, sin que importe demasiado discriminar si el enfermo es maniático, demente, imbécil, o si tiene intervalos lúcidos en el momento de la caracterización." This idea was already put forth in Alberto Molinas, "Restricción de la capacidad en las personas faltas de normal sanidad mental. Diverso fundamentos," *Revista de Ciencias Jurídicas y Sociales* (Universidad del Litoral) 10, nos. 45–46 (3a época) (1945): 141.

79. Carrillo, *Clasificación sanitaria de los enfermos mentales*, 61. "Con el sistema actual, el enfermo mental, substituído totalmente por el curador, que es quien actua, no puede hablar con el juez. Porque si el enfermo no tiene un curador de bienes de buena voluntad que los lleve ante el juez, no puede hacerse oir por este."

80. Edwin M. Bouchard, *Library of Congress Guide to the Law and Legal Literature of Argentina, Brazil and Chile* (Washington, D.C.: Government Printing Office, 1917), 95. Antonio Montarcé Lastra, *La Incapacidad Civil de los Alienados* (Buenos Aires: Libreria y Editorial "La Facultad," 1928), xv. The author notes that there was some regional variation. For example, in the city of Buenos Aires, a judge did not see the patient, whereas in the Province of Buenos Aires, the patient was present for his or her insanity proceeding. This may explain, in part, the practice of bonaerense public officials and private citizens dumping their insane into the city of Buenos Aires.

81. APJN, "Insania," "Ceilia B.," legajo 55176 (1949).

82. Carrillo, *Clasificación sanitaria de los enfermos mentales*, 57–64. Carrillo also argued for the development of partial interdiction for persons who could exercise some civil rights. A restriction of who could commit finally occurred during the dictatorship of Onganía, who also expanded police powers with regard to hospitalization.

83. Argentina. Congreso Nacional. *Diario de Sesiones de la Cámara de Diputados*: Año 1946 I, reunión núm. 2, (June 27, 1946), 121. "No hay que olvidar que si por un lado hay el fantasma de los secuestros de no alienados, de lo cual tanto se habla con exageración, del otro hay el peligro del alienado libre y sin asistencia o mal vigilado, por negligencia o ignorancia de la familia, de lo cual poco o nada se dice." Rojas's law came before Congress in 1943, 1946, and 1961 but never passed. Rojas resubmitted his bill in 1961. See Argentina. Congreso Nacional. *Diario de Sesiones de la Cámara de Diputados* I, Reunión 2a., (May 16, 1961): 137–40.

84. Nerio Rojas, *Medicina legal*, 7th ed. (Buenos Aires: Editorial "El Ateneo," 1959), 465–66. "El régimen de la internación, la inspección de los establecimientos especiales, la situación del alienado, internado o no, pero no interdicto, no están legislados entre nosotros. Es una falla lamentable, que se subsana bien o mal, gracias a reglamentos o a buena voluntad o experiencia o a honestidad de médicos y parientes."

85. Ibid., 466. "No he de ocuparme delos supuestos 'secuestros' de personas sana, otro de los prejuicios populares favorecidos sobre todo por reclamaciones de algún alienado lúcido, cuya psicosis es desconocida o negada por él y sus allegados no siempre desinteresados."

86. Mariano Ben Plotkin, "Politics of Consensus in Peronist Argentina (1943–1955)" (Ph.D. diss., University of California at Berkeley, 1992), 284.

87. Eduardo José Cárdenas, "Para internar a un enfermo mental hace la falta la intervención de un juez," *El Observador*, May 4, 1984, 33. "Pero ninguno había logrado plasmarse, debido a la resistencia opuesta por los intereses economicos de las clinicas privadas—unidas a las poderosas obras sociales—y por el inmovilismo enquistado en ciertos sectores."

88. See the 1918 exposé of the Hospital Nacional de Alienadas, Juan José Soiza Reilly, "Muerte misteriosa de una señora," *La Revista Popular* (August 5, 1918). The author alleged that the directors of the hospital moonlighted at a private clinic and diverted better-off patients to the latter institution.

89. Roberto Ciafardo, *Psicopatología Forense* (Buenos Aires: "El Ateneo," 1972), 351.

90. Little, "Society of Beneficence in Buenos Aires," 235.

91. Archivo General de la Nación—Sociedad de Beneficencia—Hospital Nacional de Alienados, legajo 208, expediente 8172, "HNA-Reglamentación de la carrera hospitalaria en el establecimiento" (April 12, 1935).

92. APJN, "Insania," "Graciana E.," legajo 22116 (1946). While accepting guardianship of the person of the patient, director Luís Esteves Balado stated that overcrowding made it impossible for him to accept responsibility for her property.

93. AGN-SB-HNA, legajo 200, expediente 2784 and 2659. See also AGN-SB-HNA, legajo 223, libro 1917.

94. APJN "Insania," "Santiago D.," legajo 14259, fol. 145, entrado 973 (1912). The three conditions for release are as follows: the illness disappears; subject is sufficiently improved so as to not pose a danger to self or others, and "Cuando lo solicitaren las autoridades que ordenaron su resolución o las personas que la pidieron voluntariamente." It seems that in the second half of the nineteenth century, hospital directors may have operated with greater independence. See Vezzetti, *La locura*, 54.

95. Cárdenas, Grimson, and Alvarez, *El juicio de insania*, 46–47. "En la gran mayoría de los casos, la policía actuaba a título de colaboración con un familiar, y no se consideraba responsable de la internación. No daba, pues, cuenta al juez. Sin embargo, en el hospital la persona figuraba como internada por la policía, y no se permitía su egreso hasta que se recibiera una orden judicial que nunca llegaba, porque ningún juez conocía el asunto."

96. See the highly polemical Alfredo Moffatt, *Socioterapia para sectores marginados: Terapia comunitaria para grupos de riesgo* (Buenos Aires: Lumen Humanitas, 1997). Also Christián Courtis, "La Locura no da Derechos," *Desbordar* 3, nos. 41–43 (October 1991): 42. Courtis notes that there is little legal literature on cases of judicial neglect or medical abuse. Likewise, medical malpractice has only recently entered into Argentine jurisprudence. Luís Frontera, "La Dictadura del Valium," *Caras y Caretas* 2212, no. 85 (July 1984): 32; Vezzetti, "Secuestrados en los manicomios"; Wilbur R. Grimson, *Sociedad de locos: Experiencia y violencia en un hospital psiquiátrico* (Buenos Aires: Ediciones Nueva Visión, 1972).

97. For an example of a recent study on the gulf between written law and its implementation, see Silvia Marina Arrom, *Containing the Poor: The Mexico City Poor House, 1774–1871* (Durham, N.C.: Duke University Press, 2000).

98. Michel Foucault, *Discipline and Punish: The Birth of the Prison* (New York: Pantheon Books, 1977). See "Panopticism."

99. The extent to which psychiatric patients have been neglected and forgotten is well documented in Jonathan Sadowsky, *Imperial Bedlam*:

Institutions of Madness in Colonial Southwest Nigeria (Berkeley and Los Angeles: University of California Press, 1999), 27. "The colonial lunatic asylums of Nigeria were simply not benign enough to be insidious. Nor would a view of colonial asylums as 'panoptic' really be apt. More to the point is how little these institutions saw, or cared to."

Chapter 4

1. A similar symbolic operation is described by Michel Foucault, *Surveiller et punir: Naissance de la prison* (Paris: Gallimard, 1975), 144.

2. On the Argentine reception of fashionable theories about the crowd, see Oscar Terán, *José Ingenieros: Pensar la Nación* (Buenos Aires: Alianza, 1986), 46.

3. Pedro Gori, "Estudios carcelarios: Una visita a la penitenciaría de Sierra Chica," *Criminología Moderna* 2 (March 5, 1899): 176.

4. Osvaldo Loudet, "El Instituto de Criminología de Buenos Aires," *Revista de Criminología, Psiquiatría y Medicina Legal* 19 (1932): 282.

5. José Ingenieros, *Criminología* (Madrid: Ed. D. Jorro, 1913), 105.

6. José Ingenieros, "Valor de la psicopatología en la antropología criminal," Archivos de Psiquiatría y Criminología 1 (1902): 4; "Nueva clasificación de delincuentes fundada en su psicopatología," *Archivos* 4 (1906): 30.

7. Quoted in Osvaldo Loudet, "Enrique Ferri y la ciencia penal," *Revista de Criminología, Psiquiatría y Medicina Legal* 16 (1929): 133.

8. Helvio Fernández had worked with Ingenieros and was by then the leading psychiatrist at the Hospice "Las Mercedes"; Loudet was also a prestigious psychiatrist and would become the main historian of Argentine psychiatry.

9. On the "criminalization" of anarchists at the beginning of the century, see E. Zimmermann, *Los liberales reformistas: La cuestión social en la Argentina, 1890–1916* (Buenos Aires: Sudamericana/San Andrés, 1994), 129.

10. O. Loudet, J. Nogués, P. Pietranera, J. Delpiano, and F. Isla, "Juicio de peligrosidad en un ex-alienado delincuente," *Revista de Criminología, Psiquiatría y Medicina Legal* 17 (1930): 407.

11. An analysis of the strategies of inmates to appear "adaptable" can be found in Lila Caimari, "Remembering Freedom: Life as Seen from the Prison Cell" (paper presented at the Conference "The Contested Terrains of Law and Order in Latin America," Yale University, April 15, 1996).

12. Penitenciaría Nacional de Buenos Aires, Instituto de Criminología, "Informe Psíquico N° 8, prontuario N° 6563, penado 669," Boletín Médico Psicológico N° 12; "Informe N° 13, prontuario N° 6201, penado 520," Boletín Médico-Psicológico, N° 17, written by Dr. Helvio Fernández. The information comes from a sample of twenty reports, written in forms that were similar to the originals designed by Ingenieros. From the legal and institutional points of view, the final summaries were the only documentation that counted. Written in plain prose, such reports were the place where the diagnosis of dangerousness was founded. Penitentiary authorities and judges making decisions about parole, about the fitness for trial of an individual, or about the ultimate destiny of a sentenced person (prison or the psychiatric hospital) saw neither the context from which these conclusions followed, nor what theoretical system had generated the questions and guided the interpretation of the answers. The final report of the director was the only document to make it to their desks, and most probably what founded the decisions about the fate of convicts. The cases examined here suggest that the recommendations of the Institute of Criminology were usually followed by judges.

13. Eusebio Gómez, "Clasificación de los condenados," *Revista de Criminología, Psiquiatría y Medicina Legal* 12 (1925): 617.

14. Ibid.

15. O. Loudet, "El médico en las prisiones," *Revista de Criminología, Psiquiatría y Medicina Legal*, 15 (1928): 373.

16. Loudet himself quoted this passage by Ferri in "La historia de clínica criminológica," *Revista de Criminología, Psiquiatría y Medicina Legal*, 21 (1934): 209; emphasis added.

17. Loudet's reports in Ministerio de Justicia e Instrucción Pública, *Memoria presentada al Congreso* (1936), 460.

18. The information about Clinical Criminological Histories designed by Loudet and used by the Penitentiary Service until the 1940s has been obtained from a sample of thirty-six such reports located in the Archivo Penitenciario de San Telmo (Buenos Aires) and the Museo y Archivo Penitenciario de la Provincia de Buenos Aires, La Plata.

19. Instituto de Criminología, Historia de Clínica Criminológica, prontuario 35.252, 1934.

20. Instituto de Criminología, standard form of the Historia de clínica criminológica, 6.

21. See, for example, Eusebio Gómez, *Estudios Penitenciarios* (Buenos Aires: Talleres Gráficos de la Penitenciaría Nacional, 1906), 45; Eusebio Gómez, *La mala vida en Buenos Aires* (Buenos Aires: Ed. Juan Roldán,

1908), 215; also Gori, "Estudios carcelarios," 180. Interestingly, this negative view was limited to male prison therapy. Despite all the anti-clerical rhetoric of criminologists and government leaders, female offenders were placed under the supervision of the Catholic congregation of the Good Shepherd, who ran all female prisons from 1890 to the 1970s.

22. Gori, "Estudios carcelarios," 180.

23. Ibid., 19.

Chapter 5

1. See Enrique Pichon Rivière, "Prólogo," *Del psicoanálisis a la psicología social* (Buenos Aires: Galerna, 1970), vol. 1. Ana Pampliega de Quiroga, "Enrique Pichon-Rivière (1907–1977)," *Revista Argentina de Clínica Psicológica* 1, no. 1 (April 1992): 77–87.

2. Roberto Arlt (1900–1942) was a novelist, dramatist, and journalist rooted in the themes and figures of Buenos Aires's culture and society in the 1920s and 1930s. He wrote novels such as *El juguete rabioso* (The rabid toy) (1926), *Los siete locos* (The seven madmen) (1929), *Los lanzallamas* (The flame throwers) (1931), and *El amor brujo* (Witchy love) (1932). He wrote also a long series of *Aguafuertes porteñas* (Etchings from Buenos Aires), originally published as articles in the newspaper El Mundo.

3. Vicente Zito Lima, *Conversaciones con Enrique Pichon Rivière sobre el arte y la locura* (Buenos Aires: Timerman Editores, 1976; reprint, Buenos Aires: Edic. Cinco, 1985), 35, 127.

4. See Enrique Pichon Rivière, "Vida e imagen del conde de Lautréamont," Ciclos, no. 2, Buenos Aires (1949); "Lo siniestro en la vida y en la obra del conde de Lautréamont" and "Psicoanálisis del conde de Lautréamont," both in Enrique Pichon Rivière, *Psicoanálisis del Conde de Lautréamont* (Buenos Aires: Argonauta, 1992). The prose poem Les Chants de Maldoror was published anonymously in 1868 and was republished in 1890. The work received little notice until the surrealists adopted Lautréamont as a founding model.

5. See Jorge Balán, *Cuéntame tu vida: Una biografía colectiva del psicoanálisis argentino* (Buenos Aires: Planeta, 1991), 122.

6. See Hugo Vezzetti, "Las promesas del psicoanálisis en la cultura de masas," in *Historia de la vida privada en la Argentina*, ed. M. Madero and F. Devoto (Buenos Aires: Taurus, 1999), vol. 3. Mariano Plotkin, "Tell Me Your Dreams: Psychoanalysis and Popular Culture in Buenos Aires, 1930–1950," *The Americas* 55, no. 4 (April 1999).

7. Hugo Vezzetti, *Aventuras de Freud en el país de los argentinos* (Buenos Aires: Paidós, 1996).

8. See Vezzetti, "Las promesas."

9. See Balán, *Cuéntame*, 102.

10. Nathan H. Hale, "From Bergasse 19 to Central Park West: The Americanization of Psychoanalysis, 1919–1940," *Journal of the History of the Behavioral Sciences* 14 (1978): 299.

11. Ibid., 303–4.

12. Enrique Pichon Rivière, "¿Qué es el psicoanálisis?" (1946) in *Del psicoanálisis a la psicología social* (Buenos Aires: Galerna, 1970), 2:69.

13. Ibid., 2:74.

14. "Y a partir del fútbol, como de las otras actividades instintivamente grupales en las que participo—vivíamos en pueblos pequeños, donde se integran con naturalidad 'pandillas' o 'barras'—ha quedado en mí, como alguna vez he dicho, la vivencia del carácter operativo de las situaciones grupales" (Zito Lima, *Conversaciones*, 28).

15. Janet Sayers, *Mothering Psychoanalysis: Helen Deutsch, Karen Horney, Anna Freud, Melanie Klein* (London: Penguin Books, 1992), 233.

16. See G. H. Mead, Mind, Self and Society: From the Standpoint of a Social Behaviorist (Chicago: University of Chicago Press, 1934), esp. part 3.

17. Zito Lima, *Conversaciones*, 101, 103.

18. E. Pichon Rivière, "Estructura de una Escuela destinada a la formación de psicólogos sociales", in *Del psicoanálisis a la psicologiía social*," (Buenos Aires: Galerna, 1970), 2, p. 311.

19. Ibid., 2:315.

20. Joel Pfister, "Glamorizing the Psychological: The Politics of the Performances of Modern Psychological Identities," in *Inventing the Psychological: Toward a Cultural History of Emotional Life in America*, ed. Joel Pfister and Nancy Schnog (New Haven, Conn., and London: Yale University Press, 1997).

21. José Bleger, *Psicología de la conducta* (Buenos Aires: Eudeba, 1963; reprint, Buenos Aires: Paidós, 1973); and José Bleger, *Psicohigiene y psicología institucional* (Buenos Aires: Paidós, 1966).

22. See Hugo Vezzetti, "Applied Psychology in Argentina: 'Psycho-hygiene' in the Early Days of its Professionalization" (paper presented at the 24th International Congress of Applied Psychology, San Francisco, August 9–14, 1998).

23. Enrique Pichon Rivière, José Bleger, David Liberman, and Edgardo Rolla, "Técnica de grupos operativos" (1960) in *Del psicoanálisis a la psicología social*, 261.

24. Fernando Ulloa, *Novela y clínica psicoanalítica* (Buenos Aires: Paidós, 1995), 63–64.

25. Servicio de Neuro-Psiquiatría del Hospital Español de Rosario, Departamento de Psiquiatría, "Curso de Psicología Social: Distintos ámbitos operacionales," August–October 1967, mimeo. I am grateful to Lic. Silvia Chiarvetti, who gave me this material.

26. Enrique Pichon Rivière, Ana P. de Quiroga, Carlos Gandolfo, and Marta Lazzarini, "Grupo operativo y modelo dramático," *Del psicoanálisis a la psicología social* (Galerna, tomo II). The course was directed by a well-known theatrical director, Carlos Gandolfo.

27. The series was published as Enrique Pichon Rivière and Ana P. Quiroga, *Psicología de la vida cotidiana* (Buenos Aires: Nueva Visión, 1985).

28. See Silvia Sigal, *Intelectuales y poder en la década del sesenta* (Buenos Aires: Puntosur, 1991), chap. 2, entitled "Los nuevos tiempos."

29. See Oscar Terán, *Nuestros años sesentas: la formación de la nueva izquierda intelectual en la Argentina, 1956–1966* (Buenos Aires: Puntosur, 1991), chap. 4, entitled "Destellos de modernidad y pérdida de hegemonía de Sur," 81–85.

30. See "Inundados: Las reacciones psicológicas ante el desastre," in Pichon and Quiroga, *Del psicoanálisis a la psicología social*, 22–31.

31. See "Miedo al asfalto," in Pichon and Quiroga, *Del psicoanálisis a la psicología social*, 111–13.

32. See "Futbol y política," in Pichon and Quiroga, *Del psicoanálisis a la psicología social*, 69–71.

Chapter 6

1. Juan Ramón Beltrán, "Psicopatología de la duda," *La Semana Médica* 39, no. 3 (January 20, 1927): 160–62. See also Juan Ramón Beltrán, "La psicoanálisis al servicio de la criminología," *Revista de Criminología, Psiquiatría y Medicina Legal* 10 (1923): 442.

2. The concept of "psychoanalytic culture" is borrowed from Sherry Turkle, Psychoanalytic Politics: Jacques Lacan and Freud's French Revolution, 2d ed. (London: Free Association Books, 1992).

3. What follows draws on an elaboration of material presented in my book *Freud in the Pampas: The Emergence and Development of a Psychoanalytic Culture in Argentina* (Stanford, Calif.: Stanford University Press, 2001), esp. chaps. 1 and 5.

4. The image of immigrants as idiots or degenerates can be seen in such late-nineteenth-century novels as Eugenio Cambaceres, *En la sangre*

(1887), or Julian Martel, *La bolsa (estudio social)* (1891). For a general discussion, see Hugo Vezzetti, *La locura en la Argentina* (Buenos Aires: Folios, 1983).

5. Francisco de Veyga, "Psicología de los delincuentes profesionales," *Anales de Psicología* 2 (1911): 96–135.

6. "Sentencia del Juez Dr. José Antonio de Oro en el proceso Godino," *Revista de Criminología, Psiquiatría y Medicina Legal* 1, no. 1 (January–February 1914).

7. On Brazil, see Silvia Alexim Nunes, "Da medicina social á psicanálise," *Percursos na história da psicanálise*, ed. Joel Birman (Rio de Janeiro: Taurus Editora, 1988), 61–122.

8. Horacio Piñero, "La psicología experimental en la República Argentina," reprinted in *El nacimiento de la psicología en la Argentina*, ed. Hugo Vezzetti (Buenos Aires: Puntosur, 1988), 43–54.

9. On the development of psychoanalysis in France, see Elisabeth Roudinesco, *La bataille de cent ans: L'histoire de la psychanalyse en France*, 2 vols. (Paris: Seuil, 1986).

10. On Italy, see Michel David, *La psicanalisi nella cultura italiana* (Turin: Boringhieri, 1966).

11. Germán Greve, "Sobre psicología y psicoterapia de ciertos estados angustiosos," reprinted in *Freud en Buenos Aires, 1910/1939*, ed. Hugo Vezzetti (Buenos Aires: Puntosur, 1989), 89–105. See Plotkin, *Freud in the Pampas*, 13–14.

12. Fernando Gorriti, *Psicoanálisis de los sueños en un síndrome de desposesión: Estudio psicosexual freudiano de 74 sueños de un alienado que terminó por curarse de este modo* (Buenos Aires: Talleres Gráficos Argentinos, 1930). In that year, Gorriti, who was interested in literature, also attempted literary criticism using psychoanalysis. See his "'La fuerza ciega' del Dr. Vicente Martínez Cuitiño desde el punto de vista freudiano," *La Semana Médica* 2 (1930): 320–23.

13. Alejandro Raitzin, "La locura y los sueños," *Revista de Criminología, Psiquiatría y Medicina Legal* 6 (1919). Raitzin's exposure to psychoanalysis was through Emmanuel Regis and Angelo Hesnard, *La psychanalyse des névrosas et des psychoses, ses applications médicales et extra médicales* (Paris: Alcan, 1914).

14. As late as in 1941, for instance, Dr. Roberto Ciafardo, a well-known psychiatrist, was appointed by the court as a forensic expert to determine the mental condition of a man accused of homicide. Ciafardo concludes his report to the court making the determination that "the somatic examination has revealed the existence of some of the

deformities that the psychiatric technique characterizes as physical stigmas of degeneration [shape of the ears, dental cavities, shape of the teeth]." *Revista de Psiquiatría y Criminología* 5, no. 28 (July–August 1940).

15. E. Eduardo Krapf, "Doctrina y tratamiento de la alienación a través de los siglos," *Anales de la Sociedad Científica Argentina* 128, no. 5 (November 1939). See also Andrew Scull, "Somatic Treatments and the Historiography of Psychiatry," *History of Psychiatry* 5, no. 18 (1994): 1–12.

16. Enrique Pichon Rivière, "Contribución a la teoría psicoanalítica de la esquizofrania," *Revista de Psicoanálisis* 4, no. 1 (July 1946), reprinted in Enrique Pichon Rivière, *Del psicoanálisis a la psicología social*, 2 vols. (Buenos Aires: Galerna, 1970–1971), 1:63.

17. Jorge Balán, *Profesión e identidad en una sociedad dividida: La medicina y el origen del psicoanálisis en la Argentina* (Buenos Aires: CEDES, 1988), 9. See also James Mapelli, *La psicoinervación: Estudio de la acción psíquica sobre las funciones vitales* (Buenos Aires: El Ateneo, 1928). Gregorio Bermann, "James Mapelli," *Revista Latinoamericana de Psiquiatría* 1, no. 2 (1952); and Jorge Balán, *Cuéntame tu vida: Una biografía colectiva del psicoanálisis en la Argentina* (Buenos Aires: Planeta, 1991), 54–55.

18. Nathan Hale, *Freud and the Americans*, 2 vols. Vol. 1: *The Beginnings of Psychoanalysis in the United States, 1876–1917* (1971; reprint, New York: Oxford University Press, 1995), 235.

19. For the Brazilian League, see Jurandir Freire Costa, *História na psiquiatria no Brasil: Um corte ideológico* (Rio de Janeiro: Campus, 1980).

20. Fernando Gorriti, "Higiene mental en la Argentina," *La Semana Médica* 35, no. 23 (June 7, 1928): 1375–82.

21. Sylvia Bermann, "Análisis de algunos datos de estadística psiquiátrica," *Acta Neuropsiquiátrica Argentina*, no. 5 (1959): 150–60.

22. During the 1930s there were outpatient psychiatric services available at the Hospital Nacional de Alienadas in Rosario and elsewhere. In 1923 Fernando Gorriti had proposed without success the creation of one such service in Hospicio. See Gonzalo Bosch, "Organización de la profilaxis de las enfermedades mentales en la Argentina," *Revista de la Liga Argentina de Higiene Mental* 2, no. 4 (1931).

23. In 1940 the Liga lost a building from the municipality for not presenting the plans for renovation in time. They claimed that they did not have the resources for carrying out the project. See Liga Argentina de Higiene Mental, *Memoria y Balance correspondiente al 11 ejercicio* (1940), 11. My appreciation to Hugo Vezzetti for kindly providing me with copies of the material concerning the Liga.

24. "Palabras pronunciadas por el Dr. Gonzalo Bosch con motivo de la inauguración de la 1ra exposición de trabajos de alienados," Liga Argentina de Higiene Mental, *Memoria y Balance Correspondiente al 12 ejercicio* (1941).

25. See, for instance, Eduardo Torres Guido, "La higiene mental en la educación familiar," RAHM 2, no. 3 (January 1943): 10–12; Esther Vodovotz, "El mimo y su importancia en la formación del carácter," RAHM 5, no. 19 (August 1946): 19–29.

26. Francisco de Veyga, "La filantropía actual," RAHM 2, no. 3 (January 1943): 3–9.

27. Mariano Plotkin, "Tell Me Your Dreams: Psychoanalysis and Popular Culture in Buenos Aires, 1930–1950," The Americas 55, no. 4 (April 1999).

28. See Turkle, *Psychoanalytic Politics*, Introduction.

29. Juan Ramón Beltrán, "La psicoanálisis y el médico práctico," *Psicoterapia* 3 (September 1936).

30. Emilio Pizarro Crespo, "Las neurosis obsesivas y las fobias: Aportaciones psicoterapéuticas y metodológicas de cinco casos clínicos," Psicoterapia, no. 2 (May 1936).

31. Emilio Pizarro Crespo, "El narcicismo: De una actitud psíquica a una enfermedad social del erotismo," *Archivos Argentinos de Psicología Normal y Patológica, Terapia Neuro-Mental y Ciencias Afines* 1 (1933–1934).

32. See Plotkin, *Freud in the Pampas*, chap. 1.

33. The journal published extensively on psychiatry in the Soviet Union and in Republican Spain. The first article of the last issue was an article by Emilio Mira y López, titled "Breviario de higiene mental" and addressed to the milicians of the Spanish Republican Army. *Psicoterapia*, no. 4 (May 1937). Soon after the last issue of the journal was out Bermann left Argentina to offer his services to the Spanish Republican Army.

34. Thomas F. Glick, "The Naked Science: Psychoanalysis in Spain, 1914–1948," *Comparative Studies in Society and History* 24 (1982): 534–71; and Thomas F. Glick, "El impacto del psicoanálisis en la psiquiatría espanola de entreguerras," in *Ciencia y sociedad en España: De la Ilustración a la Guerra Civil*, ed. Ron Sánchez, ed.; José Manuel (Madrid: Ediciones el Arquero, 1988), 205–21.

35. Luís Jiménez de Asúa, "Valor de la psicología profunda en ciencias penales (Psicoanálisis y Psicología individual)," *Revista de Criminología, Psiquiatría y Medicina Legal* 22, no. 131 (September–October 1935), 596.

36. Julio Irazusta, *Memorias: Historia de un historiador a la fuerza* (Buenos Aires: Ediciones culturales argentinas, 1975), 227.

37. Telma Reca to Robert Lambert, July 28, 1944. The Rockefeller Foundation Archives, Tarry Town, New York, Series 301, A, Box 3, Folder 34.

38. There is a long history of antagonism between communists and psycho-analysts. During the first years of the Soviet Union, in part as a result of the influence of Trotsky, who was an admirer of Freud, the state not only promoted but financially supported psychoanalytic research. After the fall of Trotsky and the raise of Stalin, psychoanalysis was all but banned in the Soviet Union and the official line of the Communist Party became that psychoanalysis was a bourgeois doctrine. "Reflexology" inspired in the theories of Ivan Pavlov was promoted instead. For a history of psychoanalysis in the Soviet Union, see Alexander Etkind, *Eros of the Impossible: The History of Psychoanalysis in Russia* (Boulder, Colo.: Westview Press, 1997).

39. See Lila Caimari and Mariano Plotkin, *Pueblo contra anti-pueblo: La poli-tización de identidades no-política durante la Argentina Peronista (1943–1955)* (Buenos Aires: Universidad Católica Argentina, 1997).

40. For a discussion of the changes introduced to public education during the Peron regime, see Mariano Plotkin, *Mañana es San Perón: Propaganda, rituales políticos y educación en el régimen Peronista (1946–1955)* (Buenos Aires: Planeta, 1993), part 3.

41. Plotkin, *Mañana es San Perón; and Daniel James, Resistance and Integration: Peronism and the Argentine Working Class, 1946–1955* (Cambridge: Cambridge University Press, 1988).

42. For a general discussion of the differences between traditional mental hygiene and mental health, see Gregorio Bermann, "De la higiene mental mítica de ayer a la higiene mental racional," in *Problemas psiquiátricos* (Buenos Aires: Paidós, 1966), 391–403; and Marijke Giswijt-Hoftra and Roy Porter, eds., *Cultures of Psychiatry and Mental Health Care in Postwar Britain and the Netherlands* (Amsterdam: Editions Rodopi, 1998).

43. For a general discussion on the diffusion of psychoanalysis in Argentina, see Plotkin, *Freud in the Pampas.*

44. By 1966 the service included forty-eight MDs, eighteen residents, sixteen psychologists, two sociologists, two psychopedagogists, and one occupational therapist. Interestingly enough, only five of these team members received any salary.

45. Mauricio Goldenberg, et al., "La psiquiatría en el hospital general. Historia y estructure del Servicio de Psicopatología y Neurología de

Policlínico Dr. Gregorio Araoz Alfaro," *La Semana Médica* no. 4014 (1966): 80–102. 18. See also Carlos Sluzki, "Informe estadístico del servicio de psicopatología y neurología del policlínico de Lanús," *Acta Psiquiátrica y Psicológica Latinoamericana* 11, no. 2 (June 1965): 145–47. Sluzki attributed the increase of neurotic patients to "a better and more adequate information of the public and the subsequent lesser resistance or prejudice towards mental disorders of the general population and of the doctors."

46. For a sociological analysis of the patients carried out by members of Goldenberg's service, see Alejandro Tarnopolsky, Gabriel del Olmo, and Dora Orlansky, "Características sociológicas de pacientes psiquiátricos en tratamiento hospitalario: Estudio exploratorio," *Acta Psiquiátrica y Psicológica de América Latina* 14, no. 3 (September 1968): 217–28. For a description of the psychotherapeutic techniques used in Lanús, see Mauricio Goldenberg, "La psicoterapia en el hospital general," in *Las psicoterapias y el psicoterapeuta*, ed. Gregorio Bermann (Buenos Aires: Paidós, 1964), 119–26.

47. Response of Goldenberg to a question formulated in the Primeras Jornadas Argentinas de Psicoterapia, Cordoba, July, 1962. In Gregorio Bermann, *Las psicoterapias y el psicoterapeuta* (Buenos Aires: Paidós, 1964), 155.

48. Ibid., 156.

49. *Testimonios para la experiencia de enseñar: Mauricio Goldenberg. Maestro, médico, psiquiatra, humanista* (Buenos Aires: Facultad de Psicología, UBA, 1996), 218. Horacio Etchegoyen, personal interview with author, Buenos Aires, November 14, 1996.

50. See Plotkin, *Freud in the Pampas*, chaps. 6 and 7.

51. The main idea behind the notion of therapeutic community was turning the whole institution, including the relationship between patients and staff, and the relationship among patients themselves, into therapeutic tools. This implied a drastic democratization of the internal structure of hospitals. In the most radicalized version of therapeutic community, which was influenced by the antipsychiatric movement, patients would have voice and vote on matters of general policies (including in some cases the admission or discharge of other patients), which were decided in general assemblies with the participation of representatives of staff and patients. For an insightful discussion of therapeutic communities and an analysis in depth of an experience carried out at the Austen Rigg Clinic in Massachusetts, see Emilio Rodrigué, *Biografía de una comunidad terapéutica* (Buenos Aires: EUDEBA, 1965). The particular experience in Lomas de Zamora is discussed by Wilbur Ricardo Grimson, "La Transformación del Hospital Psiquiátrico: Una experiencia de

comunidad terapéutica," *Acta Psiquiátrica y Psicológica de América Latina* 16, no. 4 (December 1970), 354–60. For the experience at the Roballo, see Luís César Guédes Arroyo, "Hospital Dr. A. L. Roballos: Primer centro piloto psiquiátrico regional. El hospital como comunidad terapéutica" (mimeo, 1968).

52. "Declaraciones del capitán de navío Manuel Irán Campo," *Clarín*, September 10, 1976, quoted in Hugo Vezzetti, "Situación actual del psicoanálisis," in *Cuestionamos: 1971 Plataforma-Documento, ruptura con la A.P.A.*, ed. Marie Langer (Buenos Aires: Ediciones Búsqueda, 1987), 221.

53. "El psicoanálisis en la picota," *Somos*, September 19, 1980, 6, cited in Plotkin, *Freud in the Pampas*, 219.

54. Cited by Nancy Caro Hollander, *Love in a Time of Hate: Liberation Psychology in Latin America* (New Brunswick, N.J.: Rutgers University Press, 1997), 74.

55. Ibid., 75. For discussions of the development of psychoanalysis during the military dictatorship, see Hollander, *Love*; and María Matilde Ollier, *La creencia y la pasión: Privado, público y político en la izquierda revolucionaria* (Buenos Aires: Ariel, 1998).

56. "Psicoanálisis en la picota," cited in Plotkin, *Freud in the Pampas*, 222.

Epilogue

1. As I write, the situation continues deteriorating. Yesterday, June 25th, 2002, there were violent incidents between an activist group of unemployed people ("piqueteros") and the police. Two activists died and several others were injured by the police. At this moment there are demonstrations all over the place.

2. Given the seriousness of the crisis, President Duhalde has called for early elections on March 2003. Many people oppose this change of schedule arguing that the country is not prepared for elections now and that there are not credible candidates within sight.

3. Ver Rudy, *Buffet Freud* (Buenos Aires: Planeta, 1999), y Rudy, *Freud mas o menos explícito* (Buenos Aires: Planeta, 2001)

4. This is based on impressions and conversations with several therapists who practice psychoanalytic therapy. There are not statistics available on the number of patients doing psychoanalysis or paychotherapy.

5. "La vida adentro del corralito de la angustia" *Clarín*, March 17, 2002, "Zona" supplement, P. 3.

6. *Ibid.*, P. 5

7. Lakoff, Andrew, "Pharmaceutical Reason. Subject and Psychotrope in Buenos Aires" Ph.D. Dissertation, Department of Anthropology, University of California, Berkeley, 2000.

8. Although a few psychoanalysts were in good terms with the military authorities of the dictatorship, and in spite of the fact that the military appropriated areas of the psychoanalytic discourse for their own political purposes (see chapter 6 of this volume and Plotkin, *Freud in the Pampas*, chapter 8), there is a strong association between psychoanalysis and democracy in people's minds. It is not by chance that the first democratic president after the dictatorship, Raúl Alfonsín was a member of the honorary commission of the XV Latin American Psychoanalytic Congress of 1984. See Visacovsky, *El Lanús: Memoria y política en la construcción de una tradición psiquiátrica y psicoanalítica argentina* (Buenos Aires: Alianza, 2002) 117.

9. For an analysis of these tensions at the particular location of the Aráoz Alfaro Hospital in Lanús, see Visacovsky, Sergio, *El Lanús*. See also Lakoff, "Pharmaceutical."

10. For a thorough discussion of the cultural dimension of the diffusion of psychoanalysis in Argentina, see Plotkin, Mariano, *Freud in the Pampas. The Emergence and Development of a Psychoanalytic Culture in Argentina* (Stanford: Stanford University Press, 2001), especially chapters 7 and 8.

11. Turkle, Sherry, *Psychoanalytic Politics: Jacques Lacan and Freud's French Revolution* (Second Edition,London: The Guilford Press, 1992).

12. Plotkin, *Freud in the Pampas*

13. Sartre, Jean-Paul, "Question de Méthode," in *Temps Modernes* 13, no.139 (September 1957): 339–417, and 140 (October 1957): 658–98

14. Plotkin, *Freud in the Pampas*, 175.

15. See, among many others the works by José Bleger, "Ideología y política" *Revista de Psicoanálisis*, 30, no. 2 (April–June, 1973); Bleger, *Psicoanálisis y dialéctica materialista: Estudios sobre la estructura del psicoanálisis* (Buenos Aires: Piados, 1958); León Rozitchner, "La izquierda sin sujeto" *La Rosa Blindada* 2, no. 9 (September 1966); Rozitchner, *Freud y los límites del individualismo burgués* (Buenos Aires: Siglo XXI, 1972).

16. Freud, Sigmund, "The Question of a *Weltanschauung*" *New Introductory Lectures on Psycho-Analysis* (1933), Freud, Sigmund, *The Standard Edition of the Complete Psychological Works of Sigmund Freud*, edited and translated by James Strachey et al. (London: The Hogarth Press, 1964), Vol. XXII, P. 158 and ff.

17. For a critical discussion of the usefulness of the concept of trauma, as something induced from without, to describe the military dictatorship,

see Vezzetti, Hugo, *Pasado y presente. Guerra, dictadura y sociedad en la Argentina* (Buenos Aires: Siglo XXI, 2002), 60–61.

18. Recently, there have been a wave of works on memory as a way of processing the traumas of the dictatorship. See among others, Vezzetti, *Pasado y presente*, and Guber, Rosana, *¿Por qué Malvinas? De la causa nacional a la guerra absurda* (Buenos Aires: Fondo de Cultura Económica, 2001).

19. Rozitchner, Alejandro, "Nuestro paradógico logro" *La Nación* (March 15, 2002), Section "Opinión," P. 1.

20. See, for instance, Martínez Estrada, Ezequiel, *Radiografía de la Pampa* (1933) (English translation available: Martínez Estrada, *X-Ray of the Pampa* (Austin: Texas University Press, 1971), and Scalabrini Ortiz, Raúl, *El hombre que está solo y espera* (1931).

21. See, for instance, Inda, Norberto, "El dolor de ya no ser ni tener" *Clarín* (February 28, 2002), P.23

22. Giberti, Eva, "Generaciones de psicoanalistas, política e historia" *Actualidad Psicológica*, XXVII; N.296 (April, 2002), 14–17.

23. For more details on the politicization of psychoanalysis and the emergence of Plataforma and Documento, see Balán, Jorge, *Cuéntame tu vida. Una biografía colectiva del psicoanálisis argentino.* (Buenos Aires: Planeta, 1991), and Plotkin, *Freud in the Pampas*, chapter 8.

24. Martinto de Paschero, Lucía, "Situación actual," *Actualidad Psicológica*, 27, no. 296 (April 2002).

25. When the risk index of a particular country reaches the level of 1,000 it is considered as an indication that that country is not any longer in the position of borrowing money in the international market. In June 2002, the risk country index of Argentina was never below 6,000.

26. Bleichmar, Silvia, *Dolor país* (Buenos Aires: Zorzal, third edition, 2002). The book consists of a series of articles that the author had published in newspapers and a few new additions.

27. Bleichamar, *Dolor país*, 88.

28. *Ibid.*, chapter 1.

29. "Entre la política y la subjetividad" Interview to Silvia Bleichmar, *La Nación*, Section "Cultura," April 14th, 2002, P. 6.

30. "Hay impotencia, no incertidumbre" Interview to Germán García. *La Nación*, Section "Enfoques" February 17th, 2002, P.3

31. Freud, Sigmund, *Future of an Illusion.* Vol 21 of *The Standard Edition of the Complete Psychological Works of Sigmund Freud.* Ed. James Strachey et al. (London: Hogart, 1962).

Index

Note: Page numbers for figures appear in bold type.

a memory you don't have or use for it. You would never say, for instance, "I really liked that Memento movie", you might you discussion of the movie to, "I am really liking sitting in this soft seat watching people move around on this big bright screen in front of me" and you wouldn't remember you were supposed to whisper in a movie theater if you had to say something to the person next to you, in fact, not only would you likely ignore accepted rules of theater etiquette you'd be just as likely to turn to somebody you didn't know to make your observation because you wouldn't have any idea who it was you came with. We will call this what it is, which is a bitch ass kick of a mother fucker.

Look up Indian Tribes that don't use the past tense

I read today of a man with acute retrograde amnesia. I didn't know either, but, apparently, he ~~has entirely~~ ~~lost the past tenses~~ He was war ~~not ability to remember~~ found wandering the streets of Manhattan, so lost he couldn't even give them his name. Unfortunately everyone has seen Memento, the recent movie based on exactly this premise (that you might just anyway someday wake up unable to remember a thing, perhaps including him, but confirmation of his viewership would require an exhaustive study of his receipts and credit card records as he can't remember whether he had or hasn't), so it is generally assumed that he is faking the entire thing (apparently this diagnosis of deliberate retrograde amnesia has become widely more popular since the theatrical release of the aforementioned Memento). But an insanely unlikely and ridiculously complicated psychosomatic malady. All that remembering not remember anything must be terribly exhausting. reading the article had mentioned, the little that kept rattling around in his head, was the fact that this disease had robbed this man of the past tenses. If you ~~can't think~~ don't have